T4-AFX-710

Prose Immortality, 1711–1819

Winner of the Walker Cowen Memorial Prize
for an outstanding work of scholarship
in eighteenth-century studies

PROSE
IMMORTALITY,
1711–1819

Jacob Sider Jost

UNIVERSITY OF VIRGINIA PRESS

Charlottesville & London

University of Virginia Press
© 2015 by the Rector and Visitors of the University of Virginia
All rights reserved
Printed in the United States of America on acid-free paper

First published 2015

1 3 5 7 9 8 6 4 2

Library of Congress Cataloging-in-Publication Data
Sider Jost, Jacob, 1983– author.
Prose Immortality, 1711–1819 / Jacob Sider Jost.
pages cm. — (Winner of the Walker Cowen Memorial Prize)
Includes bibliographical references and index.
ISBN 978-0-8139-3680-2 (cloth : acid-free paper) —
ISBN 978-0-8139-3681-9 (ebook)
1. English prose literature—18th century—History and criticism. I. Title.
PR769.J67 2015
828'.50809—dc23

2014029161

CONTENTS

ACKNOWLEDGMENTS

My oldest obligations are to my mentors at Goshen College, John D. Roth and Ervin Beck. At Oxford I was lucky to learn Chaucer from Carolyne Larrington and Shakespeare from Frank Romany, but not before Clare Brant hooked me on the eighteenth century in a four-person tutorial where 50 percent of the students went pro in the field (hi, Natalie!). In the Harvard English department I had an all-star team of advisors in Jim Engell, Leo Damrosch, and Leah Price. I learned an enormous amount from talking with them and reading their comments on my work, and even more from watching them teach, think, and write. To my two gracious and generous mentors beyond the committee, Elaine Scarry and Emma Rothschild: thank you.

Among other professors with open doors and helpful thoughts, I thank Nicholas Watson, James Simpson, and Amanda Claybaugh. Harvard also provided me with a fantastic graduate student community: here my greatest debt is to the eighteenth-century and romanticism colloquium and its redoubtable founding coordinator, Matt Ocheltree; thanks also to Dan Shore, Tom Fehse, Fred van der Wyck, Sarah Wagner-McCoy, Sam Foster, and Nick Donofrio. Luke Leafgren and Lindsay Noll went above and beyond the call of friendship in opening their home to me in my final year at the Society. Make new friends and keep the old: my formative grad school years were enriched throughout by dialogue with Peter Fairfield, John Leigh, Peter Hartman, Laura Yoder, Peter Dula, Mark Metzler-Sawin, Lee Good, and Janneken Smucker. Three cheers also to librarians like Laura Farwell Blake and John "Horace Rumpole" Overholt.

Finding my way in the wider world of eighteenth-century studies, I came under the influence and patronage of two major figures in the field, Adam Potkay and Stuart Sherman. Both have given me opportunities and support that the footnotes to their works in what follows cannot convey. I am also grateful for the friendship and assistance of Adam Rounce, Tony Lavopa,

Rosemary Dixon, Derek Taylor, Robert Demaria, and Billy Flesch, as well as the opportunities provided by the Yale Boswell Projects and Rare Book School.

At the Harvard Society of Fellows, I found new sources of insight in conversation with Gregory Nagy and Noah Feldman among the grownups and Marta Figlerowicz, Martin Hägglund, Timothy Barnes, Eric Nelson, and Jo Guldi among the kids. Thanks also to Diana Morse, Kelly Katz, and Wally Gilbert.

I know how lucky I am to have wonderful colleagues at Dickinson College. Particular thanks go to Siobhan Philips, Carol Ann Johnston, Wendy Moffat, and Tom Reed. Thanks also to the Dickinson College Research and Development Committee. Beyond the limestone, other institutions and organizations that deserve warm thanks for paying the bills while I was reading books include the Mellon Foundation and the American Council of Learned Societies, which generously provided dissertation completion funding; Harvard's Milton Fund; and Dunster and Lowell Houses.

Material from my first chapter, "The Afterlife and the *Spectator*," is reprinted with permission from *SEL: Studies in English Literature 1500–1900* 51, no. 3 (Summer 2011), where it appeared in a slightly different form.

The University of Virginia Press was kind enough to place this book in the illustrious company of winners of the Cowen Memorial Prize, but as I told my editor, Angie Hogan, when I got this news, it was the Hogan Prize of working with her and the Press's capable staff that I valued more.

I've got a big family, and they're a big part of my life. Thanks and love to Ruth, Timothy, Micah, Hannah, David, Laura, Pierrick, Sebastien, Rebecca, Rose, Bruce, Christian, Andrew, Daniel, Jacob, Katie, Tim, Grant, Miriam, Susy, Dan, Kathy, John, Joshua, Christine, Mary, Maggie, Hannah, Grace, Nathaniel, Miriam, Thomas, Ruth, Esther, Peter, Bethany, Elizabeth, James, Esau, Andrew, Molly, Helen, Albert, Lydia, Emily, David, Elaine, Robert, Amy, Eloise, John, and Suzanne. We remember Arthur and Esther in Columbus and Grant, Ruth, Allen, and Reuben in Lindale.

I also have my own family, which is the biggest part of my life. This book is dedicated to Felix, to Emily, and above all to Laura, with whom being there together is enough.

Prose Immortality, 1711–1819

Introduction

How do writers memorialize and preserve the dead? When John Dryden died in 1700, poets wrote elegies. When Samuel Johnson died in 1784, biographers wrote lives. This book is about what happens in between.

Few poets die at convenient times for literary periodization, but Dryden is an obliging exception. When the poet laureate succumbed to gangrene on May 1, 1700, he brought the poetic history of the seventeenth century to a close with him. Two anthologies of memorial verse appeared the same year: *Luctus Britannici: or The Tears of the British Muses; for the Death of John Dryden, Esq.*, and *The Nine Muses, or Poems Written by Nine Several Ladies upon the Death of the Late Famous John Dryden, Esq.* Neither is distinguished for the quality of its contents, but together they provide a comprehensive picture of the function and importance assumed for poetry at the turn of the eighteenth century. The title page of *Luctus Britannici* quotes a programmatic triplet from Dryden himself: "For ev'n when Death dissolve's our human Frame / The Soul return's to Heav'n, from whence it came / *Earth* keep's the Body, *Verse* preserves the Fame." Poetry is a technology of preservation, perpetuating the "Fame" of individual humans beyond death. This idea recurs throughout the collection. "A Person of QUALITY" praises Dryden for his power to immortalize British military achievements during his lifetime. Multiple poets reflect on their responsibility to perpetuate Dryden's fame, and regret that they lack his talent and thus fitness for the task. Henry Hoyle, one of the minority of elegiasts who sign their contributions, repeats Dryden's own observation in the epigraph that after death both the "soul" and the "fame" of the decedent must be accounted for: a dying poet enters into both the salvation economy of Christian theology and the annals of literary history. Hoyle piously privileges the former over the latter and charitably expresses high hopes for his subject in both: "His Soul, and Fame how e'er his body die, / Shall share unequal Immortality."[1] Verse tributes like Hoyle's, the poem implies, are the lifeblood of the deceased poet's fame.

No poetry collection wept Johnson's death in 1784; rather, the page of narrative hastened to document his life.[2] James Boswell's *Life of Johnson* (1791) was preceded not only by John Hawkins's biography and Hester Piozzi's *Anecdotes,* but by eight other life accounts published between 1784 and 1786.[3] Samuel Romilly reported that "above a year together after the death of Dr. Johnson nothing was to be heard but panegyrics of him,—lives, letters, and anecdotes."[4] It is revealing that for Romilly "panegyric" comprises not celebratory poetry or a classical funeral oration, but rather biographical and anecdotal documentation—and even includes Johnson's letters.

Indeed, the few poems that marked Johnson's passing tended not to mourn him directly but instead deplore the proliferation of biographies. Samuel Bishop writes:

> While Johnson the Lives of our Poets compos'd,
> He scarce thought how his own would be hack'd, when it clos'd.
> We've had life upon life, without end or cessation,
> A perfect biographical superfetation:
> Male, female, friend, foe, have had hands in the mess;
> And the paper announces still more in the press.—
> Not a cat, tho' for cats Fate spins ninefold the thread,
> Has so many lives, living—as Johnson has, dead.[5]

The dictionary word "superfetation" (Johnson defines it as "one conception following another, so that both are in the womb together, but come not to their full time for delivery together") suggests that the biographers by whom Johnson's life is "hack'd"—the word has both literary and anatomical connotations—can gestate an infinite sequence of Johnson clones through their books.[6] Though dead, Johnson is fated to pass "life upon life, without end or cessation."[7]

Matthew Arnold called the eighteenth century the "age of prose"; I argue that it is the age of prose immortality.[8] For the first time, writing is imagined as a way of immortalizing not only heroic acts or transcendent beauty but also the rhythms and events of daily life. "I should live no more than I can record, as one should not have more corn growing than one can get in," James Boswell muses in a diary entry from 1776. "There is a waste of good if it be not preserved."[9] If any undocumented day in the life of an Edinburgh lawyer counts as "waste," then the epitaphs and elegies that provided literary immortality to Dryden and his predecessors will no longer be adequate. When Boswell writes the *Life of Samuel Johnson* as a monument to his friend and mentor, he imagines it not as a lapidary lyric tablet but as a massive cairn of stones, individual anecdotes collected from Johnson's day-to-day existence.

Prose immortality is this book's name for the aspiration, first articulated in the eighteenth century, to use documentary writing that attends to the rhythms and events of everyday life to preserve a particular individual in such detail that he or she is felt to survive beyond physical death. Boswell's *Life of Johnson,* to which this book's final chapter is dedicated, epitomizes this paradigm. My study seeks to answer two major questions. The first is, What developments in literary form and genre are necessary for prose immortality to be possible? Without the diary, the periodical paper, and the novel, to name the three most important examples, Boswell's magnum opus could not have been written. As a history of literary form, this study builds on the seminal work of Stuart Sherman, whose *Telling Time* identifies the clock, which divides the passage of time into discrete, quantifiable units, as a central engine of literary development of the long eighteenth century. Sherman tells a powerful story of "the absorption into narrative form of the kinds of time propounded by the new chronometry, and of the emergence of new narrative time, at first (necessarily) in private writings and then in public performances."[10] I extend Sherman's insights by arguing that the very genres that reshape the eighteenth-century understanding of lived time—the diary, the periodical paper, the novel—are both called into being by and crucial in shaping conceptions of time beyond earthly human life. Hence this study's second major question: Why is the desire for prose immortality so powerful in eighteenth-century England? What cultural work does it do? Lacking his lifelong obsession with documenting himself and others as a prophylactic against annihilation and loss, Boswell would have had no reason to write the *Life of Johnson.* For Boswell, as for the figures that precede and follow him, literary immortality is important because of its close connection with the religious understanding of a personal afterlife. Prose immortality emerges at the same time as, and has close affinities with, a new eighteenth-century conception of the afterlife that emphasizes gradual, continuous moral improvement; a sociable and recognizably human heaven; and the survival of the individual personality after death. Eighteenth-century authors were obsessed with immortality in both its literary and its theological forms, and they used concepts and metaphors from each realm when thinking about the other. As a study of ideas, this book builds on a groundswell of recent scholarship, in both intellectual history and literary studies, on the close connections in Britain between religion and the program of intellectual inquiry and social and moral progress that we now call the Enlightenment. In particular, prose immortality can be understood as a literary correlative of what J. G. A. Pocock has christened "the Arminian Enlightenment," which "open[ed] the prospect that [the individual] might be saved by his own works and virtues, his own reasonable and social nature."[11] This book is accordingly indebted to Pocock and allied historians, as well as to literary scholars who have recognized the connections between theology and imaginative writing in the period.[12]

Prose immortality is a phenomenon of Britain's religious Enlightenment because the conception of the religious afterlife that it endorses works as an ecumenical, politically irenic, and socially salutary moral guarantor. For some of the figures in this study, particularly Joseph Addison, imagining an Enlightened afterlife is a constructive, forward-looking project. For others, particularly Boswell, the habits of thought that generate prose immortality emerge in response to skeptical or anti-religious currents in British thought. For Boswell, life writing provided a comforting bulwark against skeptical challenges to Christianity that threatened the belief in a stable, enduring self. Concerns about immortality—both literary and religious— drive many of the most significant generic and stylistic innovations in eighteenth-century literature: the daily time scale of Addison and Richard Steele's *Spectator*, the open-ended structure and proto-Romantic introspection of Edward Young's poetry, the realism of Samuel Richardson's novels, the hybrid verse/prose form of Laetitia Pilkington's *Memoirs*, and the anecdotal texture of literary biography practiced by Boswell.

To clarify what is new and important about these eighteenth-century forms, let us return to Dryden's mourners and the status quo ante from which, over the course of the eighteenth century, prose immortality emerges. Henry Hoyle and his fellow elegists stand in a long tradition, rooted in Greek and Latin thought, according to which human excellence of all kinds seeks to escape or overcome death, and poetry, particularly the lyric and the epic, is the preeminent means of securing immortality. As Hannah Arendt puts it, "The task and potential greatness of mortals lie in their ability to produce things—works and deeds and words—which would deserve to be and, at least to a degree, are at home in everlastingness, so that though them men could find their place in a cosmos where everything is immortal except themselves."[13] There were many variants to this fundamental idea. Poets presented themselves to kings, generals, and athletes as preservers of their names, and ambitious rulers patronized poets.[14] The emphatic final words of Sir Philip Sidney's *Defence of Poetry* curse the condemner of poetry by wishing that he be denied access to its memorial power: "If you have so earth-creeping a mind that it cannot lift itself up to look to the sky of poetry . . . thus much curse must I send you in the behalf of all poets, that . . . when you die, your memory die from earth for want of an epitaph."[15]

Poetry also provided an immortal name to the poet. Horace concludes his third book of odes with perhaps the most famous and frequently cited claim of this kind in the ancient world:

> *Exegi monumentum aere perennius*
> *regalique situ pyramidum altius,*
> *quod non imber edax, non Aquilo impotens*
> *possit diruere aut innumerabilis*
> *annorum series et fuga temporum.*
> *non omnis moriar, multaque pars mei*
> *vitabit Libitinam.*

[I have finished a monument more lasting than bronze, more lofty than the regal structure of the pyramids, one which neither corroding rain nor the ungovernable North Wind can ever destroy, nor the countless series of the years, nor the flight of time. I shall not wholly die, and a large part of me will elude the Goddess of Death.][16]

For elegiasts versed in this tradition, a poet is his or her own best monument. "'Tis true that Dryden's worth there's none so well / As Dryden's self in his own works can tell," confesses one of the mourners in *Luctus Britannici* (4). Milton's first published poem imagines that Shakespeare has built a monument by turning his readers to stone: "Thou in our wonder and astonishment / Hast built thy self a live-long Monument."[17]

Shakespeare himself follows Renaissance predecessors such as Pierre de Ronsard in celebrating neither himself nor the civic or military figures of classical encomiasts, but rather an unnamed beloved: "So long as men can breathe or eyes can see, / So long lives this, and this gives life to thee."[18]

Shakespeare imputes to poetry the power of organic reanimation that Samuel Bishop identifies with biography two centuries later: "But were some child of yours alive that time, / You should live twice: in it, and in my rhyme" (Sonnet 17.13–14). Of course, Shakespeare's deployment of the topos raises the question of what exactly is being preserved, since the sonnets are so notoriously lacking in characteristic detail about their subject that the beloved's gender was in dispute for centuries. In this respect, the sonnets are representative of the lyric immortality tradition as a whole: because of its lapidary beauty, the lyric poem can be memorized and recited ("so long as men can breathe") and read repeatedly ("or eyes can see"). But its very brevity limits how much data it can actually preserve. Indeed, Renaissance sonnet sequences like Shakespeare's tend not to preserve the beloved so much as the erotic affect of the lover, the experience of being in love.[19]

Shakespeare's sonnets, like the poems that commit Dryden's soul to heaven and his verse to posterity, feel the need to account for both (secular) immortality and (Christian) eternity. Sonnet 55 begins with a direct echo of Horace's *exegi monumentum* ode, cited above: "Not marble nor the gilded monuments / Of princes shall outlive this powerful rhyme." But it closes by imagining an end to the immortality of poetry's "living record" in the more literal afterlife of bodily resurrection on the Day of Judgment: "So, till the judgment that yourself arise, / You live in this, and dwell in lovers' eyes" (55.1–2, 8, 13–14). Shakespeare reads immortality and eternity as two separate, successive, and incommensurable forms of lastingness. Though he does not belabor the point, his conceptual framework implies that when time is over and eternity begins, sonnets will cease to be relevant.

Milton's *Lycidas* offers a more complex synthesis of secular immortality and heavenly eternity; the "pure eyes / and perfect witness of all-judging Jove" replace the "lovers' eyes" of Shakespeare as the arbitrator and guarantor of fame, which is "no plant that grows in mortal soil." Far from superseding fame, heaven (and not "the glistering foil / Set off to th' world") becomes the only place where it truly exists. As Phoebus tells the poet, "Of so much fame in Heav'n expect thy meed" (lines 78–84). Elsewhere, Milton speculates that one of the pleasures of heaven will be that "we shall ourselves be present to hear our praise" on earth after our death.[20]

Major works of both the classical and Christian traditions provide precedents for cross-pollination of this kind.[21] Medieval Catholicism, with its prayers for the dead and purgatory-shortening endowments and benefactions, had made it particularly easy for the pious to perpetuate their names on earth in ways that reinforced their prospects of eternity in Paradise. The demolition of purgatory in the Reformation placed the relationship between immortality and eternity in a new flux.

Shakespeare's model of succession and Milton's of coordination are two models available to lyric poets of the seventeenth century. Another approach, which Keith Thomas attributes not only to poets but also to the upper stratum of British society as a whole during the early modern period, was to jettison belief in eternity entirely and focus on securing eternal fame: "Among the social elite, the horror of oblivion was an obsessive preoccupation; so much so as to make one doubt whether the Christian doctrine of the afterlife can have been a living reality for those to whom posthumous fame was so overriding an objective. . . . It is hard not to feel that the highest value of these seekers after posthumous fame was essentially pagan."[22]

Thomas points to the seventeenth-century poet Margaret Cavendish, Duchess of Newcastle, who self-consciously sought the enduring poetic fame hitherto reserved for men because of her "doubt of an after being," as well as the similar reasoning of eighteenth-century skeptics, such as Edward Gibbon and David Hume, who were deeply immersed in classical thought. Leo Braudy puts the argument even more baldly: "In a secular civilization fame and the approval of posterity replace belief in the afterlife."[23]

This story has an attractive logic to it: as belief in eternity wanes, concern with immortality waxes. It also harmonizes with readings of the long eighteenth century as a period of secularization and declining religiosity, at least among intellectual elites. But it is a partial story at best. For one thing, in the long run the correlation between cultural interest in literary immortality and the eternity of the soul is direct, not inverse. Skepticism about the personal afterlife coincides, in the Romantic era and beyond, with a new conception of fame as the pre-death adulation of a popular audience—that is, celebrity in our modern sense. Christianity and classicism, the ideological underwriters of heavenly eternity and poetic immortality respectively, recede from the life-world of the secular stratum of the West in tandem. Moreover, the argument that preoccupation with fame replaces anxiety about salvation, though it applies well to Gibbon, cannot account for a range of pious authors, such as Milton, or Samuel Richardson and his circle, or James Boswell and Samuel Johnson, whose works show a marked interest in both kinds of posthumous survival.

For a range of important literary figures spanning the eighteenth century, immortality and eternity form a combined response to the threats of death and annihilation. They provide a mutually reinforcing set of images and metaphors: the republication of a book is described as the resurrection of a body, or the verdict of critics is compared to God's judgment.[24] More important, this tight braiding of literary fame and personal afterlife leads both to assume new forms. Boswell's fear of the "waste" of an undocumented life cannot be assuaged by a fourteen-line sonnet; only a diary or biography can begin to offer the textual copiousness he needs. Richardson's *Clarissa* connects this authoritative biographical record to personal salvation; the massive novel doubles as a Book of Life vindicating its heroine both to its readers and to God.

If imaginative invocations of immortality and eternity are responses to the threat of human finitude, the perceived nature of that threat will inform the shape that such invocations will take. For several of the figures examined in this study, particularly Richardson, Boswell, and Johnson, the adversary was the "atheist," "deist," "infidel" philosophical tradition that included figures such as Spinoza, Hobbes, Anthony Collins, John Toland, Matthew Tindal, and above all Hume. This new threat takes two related forms: in a general sense, the turn of the eighteenth century marks an inflection point in the larger history of irreligion and unbelief in Europe from the Reformation to the present day, the climacteric at which atheism and related positions take on an intellectual respectability and cultural prominence that makes them impossible for partisans of religion to ignore or dismiss out of hand.[25] More specifically, the British philosophical tradition from Locke to Hume and beyond places unprecedented pressure on the Christian concept of the soul, understood as an immaterial, immortal being that survives the death of the body. Though Locke explicitly disavowed the mortalist implications of his *Essay Concerning Human Understanding*, his philosophy both raises disquieting questions about the nature of the soul and shifts the lexicon of philosophical debate from the question of the "soul" to the question of the "self," thus creating the climate in which Hume's more radical conclusions can flourish a half century later.[26]

From the perspective of mainstream orthodox Anglicanism, the timing for this philosophical revolution was highly inconvenient. Reacting against the continent-wide bloodletting of the Reformation wars of religion and the widespread and traumatic millenarianism of the English Civil War period, whose belligerents saw God working actively in political and military history from blueprints located in the books of Daniel and Revelation, the late Stuart and Hanoverian English church shifted its emphasis away from

God's interventions on earth. Instead, it emphasized personal moral conduct, adopting a political quietism with a strong Erastian tincture.[27] The textual figure of Isaac Bickerstaff, who in Jonathan Swift's hands effects the satiric demolition of the astrologer John Partridge in 1708 and narrates Richard Steele's *Tatler* from 1709 to 1711, is a useful mascot for this transition from the God of portents to the God of propriety. In this latitudinarian theological context, the survival of the human soul beyond death, always a central tenet of Christianity, becomes even more crucial. With God no longer understood to intervene in the this-worldly affairs of nations, it was critical that he guarantee posthumous reward and punishment as a theodicean makeweight in the lives of individuals.[28] A robust, philosophically defensible conception of the soul and self was necessary to ensure that the system was fair, meting out consequences to posthumous entities that were demonstrably the same as prehumous moral agents. Neither Locke nor Hume inspired confidence in this regard. Moreover, it was taken for granted that attacks on the doctrine of the immortal soul were existential attacks on the moral and political order, since a true mortalist would have no reason not to do evil if he or she could get away with it in this life. Because the doctrine of immortality carried so much social and theological weight yet rested on a philosophical foundation that was so palpably sandy, doubts could inflict a visceral psychic toll on eighteenth-century Britons who were, in William James's terms, disposed to the type of the "sick soul."[29] Had James Boswell been born a century earlier, he likely would have spent his life terrified of damnation at the hands of a Calvinist God. Instead he spent his life visiting scaffolds and deathbeds worrying that mortality was equivalent to annihilation. (Though this is not to say that predestination does not continue to exert a maleficent imaginative power in this period, as William Cowper in particular illustrates.)

Charles Taylor has argued that the most characteristic feature of secular modernity is not the decline of religious practice or the divorce of religion from state power in liberal democracy, but rather the transition "from a society in which in was virtually impossible not to believe in God, to one in which faith, even for the staunchest believer, is one human possibility among many." The effect of this multiplication of possibilities is what Taylor calls "fragilization": all individuals feel pressure to justify their belief system in the face of alternatives.[30] For writers such as Young, Richardson, Johnson, and Boswell, arguments about immortality and eternity are arguments in defense of newly vulnerable convictions about the nature of the soul and the existence and providence of God.[31] In the cases of William Warburton and Boswell, the engagement with David Hume's arguments in particular is quite explicit and even personal. But even where Hume is not an explicit interlocutor, the figures of this study exemplify John Sitter's insight that "Hume, however difficult it is to demonstrate his influence upon most of his literary contemporaries, defined rather than invented many of the major mid-eighteenth-century problems of knowledge and belief—that Hume, in short, argued out problems under which most thoughtful writers labored."[32] The hysterical tone of Warburton's polemical engagement with Hume is an extreme instance of a larger, and usually more subtle, trend.

Yet it is also crucial to acknowledge the commonalities that unite the major figures of this study with their freethinking or secularizing contemporaries. For Addison in particular, reimagining the Christian afterlife as a sociable site of indefinite moral improvement was not a defensive reaction to a skeptical threat but part of a constructive and progressive intellectual program in its own right, one that exerted great influence on Hume himself.[33] Indeed, Hume's Scotland was the site of a particularly close institutional and ideological collaboration between moderate Protestantism and the Enlightenment agenda of politeness and literature.[34] In some cases the differences and disagreements that were so existentially important to those on one side or another of the eighteenth-century pious/secular divide can seem comparatively small. Turning from the lurid seventeenth-century Calvinism of *Pilgrim's Progress* to the *dix-huitième* urbanity of *The Theory of Moral Sentiments,* one has the feeling of entering another world. In contrast, Johnson's *Rambler* and Hume's *Essays* are clearly part of the same milieu, with widely overlapping assumptions, concerns, and convictions.[35] Yet for men like Johnson and Boswell, the very closeness of their own views to those of irreligious thinkers like Hume, and the resultant plausibility of their opponents' skepticism, was precisely what made it so threatening and traumatizing.[36] The disjunction between secular thinkers and religious authors can be hard to discern, but it is all the more important for that.

Moreover, it is not the case that the secular philosophers of the century represent progress, while their literary counterparts represent conservatism or stasis.[37] Concerns about immortality, both literary and personal, emerge from technological and social change and in turn drive many of the most significant literary innovations of the eighteenth century, in particular the periodical paper, the novel, and biography and autobiography. Progress and religion are allied rather than opposed concepts. This is because theology adapted itself to a world in which chronometry, journalism, capitalism, and secular politics made time increasingly quantifiable, linear, and homogeneous, as pious writers postulated an afterlife that is an extrapolation of this world, a horizontal continuation rather than a vertical transformation, "futurity" rather than the timeless *nunc stans* of scholastic eternity.

As part of this process, literary immortality shifts, particularly from the 1740s on, away from the lyric orientation of Horace, Ovid, Shakespeare, and Dryden's mourners to the anecdotal, documentary preservation of human life over and through daily time. Contrast the parade of "mighty Dead," each identified by a single characteristic deed or trait, that marches through James Thomson's *Winter* (first edition 1726), with Boswell's expansively anecdotal account of Johnson during their tour of the Hebrides in 1773:

> Socrates,
> Truth's early Champion, Martyr for his God:
> Solon, the next, who built his Commonweal,
> On Equity's firm Base: Lycurgus, then
> Severely good, and him of rugged Rome,
> Numa, who soften'd her rapacious Sons.[38]

> *Thursday, 14th October*
> When Dr. Johnson awaked this morning, he called "Lanky!" having, I suppose, been thinking of Langton; but corrected himself instantly, and cried, "Bozzy!" He has a way of contracting the names of his friends.[39]

Poetry may preserve a hero's name and deeds, provide a laundry list of an ancient or contemporary statesman's virtues, distil a lover's beauty, or even invite the reader to reanimate the creative consciousness of the poet in the moment of reading or recitation, but it cannot preserve, as Boswell's *Life of Johnson* does, the texture of everyday life with its subject. No poem could preserve Johnson's

> coat, his wig, his figure, his face, his scrofula, his St. Vitus's dance, his rolling walk, his blinking eye, the outward signs which too clearly marked his approbation of his dinner, his insatiable appetite for fish-sauce and veal-pie with plums, his inextinguishable thirst for tea, his trick of touching the posts as he walked, his mysterious practice of treasuring up scraps of orange-peel, his morning slumbers, his midnight disputations, his contortions, his mutterings, his gruntings, his puff-

ings, his vigorous, acute, and ready eloquence, his sarcastic wit, his vehemence, his insolence, his fits of tempestuous rage, his queer inmates,
old Mr. Levett and blind Mrs. Williams, the cat Hodge and the negro
Frank,

as Thomas Babington Macaulay put it when reviewing John Wilson Cro-
ker's edition of the *Life* in 1831.[40] Homeric epic celebrates the exploits of its
heroes, but it does not, as Boswell's expanded diary notes in the *Life* seek to
do, document daily routines or reproduce conversations verbatim.

For Boswell, conversation and conviviality at the Literary Club are
heaven on earth, and recording them in great detail provides a bulwark
against the hypochondriac sufferings and skeptical doubts that assaulted
him throughout his life. William Cowper, in whose life depression and the
fear of reprobation played a yet greater role, left a striking example of the
associations and anxieties that generate the prose immortality paradigm in
his final English poem, "The Cast-away." Writing in 1799, a year before his
death, Cowper recounts the story of a sailor on Commodore George Anson's naval expedition of 1740–44 who was thrown overboard in seas so
stormy that his fellows, who could hear his cries and see him swimming
strongly, were able to offer no assistance. The poem was not published in
Cowper's lifetime, and the antepenultimate and penultimate stanzas explain why:

> No poet wept him, but the page
> Of narrative sincere
> That tells his name, his worth, his age
> Is wet with Anson's tear,
> And tears by bards or heroes shed
> Alike immortalize the Dead.
>
> I, therefore, purpose not or dream,
> Descanting on his fate,
> To give the melancholy theme
> A more enduring date,
> But Mis'ry still delights to trace
> Its semblance in another's case.[41]

The poem's final stanza explains wherein the "semblance" between the narrator and the sailor consists: Cowper believed himself to be predestined
for damnation—in this conviction, he refused to pray or enter a church for

the last twenty-seven years of his life—and thus he and the drowned man "snatch'd from all effectual aid . . . perish'd, each, alone."[42] "The Cast-away" explicitly renounces the long-standing prerogative of lyric poetry to give "a more enduring date" to human heroism and greatness, deferring instead to "the page / Of narrative sincere" that can transmit the pertinent biographical details (the "name," "worth," and "age" of the sailor, all omitted from the poem) to the drowned man's superior officer, who in turn writes the book that conveys the story to the British reading public and Cowper himself.[43] The genres of ship's log and travel narrative are, for Cowper, the new sites for immortality. And this renunciation of poetic immortality is an allegory for Cowper's conviction of his own reprobation: poet and poem alike are imagined to perish. "The Cast-away" is a dark obverse to the more sanguine tenor of *Sir Charles Grandison* or the *Life of Johnson,* but it operates on the same assumptions: prose is the site of immortality, and textual survival on earth doubles beatification in heaven.

The apparent triviality of Boswell's anecdotal data in the *Life of Johnson* can lead to critical misunderstanding. When Marshall Brown sniffs in *Preromanticism* that "any period that counts a thousand pages of table talk masquerading as a biography . . . among its lasting monuments has talked too much around the main point," he ignores the fact that Boswell is offering a serious and conscious redefinition of what a monument should be.[44] Faced with Hume's sapping operation against the philosophical doctrine of the unified, stable self and the theological doctrine of the sempiternal soul, Boswell's prose monument cannot offer a literal refutation (though the "let's prove Hume wrong" genre was popular among clergymen of the mid-eighteenth century) but presents instead an imaginative rebuttal, at the same level of rigor as Boswell's story of Johnson "refuting" Berkeleyan idealism by kicking a stone.[45] If there is no such thing as the self, Boswell's massive hoard of autobiographical papers asks, what has been keeping a diary these thirty years? If all that we are ends with death, why is it that writing down Johnson's life can preserve him so vividly, so fully? Prose immortality reproduces the logic of Weber's theory of the Protestant work ethic. If you do not know whether or not you are saved, you work hard to prove to yourself that you are; if you do not know whether you have a unified and stable self, a continuous being capable of surviving death, you write down your day-to-day life to prove to yourself that you do.

Prose immortality also takes the epistemology of empiricism, with its interest in collecting and organizing sense data, and enlists that epistemology in the service of its own theological ends. Indeed, Boswell attributes his zeal to preserve details of Johnson's dress and demeanor in the *Journal of a Tour of the Hebrides* to the authority of Boswell's old teacher Adam Smith: "Let me not be censured for mentioning such minute particulars. Everything relative to so great a man is worth observing. I remember Dr. Adam Smith, in his rhetorical lectures at Glasgow, told us he was glad to know that Milton wore latchets in his shoes instead of buckles."[46]

The literal-minded reader might register a protest here: surely literary reputation and the theological afterlife are apples and oranges, and documenting continuities in language or imagery between the two does nothing to change this fact. Does this study offer nothing but "new-historicist homologies," in Christian Thorne's damning phrase, in which "the simile is the chief argumentative figure," and puns bear the weight of historical argument?[47] A first-order answer would be that this study does not, in general, undertake to be wiser than its subjects, and does not seek to draw connections (between republication and resurrection, between the epistolary novel and the Book of Life, between friendship in collaborative writing and friendship in heaven) where they do not. The similes in question are the texts'; they are not mine. A second-order answer comes from an anecdote in Boswell's *London Journal,* the diary Boswell kept during a year spent sampling the pleasures of metropolitan life before settling down to the legal career marked out for him by his dominating father. George Dempster and Andrew Erskine, two of Boswell's Scottish cronies in London, tricked him with a forged letter from David Hume, which combines "genteel compliments" for Boswell with a recommendation of its bearer, a cousin of Dempster's for whom Boswell entertained "a very great antipathy."[48] Boswell, in his late teens, still viewed Hume as an attractive celebrity, not a perturbing skeptic, and his pride was immensely swollen by "Hume's" compliments and correspondingly crushed when his companions revealed their deception. Boswell's response to his disappointment, astonishingly, was to write a letter to the real David Hume enclosing the forgery, telling the whole story, and asking Hume to correspond with him: "You will give me a triumph over my facetious tormenters when they find that I really possess what I was so vain of in imagination; and in short you will give much happiness to your, &c., James Boswell." Hume, in no very good humor with Boswell because of an unrelated piece of cheekiness (Boswell had repeated in print a remark Hume had allegedly made in private), sent a testy reply a week later. Imagination, for Boswell as for Keats, is like Adam's dream; he wakes to find it truth.

The wish-fulfilling logic that transmutes a forged letter from Hume into the real thing is the same logic that infers the existence of heaven from man's desire for fame. Indeed, the idea that the afterlife must exist because we long for it, known as the "argument from desire," had a long and respectable intellectual pedigree in the eighteenth century.[49]

The chapters that follow trace the emergence of the paradigm of prose immortality and cognate changes in the conception of the Christian afterlife over the course of the eighteenth century. This story begins with chapters on *The Spectator* (1711–12) and Edward Young's *Night Thoughts* (1742–45), two texts that use periodical publication and a concatenative, non-narrative form to imagine the afterlife in terms borrowed from modern chronometry and secular time. As a periodical paper, the *Spectator* is diurnal; as a succession of poetic "nights," Young's poem is nocturnal. Both texts combine consideration of literary immortality with a concern for preparing their reader for an eternity of progressive development. I then offer a brief intellectual-historical sketch of what was at stake in mid-century arguments about the afterlife before turning to Samuel Richardson's two most ambitious novels, *Clarissa* (1747–48) and *Sir Charles Grandison* (1753). These texts represent two different attempts, the former tragic and the latter comic, to integrate the new conception of immortality developed by Addison and Young into narrative prose. *Clarissa* forces readers to imagine its heroine entering into heaven, while *Sir Charles Grandison* draws attention to the afterlife through a typology that unites "changing one's state" from singleness to marriage and "changing one's state" from life to immortality. Finally, I look at authors who theorize and practice afterlife writing, using prose to preserve themselves and others in texts that reflect anxieties about personal survival: Laetitia Pilkington's *Memoirs* (1748–54), the essays and other writings of Samuel Johnson, and James Boswell's *Life of Johnson* (1791). I close with a brief discussion of Keats and the dream of an anecdotal biography of Shakespeare, which I read as an expression of the curiosity and desire aroused by the prose immortality paradigm. Keats speaks for many late-eighteenth-century figures when he yearns to know more about Shakespeare than the surviving sixteenth- and seventeenth-century record can provide.

I proceed chronologically, and inasmuch as the authors examined in earlier chapters were in nearly all cases well known, not only textually but also personally, to their successors, I posit a coherent cross-generic tradition that runs through the periodical paper, long poem, novel, memoir, and biography, and from the final years of Queen Anne to the French Revolution. It is no coincidence that it is also a "canonical" tradition. Some of the authors considered here were born into the genteel-clerical elite of the long eighteenth century (Addison, Boswell), while others began in the upper station of low life (Richardson, Johnson). But, with the exception of Laetitia Pilkington, they all positioned themselves and each other as writers at the moral and social center of British society. Their desires for literary immortality found willing collaborators in eighteenth- and nineteenth-century figures looking to build a national-linguistic canon.

Vita brevis, ars longa; much more can and should be written about the intersection of literary and Christian immortality in eighteenth-century authors beyond the orbit of this study: in spiritual autobiographies and Calvinist devotional writings; in the novels of Defoe, Fielding, Sterne, and Smollett; in the narrative and homiletic works of the Methodist movement, including Charles Wesley's *Arminian Magazine;* and even in secular memoirists and life writers such as Lord Hervey, Lord Chesterfield, and Horace Walpole. This study does in a few places gesture to the reception of ideas about immortality and textual preservation beyond the main stream of its narrative, usually to show that eighteenth- and nineteenth-century readers' responses to texts anticipate my own: such responses include Benjamin Franklin's reading of the *Spectator,* William Blake's illustrations of *Night Thoughts,* Goethe's aspiration to write a novel like *Clarissa,* and Oliver Wendell Holmes's annual rereading of Boswell.

The legacy of prose immortality in my own early-twenty-first-century time of writing is an ambiguous one. On the one hand, the nineteenth through twenty-first centuries have yielded technologies, from the Dictaphone to the online social media profile, that can create a documentary record of daily human life more vivid, detailed, and chronometrically exact than even Boswell could have dreamed. We share the eighteenth century's appetite for minute self-documentation, and are thus in some sense heirs to the developments that this book chronicles. At the same time, aspirations for posthumous fame have largely given way to the desire for this-worldly celebrity or social-technological connectedness among both religious and nonreligious members of the secular West. Boswell's impulse to create a record that will last through time has given way to the practice of diffusing minute updates to our physical or mental status across space to a network of readers and viewers. In part, then, the object of this study is to demonstrate that a characteristically modern impulse with its roots in the eighteenth century—the longing to document even the most seemingly minor parts of our lives—was undertaken by our predecessors for reasons fascinatingly different from our own. We, of all people, are the literary afterlife that they have. They have given us so much, and we owe it to them and to ourselves to understand what their wishes and desires were.

Part One

DAILY TIME
AND
HORIZONTAL
FUTURITY

1

The Afterlife and the *Spectator*

When Richard Steele began his pioneering periodical, the *Tatler,* in 1709, he borrowed from Jonathan Swift both the name of his narrator, "Isaac Bickerstaff, Esq.," and the comic doctrine that life and death are in the eye of the beholder, questions of degree rather than irrevocable absolutes.[1] Swift's Bickerstaff had predicted the astrologer John Partridge's death and then indignantly rebutted Partridge's claims to be still alive.[2] Steele's Bickerstaff claims the power to "confute other dead Men, who pretend to be in Being" but are "actually deceased." Swift's satire, against the pretensions of astrology and Partridge's anti–High Church demagogy, is broadened to a general program of moral improvement, as the *Tatler* gives "all Men fair Warning to mend their Manners," since "they who are good for Nothing shall find themselves in the Number of the Deceased."[3]

Recent studies of Addison and Steele, and of the *Tatler* and the *Spectator* in particular, have shied away from matters of life and death. Extensive attention has been paid to Addison's role as a founding figure of English literary criticism, and numerous scholars have written to amplify or critique Jürgen Habermas's use of the *Spectator* as a founding site of the public sphere.[4] Sometimes stated and often implied in these accounts has been the claim, as Erin Mackie puts it, that the *Spectator* is backed by "a secure secularism and a tacit acceptance of the basic principle of consumption: that human desires are valid."[5]

I argue that the secularism of the *Spectator* is not as secure as recent studies have assumed. The paper's formal innovations and enormous influence in the eighteenth century are interventions in the theological world of late

Stuart and Hanoverian Britain, and specifically in that world's understanding of the afterlife. Addison and Steele's didactic jokes about the living dead double in a comic register their more serious accounts of the relationship between life, death, and immortality, in which the value and purpose of the first two are grounded in a confident belief in the third. The *Spectator* is part of a culture-wide program of moral improvement and reform that includes an outpouring of didactic writing in the decades following the Glorious Revolution.[6] For the writers of the *Spectator,* daily life as lived and documented sets the human being on a trajectory that continues into the afterlife. A well-lived life in the day-to-day is the guarantor of a happy futurity. The periodical paper, with its daily increments of edifying content, is, conveniently, the perfect technology for readers seeking to work out their salvation with diligence.

The periodical paper is among the textual genres that create what Walter Benjamin calls "homogeneous, empty time," a characteristically modern sense of time as quotidian, sequential, unstructured, and linear.[7] Journalistic clock time replaces Partridge's astrological time. But even while it creates this new sense of empty time, the *Spectator* provides a new kind of plenitude, a daily regimen of moral formation that can be extrapolated into "futurity." The *Spectator* reimagines the Christian afterlife not as a judgment, but as a continuation of life lived on earth. In other words, the *Spectator* trains the reader to fill empty time with progress toward eternity. It is no coincidence that the *Spectator*'s own material, literary-historical afterlife doubles its rhetorical program. Republication and canonization extend its papers from a life of daily publication into an afterlife of more permanent, collected volumes and rereading. Though Addison and Steele, having renounced prognostication, could not foresee the enormous influence and prestige of the *Spectator* in its eighteenth- and nineteenth-century reception, their work strives for and anticipates that reception. The "periodical eternity" of the *Spectator* grew into a powerful presence for its eighteenth- and nineteenth-century readers.

The *Spectator* and the Emptiness of Time

Benjamin's "homogeneous, empty time" has provided scholars with a powerful concept for articulating what is distinctive about time in the modern West. As Stuart Sherman points out, however, Benjamin and theorists such as Benedict Anderson who have built on his insights see the emptiness of time as something waiting to be filled: "by 'progress' in Benjamin's argument, by 'nation' in Anderson's." Sherman proposes his own source of fullness, arguing that for diarists like Samuel Pepys, time is filled by "narrative portioned to the new time's terms[,] . . . a plenum of narrative within each day, and a plenum of narrated days within the calendar."[8] Charles Taylor, meanwhile, uses the concept of narrative in a rather different way to argue that "homogeneity and emptiness don't tell the full story of modern time-consciousness," because "we have forms of narrativity, gathered around notions of potential and maturation, which make different time-placings significant."[9]

What is relevant here is that the *Spectator* contains all of the hallmarks of modern homogeneous, empty time, including the simultaneity emphasized by Anderson and the absence of a "higher" time—the time of prophecy on fulfillment still present in the astrological predictions of John Partridge—emphasized by Taylor. The *Spectator* was the first periodical paper to be published daily in English. With the exception of the *Daily Courant*, a newspaper begun shortly before, it was the first truly daily publication in English *tout court*.[10] As Sherman has argued, time, rather than narrative or theme, was its organizing principle.[11]

The conviction shared by Benjamin, Anderson, Sherman, and Taylor, that the "empty time" characteristic of modernity necessarily contains the potential to be filled with something, serves as a helpful point of departure for describing exactly how time functions in the *Spectator*. Taylor's concept of "forms of narrativity, gathered around notions of potential and maturation" may be the most useful in articulating how the *Spectator* represents time that has in a sense been emptied, denuded of messianic or supernatural meaning, but can nevertheless be full. But the notions of potential and maturation in the *Spectator* are not narrative per se, but moral. In its diurnality, the periodical does not record a "story" of lived time the way, for instance, Pepys's diary does. Rather, its successive papers constitute a regimen of moral improvement for its readers.

The narrative arc of the *Spectator*, in fact, is found not in the papers themselves, but in the reader, who, the periodical implies, is to be informed, entertained, and above all improved over the course of its run. Over time, the *Spectator*'s moral regimen is cumulative; as I will argue in greater detail below, the moral weight of each individual *Spectator* compounds the *Spectators* that have gone before. And its regimen is teleological. Taylor's word "maturation" is apposite here, because it refers to both the process (the reader's "maturing") and the end (the reader's "having matured") of the interaction between the *Spectator* and its audience. As the German proverb has it, *der Weg ist das Ziel,* the way is the goal. The reader undertakes the paper's program in daily time, and each day the reader proceeds through that time toward eternity.

Periodical Eternity

The nature of the afterlife has occupied Christian thinkers from the authors of the New Testament forward, and history records an enormous variety of theories, accounts, and depictions of life after death. The *Spectator,* like innumerable Christian texts before it, frequently directs its readers' attention to the afterlife, also called "immortality" or "futurity." Scholars eager to establish the paper's secular credentials, or simply uninterested in noting its use of religious discourse, have not emphasized this element, but its quantitative presence and thematic force in the *Spectator* are undeniable.[12]

Indeed, the periodical offers an innovative and influential theory of the afterlife. To understand the originality of its depiction, some broader context is necessary.[13]

In its most basic form, the Christian doctrine of the afterlife from the late Middle Ages to the beginning of the eighteenth century was as follows: At death, the soul is separated from the body. At some future point, they will be reunited in the Resurrection to face God's Last Judgment. Thereafter the judged will spend eternity either with God in heaven or without him in hell. Heaven and hell were understood in terms of a vertical hierarchy still familiar today, with heaven located above the earth, and hell below.

Within this basic framework existed enormous variation. The fate of the soul in the interim between death and resurrection was an important point of controversy. Positions ranged from mortalism, the doctrine that the soul slept unconscious or was even annihilated before being re-created by God on the Last Day, to sophisticated systems of purgatory, in which imperfect Catholics could expiate sins which they had repented of but could not do complete penance for on earth, aided by prayers, masses, and pious legacies provided for by their wills—not to mention the indulgences that the church had the power to grant. In between these extremes lay the belief that the soul entered immediately into salvation or perdition at death, with the Last Judgment serving as something of a formality.

The criteria for a favorable divine judgment were also disputed. For strict predestinarian Calvinists and Jansenists, salvation lay entirely in the inscrutable will of God, and the prospects for any given individual ranged from uncertain to bleak. For the broad stream of post-Tridentine Catholics, dying without mortal sin was sufficient to reach heaven eventually. This meant that the timing of death could be highly significant, hence Hamlet's reluctance to kill Claudius while the latter is in prayer, "in the purging of his soul / When he is fit and seasoned for the passage" (*Hamlet* 3.3.85–86). Catholics, as well as Arminians and other Protestants who resisted the stark logic of predestination, could hope for an efficacious last-minute repentance. An epitaph, reported by William Camden in 1605, records the testimony of a wicked man that "Betwixt the stirrop and the ground, / Mercy I askt, mercy I found."[14]

Finally, Christians differed on what the afterlife was actually like. Most thought of hell in terms that can be traced back to antiquity and that remain recognizable today: fire, torment, darkness, being underground. But visions of heaven were more varied. In particular, some theologians (Richard Baxter, for example) emphasized what Colleen McDannell and Bernhard Lang call a "theocentric heaven," derived in the first instance from the book of Revelation, in which human pleasures and relationships were subsumed in the overwhelming presence of God, toward whom the saved directed their undivided, worshipful attention.[15] Others (see, for instance, the second part of Bunyan's *Pilgrim's Progress*) imagined a more humanized heaven in which licit human pleasures and relationships, particularly ties of kinship, marriage, and friendship, continued in a new form.[16]

The *Spectator* is at the vanguard of an eighteenth-century revision of the fundamental shared assumptions described above, offering a different understanding both of the prospect of future judgment and of the hierarchy of heaven above and hell below. Divine judgment recedes in importance, and the metaphor underpinning the paper's frequent discussions of the afterlife is no longer vertical, but rather horizontal; existence after death is seen as a continuation of a trajectory begun on earth, an extension to its logical conclusion of a regimen of habits created in daily life. While references to "heaven" as the site of human immortality are not uncommon in the *Spectator*, "hell" appears very rarely, unless used metaphorically or otherwise cordoned off from its traditional Christian doctrinal denotation.[17] And the dominant metaphor is not of reward above and punishment below, but rather a "beyond" toward which the entire course of lived life tends, one day at a time. The "Vision of Mirzah" in *Spectator* 159, for instance, includes an endless archipelago of delightful islands, "the Mansions of good Men after Death," who are "distributed" among them "according to the Degree and Kinds of Virtue in which they excelled" in life (2:125). Using a landscape as an allegory for human time, Addison connects life to its continuation via the horizontal metaphor of a stream running to islands in the ocean, rather than the vertical topology of earlier allegorical texts such as *The Divine Comedy,* or *The Pilgrim's Progress,* whose heavenly city is "higher than the clouds," and in which Ignorance learns to his cost that habits and practices built over time are worth nothing, and "there [is] a way to Hell, even from the Gates of Heaven."[18] For the *Spectator,* the human afterlife is not so much beyond time as an extrapolation of it.

This view finds its most explicit statement in *Spectator* 447, by Addison. After an extended discussion of custom as "a second nature" that has "a wonderful Efficacy in making every thing pleasant to us," the narrator draws the implications for moral life:

> The last Use which I shall make of this remarkable Property in Human Nature, of being delighted with those Actions to which it is accustomed, is to shew how absolutely necessary it is for us to gain Habits of Virtue in this Life, if we would enjoy the Pleasures of the next. The State of Bliss we call Heaven will not be capable of affecting those Minds, which are not thus qualified for it; we must, in this World, gain a Relish of Truth and Virtue, if we would be able to taste that Knowledge and Perfection, which are to make us happy in the next. The Seeds of those spiritual Joys and Raptures, which are to rise up and Flourish in the Soul to all Eternity, must be planted in her, during this her present State of Probation. In short, Heaven is not to be looked upon only as the Reward, but as the natural Effect of a religious Life. (4:72)

Addison echoes the Bible, including Jesus's words to Andrew and Philip in John 12:24 ("Except a corn of wheat fall into the ground and die, it abideth alone: but if it die, it bringeth forth much fruit") and, particularly, Paul's account of the resurrection in 1 Corinthians 15:35–38, 42–44:

> But some man will say, How are the dead raised up? and with what body do they come? Thou fool, that which thou sowest is not quickened, except it die: And that which thou sowest, thou sowest not that body that shall be, but bare grain, it may chance of wheat, or of some other grain: But God giveth it a body as it hath pleased him, and to

every seed his own body.... So also is the resurrection of the dead. It is sown in corruption; it is raised in incorruption: It is sown in dishonour; it is raised in glory: It is sown in weakness; it is raised in power: It is sown a natural body; it is raised a spiritual body.

Addison adopts Paul's metaphor of germination as resurrection, but he reverses the meaning. In the first letter to the Corinthians, the emphasis is on discontinuity. The sequence of antonyms in 15:42–44 underlines the total alterity of the resurrected self, which is imagined as a plant, from the mortal self, imagined as a seed. For Addison, the point is continuity, heaven as the "natural Effect" of a religious life. In his metaphor, the soul is an enduring field or portion of earth, in which "Joys and Raptures" are the seeds planted in this world to bloom in the next. No longer a homogeneous site of unearthly bliss, heaven becomes personalized, customized, an extension of the unique qualities of the individual self as developed in earthly existence.

Spectator 447 presents most clearly and systematically the model of a horizontal afterlife extrapolated from the habits and practices of mortal life, but similar statements can be found over the entire course of the paper. *Spectator* 90, also by Addison, describes the Platonic doctrine that "every Passion which has been contracted by the Soul during her Residence in the Body, remains with her in a separate State" (1:381). The body's inability to satisfy these passions thus constitutes its punishment after death; the terms and conditions of the afterlife are, as it were, established on earth. Addison's *Spectator* 93 focuses on the importance of using time virtuously, particularly filling up the "empty Spaces of Life": "If we consider further, that the Exercise of Virtue is not only an Amusement for the time it lasts, but that its Influence extends to those Parts of our Existence which lie beyond the Grave, and that our whole Eternity is to take its Colour from those Hours which we here employ in Virtue or in Vice, the Argument redoubles upon us, for putting in Practice this Method of passing away our Time" (1:396).

Another framing of this relationship between time and eternity can be found in number 111, which argues for the immortality of the soul using what Robert Walker calls "the argument from desire," or, as Addison puts it, "the perpetual Progress of the Soul to its Perfection, without a Possibility of ever arriving at it." Given the infinite potential in the human soul, it is impossible to believe that a beneficent creator would make the soul "perish at her first setting out, and in the very beginning of her Enquiries" (1:456–59).[19]

Emphases vary, but the underlying argument is repeated again and again: the afterlife continues and extends life as lived on earth. Because earthly life takes place in horizontal, daily time, our choice of virtuous habits, cemented by repetition, creates gradual moral improvement within us and thereby determines the cast of our life in eternity.[20] In the context of this repeated theme, even papers whose focus is not explicitly on eternity have their morals weighed down by it, as is the case of number 317, in which Mr. Spectator exhorts his readers "to keep a Journal of their Lives for one Week" to "incline them to consider seriously what they are about," and number 323, in which Mr. Spectator prints the journal of a leisured gentlewoman, supposedly written after reading number 317, and ironically exhorts the author to "consider what a pretty Figure she would make among Posterity, were the History of her whole Life published like these five days of it" (3:156, 185).

In its attention to habit and in its view of the afterlife as a trajectory, rather than a judgment, the *Spectator* can draw on a deep classical tradition that emphasizes gradual moral formation and the importance of building habits. The word "ethics," after all, comes from *ethos,* a Greek word that means "habit" as well as "character" or "manners." In *Spectator* 447, Addison cites a precept given by Pythagoras to his disciples: "Pitch upon that Course of Life which is the most Excellent, and Custom will render it the most Delightful" (4:71). In the same vein, he paraphrases a maxim of Hesiod that the Gods "have placed Labour before Virtue" (4:72). But the *Spectator* also refines and extends a new theological emphasis that had become current in latitudinarian Anglicanism toward the end of the seventeenth century. Later in *Spectator* 447, Addison traces his "Notion of Heaven and Hell" not only to "several of the most exalted Heathens" but also to "many Eminent Divines of the last Age," citing by name John Tillotson, William Sherlock, and John Scott (4:73). In the preface to his *Christian Life,* John Scott states that "the Practice of every Vertue is an essential Part of the Christian Life, and a necessary Means to the blessed End of it . . . in the Practice of it we do naturally grow up to the heavenly State."[21] Sherlock makes a similar claim: "If we die with Christ, we shall rise with him also into immortal Life, which is begun in this world, and will be perfected in the next."[22] Indeed, he anticipates the Bickerstaff/Partridge comedy by proclaiming that sinners are not really alive, even on earth (171–75). This leads Sherlock to place weight on daily moral and spiritual practice, on making "Religion, and the care of our Souls, the work of every day, as much as eating and drinking to preserve our bodily health and strength" (215, see also 258–59). Yet ultimately he ends with the more traditional "betwixt the stirrop and the ground" theology: "When God comes to judge the World, he will judge Men as he finds them; he will not inquire what they have been, but what they are" (271). Tillotson, meanwhile, closely anticipates Addison: "Our souls will continue forever what we make them in this world. Such a temper and disposition of mind as a man carries with him out of this world he will retain in the next."[23] Tillotson's theology is by no means hegemonic in the eighteenth century, but given the enduring popularity of his works (160 publications between 1695, the year following his death, and 1757), it is indisputably influential.[24]

Earlier texts by Addison and Steele place them in this Anglican cultural stream, emphasizing moral formation over time rather than Catholic absolution or Calvinist election. Steele offers the life of Paul as an exemplum in *The Christian Hero* (1701), focusing not on the saint's martyrdom but on the daily life that led to it: "Shall we search Antiquity for the Period and Consummation of his Illustrious Life, to give him the Crown and Glory of Martyrdom? That were a needless Labour. . . . We may . . . dismiss him with the just Eulogy in his own spritely Expression that he *Dy'd daily*."[25] But the *Spectator* marks a crucial stage in the development of this conception because it embodies formally what Scott, Tillotson, and to a lesser extent Sherlock argue rhetorically. Before *Spectator* 447 invokes Pythagoras and Tillotson on the virtues of habit, it begins with a story about an "Ideot that chancing to live within the Sound of a Clock, and always amusing himself with counting the Hour of the Day whenever the Clock struck, the Clock being spoiled by some Accident, the Ideot continued to strike and count the Hour without the help of it, in the same manner as he had done when it was entire" (4:70). The first use of habit that the *Spectator* discusses comprises bending the rhythms of the human body to the divisions of chronometry. By the same token, the *Spectator*'s daily publication schedule means that it performs the regimen of moral improvement, the daily work of achieving a blessed afterlife, which its predecessors merely recommend.

As mentioned above, the *Spectator* is the first truly daily periodical paper. Stuart Sherman quotes the poet John Gay expressing wonder at the simple fact of the paper's endurance, day after day: "We had at first indeed no manner of Notion, how a Diurnal Paper could be continu'd in the Spirit and Stile of our present SPECTATORS; but to our no small Surprize, we find them still rising upon us."[26] The *Spectator*'s relationship to time was a crucial part of its novelty and popularity, and it made significant demands upon its authors' own time.[27] The diurnal and sabbatarian rhythms of calendrical time are as basic to the form of the *Spectator* as the half-folio page itself, and, as with all literary texts, form overflows inexorably into content. Mr. Spectator makes daily repetition a cornerstone of his oft-cited programmatic statement of purpose in *Spectator* 10:

> I shall endeavour to enliven Morality with Wit, and to temper Wit with Morality, that my Readers may, if possible, both Ways find their Account in the Speculation of the Day. And to the End that their Virtue and Discretion may not be short transient intermitting Starts of Thought, I have resolved to refresh their Memories from Day to Day, till I have recovered them out of that desperate State of Vice and Folly into which the Age is fallen. The Mind that lies fallow but a single Day, sprouts up in Follies that are only to be killed by a constant and assiduous Culture. (1:44)

This passage is in part a well-tuned sales pitch: the reader cannot afford to miss a single day. But Addison's account of Mr. Spectator as a gardener who must weed every day also sows the metaphorical seeds that come to full fruition in the account of immortality in *Spectator* 447.

The *Spectator* repeats its lesson about the value of repetition: the image of weeding a garden each day is transformed in number 134 into a daily medicinal prescription, in which the *Spectator* is imagined as a series of "daily Refreshments" that "offer an infallible Cure of Vice and Folly, for the Price of One Penny" (2:29–30). The advertisement section at the end of the paper, in which nostrums and patent medicines for physical rather than moral ills figure prominently, here spills over into the main section.[28] In number 215, meanwhile, Mr. Spectator is a sculptor, who "from Day to Day contribute[s] something to the polishing of Men's Minds" (2:341).

This is only one of many instances in which the *Spectator* puts its theoretical program into practice: having used repetition to convince his readers that repetition is morally formative, Mr. Spectator uses repetition to teach them a wide variety of other lessons as well.[29] Over the course of the series, these moral exhortations build up a cumulative weight. This is not created by means of narrative concatenation; although many papers can be linked with one or two others to form micro-dialogues or micro-narratives, the papers do not add up to a single story from which, taken as a whole, one "particular Moral" can be inferred.[30] Nor do the papers effect moral improvement through repetition of formula or liturgy, like the Book of Common Prayer or other devotional manuals popular at the turn of the eighteenth century. Rather, the *Spectator* attempts to effect moral amelioration by means of repetition with difference. Each *Spectator* reminds the reader, usually implicitly, of preceding papers on its topic, while informing the reader with a new exhortation or admonition. By the end of the series, the papers show awareness of the method at work: "You have often," the correspondent of number 503 begins, "mention'd with great Vehemence and Indignation the Misbehavior of people at Church; but I am at present to talk to you on that subject" (4:284). With each new paper, the reader too becomes aware of the precedent and cumulative weight created by all the papers that have gone before, even if none is mentioned by name. At the same time, the lack of a single narrative thread means that the paper can appeal to casual or sporadic readers as well, though they may be aware that they are missing some of the intertextual richness of a given paper. The principle of cumulative moral formation thus cleverly makes the *Spectator* a paper that both offers something to everyone and promises added value to loyal customers. The more *Spectators* one has read, the more edifying each individual *Spectator* becomes. For readers who have assimilated the *Spectator*'s theology of eternity as a continuation of earthly habits, the stakes are high. Every day, "homogeneous, empty time" is filled with another *pensum* of personal improvement, and the reader's prospects for eternity improve accordingly.

"The Monument": Publication and Futurity

The *Spectator* does not merely promote a regime of moral self-improvement in time; as a literary artifact, it also embodies the relationship between life and afterlife that it inculcates in its pages. The coordination of multiple temporalities is the periodical paper's generic stock in trade, after all. In most literary genres, the author's time of composition is unmoored from the time of publication, which itself has no necessary connection to the reader or audience's time of reception. In contrast, the daily sequence of the original *Spectator* papers is tethered as solidly as writing can ever be to the passage of time from March 1, 1711, to December 6, 1712. In coffee shops, private homes, and Queen Anne's palace, publication and reception were all but simultaneous as the papers were devoured hot from the press.[31] Although some papers were reworked from earlier material, the paper's time of composition is closely coordinated with its audience's time of reading and the passage of time itself, as its letters from correspondents, comments on current events, and puffs of contemporary performances and publications indicate.[32] In the date at the top of each paper, the *Spectator*'s time of reception is located in the wider passage of modern calendrical time.[33] As I have argued, the organizing principle of the *Spectator*'s sequence is not narrative, like a story in which the beginning comes before the end, or associational, like a commonplace book or anthology that is organized by theme: rather, it is purely temporal. Of course, this concatenation of composition, publication, and reception is a feature of many periodical genres, inherent in newspapers like Steele's *London Gazette,* as well as the *Tatler* or the *Spectator.* Unique and significant about Addison and Steele's periodical essays, particularly the *Spectator,* is the way they construct and invite not only contemporary reading but also an afterlife of rereading.

Confidence in its own lastingness is a feature of the *Spectator* from its opening months; as early as *Spectator* 78, in fact, Steele expresses the conviction (in the mouth of an anonymous correspondent) that the paper "will always live" (1:334). *Spectator* 101, in which an "Imaginary Historian" of a succeeding century praises Mr. Spectator, notes that the essays are "still extant" three hundred years later—in 2011, that is. The Imaginary Historian does not explain how he came by his copies of the *Spectator,* but readers of the original folios might have found a clue at the head of the paper's fourth column, which advertises that "Compleat Setts of this Paper for the Month of May" are available for sale by a variety of purveyors. One seller also has sets of March and April, that is, the paper's complete run to date. In fact, the first notice of this kind appeared in *Spectator* 29, on April 3, offering complete sets for March, and these advertisements appeared frequently thereafter. From its earliest numbers, the *Spectator* invited not only daily consumption but also accumulation, acquisition of a complete set.[34] Within the first few months of the paper's run, moreover, Addison, Steele, and the publishers Jacob Tonson and Samuel Buckley began negotiations for the publication of the *Spectator* in volumes, a form that number 307 explicitly links to literary immortality: "Your Speculations are now swelling into Volumes," a correspondent tells Mr. Spectator, "and will in all probability pass down to future Ages" (3:105). Papers 1 through 169 had indeed been published in two octavo volumes on January 8, 1712, the same day that number 269 appeared in half folio, and the octavos were followed by a duodecimo edition ten days later. With the beginning of volume publication, advertisements for assembled sets ceased. Volumes 3 and 4 followed as 1712 and the *Spectator*'s daily publication were both drawing to a close, and the final three volumes of the original 555-paper run came out in April 1713 (1:lxxii–lxiii). These volumes conspicuously reproduce the dates of original publication; the date is placed in larger print above the motto in the first volume edition, as opposed to smaller print below, as in the original folios. Yet volume publication necessarily unmoors the *Spectator* from its periodical time-scheme, inviting rereading. Even before Mr. Spectator has printed himself out from day to day, bound volumes give him an afterlife.[35]

There is a clear analogy between the *Spectator*'s publication history—first in daily installments connected by the passage of time, then in monthly sets of these installments, and finally in collected volumes in which the installments are reprinted sequentially, their dates prominently displayed, but no longer structured by diurnality—and its theology of daily moral formation creating a posthumous trajectory. The paper explicitly canvasses this analogy between literary posterity and personal immortality. *Spectator* 166 describes writing as humanity's only way of achieving permanence on earth: "There is no other Method of fixing those Thoughts which arise and disappear in the Mind of Man, and transmitting them to the last Periods of time; no other Method of giving a Permanency to our Ideas, and preserving the Knowledge of any particular Person, when his Body is mixed with the common mass of Matter, and his Soul retired into the World of Spirits" (2:154). It then goes on to link this earthly version of immortality to its spiritual counterpart: "I have seen some Roman-Catholick Authors, who tell us that vicious Writers continue in Purgatory so long as the Influence of their Writings continues upon Posterity" (2:155). As the original run of the *Spectator* draws to a close in the final months of 1712, a letter from an unnamed correspondent continues this line of thought, in terms that clearly pertain to the paper's legacy: "When Men of worthy and excelling Genius's have obliged the World with beautiful and instructive Writings, it is in the nature of Gratitude that Praise shou'd be return'd them. . . . They are admitted into the highest Companies, and they continue pleasing and instructing Posterity from Age to Age" (551, 4:471–72). "They" refers unambiguously back to "Men"; the paper thus conflates authors and their works, making the former the interlocutors and instructors of those who read the latter in posterity. The metaphorical equation of works and authors is a commonplace, of course, but it is particularly appropriate to Mr. Spectator/*The Spectator,* who himself hovers conspicuously between personhood and textuality.

Two papers later, another letter confirms that the *Spectator*'s destiny is indeed the "pleasing and instructing" of "Companions." A group of Oxonians, with the rallying cry "O Spec, live for ever," has convened a club to preserve Mr. Spectator: "To speak plain, there are a number of us who have begun your Works afresh, and meet two Nights in the Week in order to give you a Rehearing. We never come together without drinking your Health, and as seldom part without general Expressions of Thanks to you for our Night's Improvement" (553, 4:486). The members of Mr. Spectator's own club (Sir Roger de Coverley, Will Honeycomb, Sir Andrew Freeport, and so on) have variously died, married, retired, gone into business—they have in turn met the ends that conclude tragedies, comedies, Bildungsromane, and other narrative genres. But as Mr. Spectator himself withdraws from the stage, his essays enter a posterity in which they can be reheard eternally. Indeed, this rehearing is imagined to happen in a reduced version of the same periodical schedule ("two Nights in the Week" rather than six mornings) on which the *Spectator* was first published. Enabled by volume publication, the *Spectator* can model as a literary effect the periodical eternity that its essays have commended throughout as a philosophical doctrine. Unlike other published works that lay claim to literary immortality, the *Spectator's* volumes, with their papers' original dates prominently displayed, point insistently back to the day-to-day schedule in which those papers were originally published. Printing himself from day to day, Mr. Spectator has constructed his own immortality.

Conclusion: The Afterlife of the *Spectator*

The final *Spectator* paper, number 555, presents its readers with something new: an author's signature. In that paper, Richard Steele takes his leave in propria persona, handsomely acknowledging his chief collaborator, without, at Addison's own request, identifying him by name. Steele praises Addison as follows: "I am indeed much more proud of his long continued Friendship, than I should be of the Fame of being thought the Author of any Writings which he himself is capable of producing. I remember when I finished the *Tender Husband,* I told him there was nothing I so ardently wished, as that we might some time or other publish a Work written by us both, which should bear the Name of *the Monument,* in Memory of our Friendship" (4:492–93). In the first sentence quoted, Steele downplays literary fame, which he subordinates to "long continued Friendship." But in the second, he synthesizes the two into a literary *"Monument"* that will commemorate friendship over time by virtue of its collaborative composition. That synthesis, a literary artifact whose enduring fame will preserve its creators' friendship, is, of course, the *Spectator*. Steele's final number makes an audacious claim: he imagines that daily periodical papers, sold for a penny, perhaps reused to line pie pans, can cumulatively erect a monument, an assertion that historically belonged to self-consciously permanent literary texts like Horace's odes or Shakespeare's sonnets. At the same time, this is a claim that has run throughout the paper. Eternity, both personal and literary, is built day upon day.

Addison and Steele's periodical was spectacularly successful in achieving the reception it imagined for itself. *The Conscious Lovers,* a play by Steele staged in 1722, three years after Addison's death, features a character reading *Spectator* 159 (which he describes as "This charming vision of Mirza") and rhapsodizing that "these moral writers practice virtue after death" and that "such an author consulted in a morning sets the spirit for the vicissitudes of the day better than the glass does a man's person."[36] A decade after the end of the paper's original run, Steele imagines Addison living on as his papers are reread morning after morning. James Boswell, who read the *Spectator* repeatedly and alludes to it frequently in his journal, used the paper's technique of repetition with difference in the monitory "memoranda" he kept as a discipline for moral formation.[37] Similarly, Benjamin Franklin records rereading and even rewriting the *Spectator* in order to undertake the regime of self-culture that the papers offer.[38] Franklin's "Epitaph," written at the age of twenty-two, a few years after the era when his *Autobiography* records him reading the *Spectator* most frequently, perfectly expresses the relationship between publication and immortality that I have traced through the periodical:

> The Body of
> B. Franklin,
> Printer;
> Like the Cover of an Old Book,
> Its Contents torn out,
> And stript of its Lettering and Gilding,
> Lies here, Food for Worms.
> But the Work shall not be wholly lost:
> For it will, as he believ'd, appear once more,
> In a new & more perfect Edition,

Corrected and amended
By the Author.[39]

The Oxford students' cry of "O Spec, live for ever" cannot be far from Franklin's mind (553, 4:486). A century later, translating selections from the *Spectator* into Latin was a weekly exercise for undergraduates at Oxford.[40] Steele's fantasy of erecting a classical monument like that of Horace had come true. As its popularity from 1711 to 1712 and its enduring influence thereafter, through not only Boswell and Franklin but also Jane Austen, Thomas Babington Macaulay, and William Makepeace Thackeray, bear witness, the *Spectator* was written to be both of an age and for all time.

2

Night Thoughts
on Time, Fame, and Immortality

Edward Young was a lifelong disciple and admirer of Joseph Addison; he prefixed commendatory verses to *Cato* in 1713 and made Addison's Christian deathbed scene the centerpiece of his *Conjectures on Original Composition* (1759) nearly a half century later.[1] His magnum opus *Night Thoughts* both continues and revises the *Spectator*'s exploration of time and eternity through cumulative publication. At the time of its appearance in print over the period 1742–46, *Night Thoughts* was unprecedented in being structured not as a set number of books, cantos, or sections, but as an indefinitely continued sequence of "Nights." Its nocturnality is both the counterpart of Addison's diurnality (daily, immanent time of moral self-formation) and the negative shadow of the Christian eternity with which it is obsessed. For Young, time is mankind's only proper possession: "Nothing else / is truly Man's; 'tis Fortune's."[2] In contrast both to distant predecessors like Dante, who imagines hell, purgatory, and heaven as physical spaces in the universe, and to contemporaries like Tobias Swindon or William Whiston, who made the location of hell a subject of Newtonian scientific investigation, Young insistently conceives of the afterlife in temporal, rather than spatial, terms.[3] Young is concerned with what comes after this world, not what sits above it, and conceives of the human afterlife most fundamentally as an extension, not an ascension.[4]

As a long poem with little plot, *Night Thoughts* is not an obvious quarry for material to build an argument about the reinvention of literary immortality in narrative prose. Yet, as one of the most famous, widely read, and lasting poems of the mid-eighteenth century, it has internalized assumptions about time and immortality that connect its themes more closely to Addison or Samuel Richardson than to its classical or Miltonic predecessors. *Night Thoughts* juxtaposes personal and literary immortality, seeing the desire for fame both as a prefiguring type of the desire for eternal life and as a temptation that must be properly sublimated into piety. Even more important, it reimagines the epic in periodical terms, locating the search for eternity in a modern sense of time. It replaces formal and narrative poetic closure with open-endedness and succession. Moreover, Young's other works show that these links to the emerging prose immortality paradigm are not accidental. This chapter first examines *Night Thoughts,* then turns to the *Conjectures on Original Composition,* in which Young, writing in the genre of the critical essay, invokes Addison as an exemplary case for the ultimate unity of literary fame and Christian immortality. In self-consciously documenting and preserving Addison's pious deathbed performance for future generations, the *Conjectures* builds on the narrative techniques of Richardson and anticipates Boswell's *Life of Johnson* by establishing conduct in life, not poetic achievement, as the currency of monumental posthumous preservation.

On Not Reading *Night Thoughts*

Night Thoughts is a poem that needs an introduction. It has been customary since at least 1922 to preface critical discussions of Young's poem with a comment on its post-canonical status.[5] In the century following its publication, *Night Thoughts* enjoyed massive popularity and considerable critical acclaim. Goethe read *Night Thoughts* to learn English.[6] Blake illustrated the entire poem in a sequence of more than five hundred plates, and imitated its structure by dividing *The Four Zoas* into nine "Nights." As late as 1838, the clergyman-cum-critic James Montgomery could claim that "there are but four universally and permanently popular *long* poems in the English language,—'Paradise Lost,' 'The Night Thoughts,' 'The Task,' and 'The Seasons.'"[7] The fall of *Night Thoughts* to critical penny-stock status in the nineteenth century, with George Eliot invariably cited as the decisive short seller, was steep and by all appearances permanent.[8] A trickle of ongoing scholarly attention to *Night Thoughts* is an epiphenomenon of the increased volume of humanities research generally, rather than a sign of a Young revival. Indeed, the most interesting recent studies of *Night Thoughts* take its decline in critical prestige as an explanandum, casting Young either as the victim of reductive literary periodization that leaves him too Romantic to be an Augustan and too early to be a Romantic, or as an active harbinger of "the emerging cult of sensibility and sincerity" that was later to damn him.[9] And virtually all recent treatments of the poem, regardless of their own assessment, begin with some version of this paragraph, justifying themselves in advance for troubling the reader with Young in the first place. *Night Thoughts* carries no current critical calling cards: not part of the late-twentieth-century Western Canon, not a strategic resource for any school of identity studies, not an obvious antecedent of any important contemporary stream of thought.

My brief for *Night Thoughts* in this chapter is accordingly how it is a handmaiden to a larger eighteenth-century story about time and immortality. All literary evidence in a scholarly book must in some sense stand in this relationship of means to the book's arguments rather than an end in itself. Ordinarily, however, this instrumental use of the literary text is yoked to a reciprocal sense that the scholarly book is a means to greater understanding or appreciation of the work itself. But the critic who uses *Night Thoughts* as evidence, completing the first half of this gyre, must acknowledge the places in which the poem explicitly disavows the second half. Young's poem asks, at the end of its eighth *Night,* to be used as a means to salvation and then discarded, "well-pleas'd the Verse / Should be forgot, if you the Truths retain; / And crown her with your Welfare, not your Praise" (8.1389–91). Scholars who open their analyses of *Night Thoughts* with conscious reflection on why we should read *Night Thoughts* at all are paying Young the tribute of bringing to his work the same question that he did. We concur with Young in seeing *Night Thoughts* as a means—though we may use it to different ends than those he recommends.

Lorenzo, to Recriminate Is Just: Fame and Immortality

The long line of readers who have questioned the poem's continuing relevance and value are echoing a complex and defensive engagement with the prospect of literary fame already written into *Night Thoughts* itself. A scholarly work on literary immortality must include many prophesies happily fulfilled: we have already seen Mr. Spectator looking forward to an "Imaginary Historian describing the reign of *ANNE*" after "three hundred years," and we can commune with the narrator of *Tom Jones* when he modestly predicts that his books "will most probably outlive their own infirm Author, and the weakly Productions of his abusive Contemporaries."[10] *Night Thoughts,* in contrast, prophesies its own oblivion in the lines that follow those cited above:

> But *Praise* she need not fear; I see my Fate
>
> .   .   .   .
>
> Since many an ample *Volume,* mighty *Tome,*
> Must die; and die Unwept; O Thou minute,
> Devoted *Page!* go forth among thy Foes;
> Go, nobly proud of Martyrdom for Truth,
> And die a double Death: Mankind, incens'd,
> Denies thee long to live: Nor shalt thou rest,
> When thou art Dead, in *Stygian* Shades arraign'd
> By LUCIFER, as Traitor to his Throne. (8.1392, 1394–401)

Young preemptively casts his poem as not long for this world.

Young's pessimism about the literary future of *Night Thoughts* is particularly pronounced here in its eighth and penultimate *Night;* the enthusiasm of the book-buying public had waned as the poem modulated from the short threnodies à clef of *Nights* 1–4 to the longer and more abstract theological treatises of *Nights* 5–7, apparently to the point where Young thought of his readers as persecuting "Foes." However, the poem contains a similar sentiment as early as *Night the Second,* in a finely turned compliment to Young's physician, Richard Mead:

> That *Time* is mine, O Mead! to Thee I owe;
> Fain would I pay thee with *Eternity:*
> But ill my Genius answers my Desire,
> My sickly Song is mortal, past thy Cure.
> Accept the Will; It dies not with my strain. (2.39–43)

As a noted book collector and amateur of the classics (he was a close friend of Richard Bentley), Mead is presented with the flattering implication that his critical acumen could do as much for the poem, were it more deserving, as his medical expertise had done for its author during a critical illness in the summer of 1740. Young's accurate prophecy that he cannot guarantee literary "eternity" is a stroke of bad luck for Mead, whom modern readers of eighteenth-century literature are more likely to encounter instead as the sexually deviant "Dr. Kunastrokius" in *Tristram Shandy*.[11] In the opening lines of *Night the Seventh,* Young compresses the opposition of futile poetic lastingness to the true immortality promised by Christianity into a single ironic line addressed to another friend, recently deceased: "POPE, who couldst make immortals! art thou dead?" (7.6).

On the basis of these passages, one might argue that *Night Thoughts* simply reverses the polarity of Addison's union of fame and the Christian afterlife in the *Spectator* a generation before; instead of attracting each other, earthly immortality and heavenly eternity become mutually repellant. Far from inviting rereading, *Night Thoughts* becomes a self-destructing text, which properly understood directs its reader to higher things than the mere reading of poetry. This analysis is consonant with recent criticism that meets nineteenth- and twentieth-century attacks on Young as otherworldly and falsely sublime head on by emphasizing his commitment to the utter alterity of God and consequent nullity of the created world. As Blanford Parker wittily puts it, "[George Eliot] said that [Young] could not see God in a leaf or a child. In fact, Young believed in a doctrinaire way that man could not in the final analysis see God in anything."[12]

But *Night Thoughts* overlays this either/or (or if/not) opposition of literary fame and Christian immortality with a tentative but repeated both/and alignment of the two. For Young the human desire for fame is a proof of our immortal nature: "We wish our Names *eternally* to live. / Wild Dream! Which ne'er had haunted human Thought, / Had not our Natures been eternal too" (7.359–61). From this expression of the argument from desire it follows that earthly fame is a prefiguring type of eternity: "Fame is the Shade of Immortality, / And in itself a shadow" (7.365–66). What is true of life in general, that it is "An End deplorable! a Means divine!," applies to fame in particular: "Nor absolutely vain is Human Praise, / When Human is supported by Divine" (3.407; 7.402–3). Or, elsewhere: "LORENZO! to recriminate is Just. / Fondness for Fame is Avarice of Air. . . . Praise no Man e'er deserv'd, who sought no more" (5.1–2, 4). Young harshly dismisses fame sought for its own sake, but insists that by not wanting fame, we can acquire it legitimately. Young subsumes fame under the paradoxical providential logic of Matthew 6:31–33, according to which the faithful receive the things they need by not seeking them: "Therefore take no thought, saying, What shall we eat? or, What shall we drink? or, Wherewithal shall we be clothed? (For after all these things do the Gentiles seek:) for your heavenly Father knoweth that ye have need of all these things. But seek ye first the kingdom of God, and his righteousness; and all these things shall be added unto you."

It is tempting, despite a defense by his biographer Harold Forster, to convict Young of bad faith in applying this principle not only to his own pursuit of fame but also to his ecclesiastical career, in which much patronage was added unto Young but only after he spent years aggressively seeking it.[13] One might jeer him for wondering in *Night the Fourth*

> Why all this Toil for Triumphs of an Hour?
> What, tho' we wade in Wealth, or soar in Fame?

and declaring that

> If this Song lives, Posterity shall know
> One, tho' in *Britain* born, with Courtiers bred,
> Who thought even Gold might come a Day too late;
> Nor on his subtle Deathbed plan'd his Scheme
> or future Vacancies in Church, or State (4.97–98, 101–5)

only to dedicate the *Night* to the son of the Earl of Hardwicke, who had not only ruled in Young's favor in a financially important lawsuit but was also close to the reigning dispensers of church preferment.[14] But the argument from desire (which *Nights* 6–7 apply not only to ambition for fame but to avarice for wealth) leaves Young impaled on a genuine dilemma. Insatiable concupiscence is God's paradoxical gift to fallen humanity, because it enables man to recognize that the earth is not his home ("Man's misery declares him born for bliss" [7.60]). Yet desire must be continually rerouted from shadowy earthly objects to their substantial heavenly counterparts. To be weighed favorably in the balance, Young's Christian must always be found in the act of wanting.

The five lines cited just above show this rerouting at work. The conditional "If this song lives" prefaces the narrator's self-presentation as an edifying exemplum; the claim to poetic immortality that was boastful in pagan poets is here rehabilitated as a simple prerequisite for the poem's continuing moral power. It is licit to imagine, if not to claim, posthumous poetic fame as a means to help others contemplate their mortal end. (Note, too, that for all the diffidence of Young's conditional "if," he chooses the indicative "lives" over the subjunctive "live," showing at least measured confidence in the shelf life of his poem.) *Night the Fifth* imagines itself with similar ambivalence as "a Garland for *Narcissa's* Tomb; / And, *peradventure,* of no fading Flowers" (5.293–94, emphasis to "peradventure" added). Elsewhere, Young aspires to poetic fame under erasure, expressing a wish that he simultaneously dismisses as inadequate:

> O that my Song could emulate my Soul!
> Like her Immortal. No,—the Soul disdains
> A Mark so mean . . .
>
> .   .   .   .
>
> Let not the *Laurel,* but the *Palm* inspire. (6.71–73, 75)

Indeed, this dialectic runs throughout the poem in the figure of its addressee, the worldly and skeptical Lorenzo. This silent interlocutor never converts, and the poem never stops pursuing him ("Lorenzo! 'tis not yet too late: Lorenzo!" it insists thirty lines from the end, at 9.2404). "Lorenzo," one of the many pseudo-classical or Italianate names (Narcissa, Philander, Lucia, Clarissa, Florello, Lysander, Aspasia) that populate the poem, stems etymologically from the "*Laurel*" which *Night the Sixth* subordinates to the palm of Christian martyrdom and victory. Just as Petrarch's Laura, whose name is also derived from the bay tree, stands for both the object of the poet's love and the laurels he seeks by praising her, so Lorenzo's name denotes a lost soul but connotes sought-for poetic fame.

"*Time* Is Dealt Out by Particles"

This is not to say that the passages of *Night Thoughts* that recuperate literary fame as a type or anticipation of its heavenly counterpart provide a correct reading of the poem and that the passages that degrade it as a worldly presumption do not. *Night Thoughts* does not move conclusively from one view to the other over the course of its nine nights; it presents each perspective in various places. This conceptual Cubism is characteristic of the poem as a whole. At the level of imagery and metaphor in particular, *Night Thoughts* contains contradictory multitudes, repeating a core set of metaphorical vehicles (such as the moon, the sun, feathers, pregnancy, tombs) with shifting tenors, so that no individual symbol has a single, stable meaning.[15] Even the basic symbolic opposition of night and day oscillates in this way. In *Night the Fifth,* the sun makes the stars invisible just as prosperity induces forgetfulness of God:

> As glaring *Day*
> Of these unnumbered Lustres robs our Sight;
> *Prosperity* puts out unnumbered Thoughts
> Of Import high, and Light divine to Man. (5.306–8)

A little over six hundred lines later, the simile is precisely flipped: "*Gold* glitters most, where *Virtue* shines no more; / As Stars from absent Suns have leave to shine" (5.966–67).

Night Thoughts repeatedly vacillates between consolation and grief, conversion and doubt, ultimately eschewing definitive closure. It is repetitive like the *Spectator,* but not self-consciously cumulative. There is an aleatory *sortes youngiana* quality to finding evidence for claims about *Night Thoughts,* because many of its arguments and topoi are as likely to occur in the first book as the last. Though the final lines of *Night the Ninth* look forward one final time to the suspension of time in God's final judgment ("When time . . . in nature's ruin lies entomb'd / And midnight, universal midnight, reigns!"), the poet never passes into Christian immortality and his interlocutor, Lorenzo, never converts (9.2431–34). Young imagines *Night Thoughts* as a poem that need only end with the poet's life, because of its inexhaustible theme: "Wrapt in the Thought of *Immortality* / . . . Long Life might lapse, Age unperceiv'd come on; / And find the Soul unsated with her Theme" (6.66, 68–69). Despite its single-minded focus on eternity, *Night Thoughts* is thus a fundamentally periodical poem, with neither the lapidary self-containment of lyric nor the narrative arc of epic predecessors like *Paradise Lost* (or, indeed, descendants like *The Prelude*). It merely reverses the diurnality of secular periodical forms like the newspaper into religious nocturnality.

In his reading of *Night Thoughts,* Shaun Irlam perceptively argues that for Young "the transcendence of time must occur within time" and that "Young has therefore arrogated to himself a particularly urgent and formidable task, the representation of time; the poem thus becomes a search after the proper idiom for time, a rhetoric of temporality."[16] Irlam does not, however, note that time is the organizing structural principle of *Night Thoughts;* the poem is divided not into books but into a sequence of "nights" of varying but, in general, ever-increasing length. The organizing principle of the "book" dates back to the ancient world and referred to the quantity of text recorded on an individual papyrus scroll; fundamentally a spatial metaphor, the book divides the long poem into standardized quanta.[17] Even when a poem in incomplete, book divisions gesture toward a projected whole whose completeness will be verified by epic precedent, completed plot, or symbolic significance.[18] When a poem has appeared as complete, the publication of additional books may require explanation; hence Pope's need to claim in the *Advertisement* to the 1743 *New Dunciad* that "the author of the three first books had a design to extend and complete his poem in this manner," rearranging the plot of the poem to accommodate a fourth book.[19] Young's "nights," in contrast, are structured around a purely temporal metaphor, unconstrained by plot, symbolic design, or tradition. In this respect the *Night Thoughts* may be distinguished not only from the *Dunciad* but also from Thomson's *Seasons,* the third major long poem that takes its final form in the 1740s. Thomson's temporal system of organization limits the whole to a four-part structure—there are only four seasons in a year. When he expanded the poem in 1730 and again in 1744, he did so by enlarging its existing divisions rather than appending new ones.[20] Young's poem is structured by pure sequentiality; night simply follows night. This is a feature not only of the poem's structural organization but also of its publication over the period of June 1742 to January 1746. Readers holding the anonymously published first folio edition turned a title page offering *The Complaint, or Night-Thoughts on Life, Death, & Immortality* to find, immediately above the opening apostrophe to sleep, that they were holding *Night the First.* Young's correspondence shows that he had written at least the end of his second *Night* the month before the first was published, but the first edition makes no mention of any sequel.[21] The reader is thrown into a succession, with no generic or narrative guideposts to suggest which night will be the last.

Night the First makes this uncertainty precisely constitutive of the human condition:

> Time is dealt out by Particles . . .
>
> . . . .
>
> There's no Prerogative in human Hours:
> In human hearts what bolder Thought can rise,
> Than man's Presumption on To-morrow's dawn?
> Where is To-morrow? In another world. (1.366, 371–74)

Not only does the shared precariousness of life and poem lie implicit in the irregular publication of the eight nights that follow, but it is revisited explicitly in the preface to the first edition of *Night the Fourth,* which the preface describes as a "pausing Place for the Reader, and the Writer too," since "it is uncertain, whether Providence, or Inclination, will permit him to go any farther" (36). It has already been noted that the shorter, earlier *Nights,* whose three episodes of grief aroused biographical speculation in readers, sold better than their longer, later counterparts. But the poem outlasts its episodes. The true plot of *Night Thoughts* is not in its brief elegiac descriptions of deathbeds and graveyard scenes. Rather, it is in the daily (and nightly) battle to achieve salvation.

Night Thoughts thus imports the daily sensibility of the periodical essay and newspaper, both genres that originated within living memory of its first readers, into the long poem. The poem is not literally tethered to the passage of calendar days as these two prose forms, and their private predecessor, the diary, are; but its undated nights follow the same abstract sequential principle as their numbered days.

A comparison to *Paradise Lost* sheds further light on the structure of *Night Thoughts.* Young follows Milton closely in placing an appeal for divine (Christian) inspiration among its opening lines. Milton's

> Thou from the first
> Wast present and with mighty wings outspread
> Dove-like satst brooding on the vast Abyss
> And mad'st it pregnant: What in me is dark
> Illumin (*Paradise Lost* 1.19–23)

becomes

> O thou! whose Word from solid *Darkness* struck
> That spark, the Sun; strike Wisdom from my soul;
>
> . . . .
>
> . . . transmit one pitying ray
> To lighten, and to chear. (1.38–39, 43–44)

Milton turns from his invocation to his fabula, joining the fallen angels in medias res. Young follows his longer plea with a twofold self-reflexive turn. First, in a move that he will repeat in the *Conjectures,* he aligns poetic inspiration with personal virtue: "Nor less inspire my *Conduct,* than my *Song*" (1.48). Second, Young locates his poem in its imagined moment of nocturnal composition:

The Bell strikes *One:* We take no note of Time,
But from its Loss. To give it then a Tongue,
Is wise in man. (1.54–56)

The loss of time is, of course, the theme of *Night Thoughts,* and the connection between the poem's speaker and the clock is evident in the pun on the "tongue" of the time-marking church bell even before we notice that these two sentences contain precisely twenty-four consecutive monosyllables. Young's monitory poem is a timekeeper. In its fictional representation of both the moment and the process of its own composition, *Night Thoughts* anticipates both *Clarissa* and *Tristram Shandy.* In all three cases, writing is a means for the fictional narrator/protagonist to escape or transcend death.

While the subtitle of *Night Thoughts, On Life, Death, and Immortality,* signals its preoccupation with the afterlife, the poem itself repeatedly connects that afterlife to human, earthly time. Thus Young describes our final judgment as the publication of a private diary that has been faithfully recorded over the course of our lives:

The sly Informer [Conscience] minutes every Fault,
And her dread Diary with Horror fills:

. . . .

Unnoted, notes each Moment misapply'd;
In leaves more durable than leaves of Brass,
Writes our whole History; which *Death* shall read

. . . .

And *Judgment* publish: Publish to more worlds
Than this; and endless Age in groans resound.
(2.262–63, 273–75, 277–78)

Young is remembering Revelation 20:12, in which "the dead were judged out of those things which were written in the books, according to their works." But he has reimagined those books as diaries, each recorded by an individual conscience, rather than as the court records of a judging God. Both the etymology of "diary" (from *dies,* "day") and the pun on "minutes" underline the connection between time and "*Judgment,*" which is itself imagined as one of the publishers who printed exemplary Quaker diaries or scandalous memoirs in the first half of the eighteenth century. Young's "dread Diary" of conscience is also a recasting of the poetic monument of Horace's *Ode* 3.30: the *monumentum aere perennius* has become "leaves more durable than leaves of Brass."[22] In this reconception, immortality is won through daily documentation rather than lyric poesis, and enjoyed (or repented of) in an afterlife of Christian eternity rather than literary posterity.

The *Spectator* imagines the afterlife as a continuation of life lived on earth; *Night Thoughts* appropriates and transforms this line of thought by depicting life as a prelude, an insubstantial anticipation of the more real world to come: "*This* is the bud of Being, the dim Dawn.... / *Life's* Theater as yet is shut, and Death, / Strong Death alone can heave the massy Bar" (1.121, 123–24). Far from being inconceivably other, eternity is imagined as being like life, only more so:

> Thy *Nature*, Immortality! who knows?
> And yet who knows it not? It is but Life
> In stronger Thread of brighter Colour spun,
> And spun for ever. (6.76–79)

Moreover, virtue—a life oriented toward immortality—alone gives direction to earthly existence, which the poem imagines as otherwise a state of "languid, leaden Iteration" (3.369). Two decades after Swift's Struldbruggs and a century and a half before Nietzsche's eternal recurrence, Young repudiates the idea of everlasting life on earth as torturous, Sisyphean, bestial, and above all endlessly repetitive:

> For what live ever Here?—With labouring Step
> To tread our former Footsteps? Pace the Round
> Eternal? To climb Life's worn, heavy wheel,
> Which draws up nothing new? (3.329–32)

"*Virtue*," in contrast, "gives / To Life's sick, nauseous *Iteration*, Change; / And straitens Nature's Circle to a Line" (3.366, 368–70).[23] Human nature is infinitely perfectible, and the virtuous soul begins this endless process of perfection on earth:

> ... nobler Minds
> Which relish Fruits unripen'd by the *Sun*,
> Make their Days various; various as the Dies
> On the Dove's Neck, which wanton in *his* rays.
>
> . . . .
>
> Each rising Morning sees still higher rise;
> Each bounteous Dawn its Novelty presents

To worth maturing, new Strength, Lustre, Fame
While Nature's Circle, like a Chariot wheel
Rowling *beneath* their elevated Aims,
Makes their fair Prospect, fairer every Hour;
Advancing *Virtue,* in a Line to Bliss. (3.378–81, 387–93)[24]

Far from forcing the pious reader to renounce the world, virtue in Young makes daily life an active good: "Dawn . . . presents . . . new Strength, Lustre, Fame"; "Nature's Circle . . . makes their fair Prospect, fairer every Hour." Units and moments of earthly time become agents of salvation (note as well that "Fame" once again becomes a good when properly subordinated to greater goods). The chiasmus of "Days various; various as the Dies / On the Dove's Neck" emphasizes this point by reinforcing its simile with a Latin pun: "Dies" are both pigments and *dies,* or days. Diurnal life is beautifully reified as the iridescent feathers of a bird (while another English meaning of "dies," though ungrammatical here, reminds the reader of the end to which all life tends). Young leaves the connection implicit in *Night the Third,* but his logic of eternity redeeming time may be applied to the periodical structure of *Night Thoughts* itself. In this reading, it appears repetitive and lacking in narrative arc to exoteric readers only, to Lorenzos or other "Foes" (likely including many twenty-first-century readers). The esoteric convert will find each newly published *Night,* like each new-dawning day, an advance on the last.

See in What Peace a Christian Can Die

Virtue, for Young, is an ongoing, daily practice. But he attaches heightened significance to the deathbed, that "Detector of the Heart" where spectators behold the virtuous man "just rising to a God" (2.639, 630). Young expresses a widely held view when he holds that the moment of death is an infallible touchstone, when dissimulation becomes both fruitless and impossible: "*Here* tir'd *Dissimulation* drops her Masque. . . . *Here* Real, and Apparent, are the Same" (2.640, 642). This is the view that made the Earl of Rochester's deathbed conversion so crucial to his eighteenth-century reception, left Boswell so disturbed by his visit to the complacently dying Hume, and rendered Adam Smith's record of Hume's death and various authors' conflicting accounts of Johnson's final hours so fraught.[25] Young's lines also anticipate the cornucopia of deathbed scenes in *Clarissa* (Clarissa, Lovelace,

Belton, Sinclair, Lord M, Belford's uncle, Anna Howe's "cousin Larkin"), each of which carries its own nuanced moral message.

Written thirteen years after the end of *Night Thoughts,* Young's *Conjectures on Original Composition: In a Letter to the Author of Sir Charles Grandison* combines literary criticism (a parting shot in the subsiding quarrel of the Ancients and Moderns) with a handful of death-centered biographical anecdotes. The piece is our source for Swift's prescient statement, pointing at a withering elm, that "I shall be like that tree, I shall die at top," and of Pope's deathbed literary projecting: "I heard the dying swan talk over an epic plan a few weeks before his decease."[26] The avowed purpose of the essay, in fact, is to recount Addison's dying words to his stepson, "See in what peace a Christian can die" (45). The *Conjectures* asserts throughout that poetry offers "a name immortal," but it is saturated with the death of poets (23, 29). Like the *Spectator* a half century before and the *Life of Johnson* a generation later, the *Conjectures* describes itself as a monument. After the first paragraph of the text promises his addressee "a serious Thought" that will "strike the careless Wanderer . . . with useful awe," just as "monumental Marbles scattered in a wide Pleasure-Garden . . . will call to Recollection those who would never have sought it in a Churchyard-walk of mournful Yews," Young follows his account of the dying Addison in his final pages by identifying it as "the *monumental marble* . . . to which I promised to conduct you" (3, 48). Young's essay enters the *et in arcadia ego* tradition, in which the presence of a tombstone in a garden recalls its viewers from their pastoral pleasures to mindfulness of death.[27]

Young signals from the beginning that his *Conjectures* will modulate from critical speculation to Christian exhortation, and the opening of his essay constructs these two modes as distinct, even incongruous: "monumental Marbles" have their effect precisely because they are out of place in "a wide Pleasure-Garden." Yet, like Wallace Stevens's jar, which "made the slovenly wilderness / Surround that hill" on which it was placed, Young's pious monument to Addison is fundamental to the meaning of the critical-aesthetic *locus amoenus* where he erects it.[28]

Biography is a natural companion to Young's critical project because literary merit in the *Conjectures* must be understood in biographical-historical terms. Originality and imitation are comprehensible as critical terms only if we know when an author lived and whom he read. Likewise genius, "the Power of accomplishing great things without the means generally reputed necessary to that end," can only be assessed if we know what means, particularly what predecessors, were at an author's disposal. By this reasoning, genius may indeed exist independently of any literary output whatsoever; echoing Gray's *Elegy,* Young speculates that "many a Genius, probably, there has been, which could neither write, nor read" (17).

Criticism must be biographical in another sense: Young sees the work of art (what the essay calls a "composition") as an expression of its creator's moral nature: "*Tully, Quintillian,* and all true critics allow, that virtue assists Genius, and that the writer be more able, when better is the man." Young reasons that the Christian dispensation must, with time, produce compositions that surpass the classics "*since,* as the moral world expects its glorious millennium, the world intellectual may hope, by the rules of analogy, for some superior degrees of excellence to crown her latter scenes. . . . Why should it seem altogether impossible, that heaven's latest editions of the human mind may be most correct, and fair" (32). The simile of human being as book (and the related simile of book as human offspring or progeny) runs through every text discussed in this monograph, from the *Spectator* to the *Life of Johnson;* here, Young combines the figurative association of the two with their literal causal relationship: as God over time makes men, metaphorically speaking, into better "books," men will make better books.[29]

In Addison, this biographical and moral conception of genius reaches its logical conclusion when literary creation and deathbed conduct collapse into a single whole: "His compositions are but a noble preface; the grand work is his death. . . . How gloriously has he opened a splendid path, thro' fame immortal, into eternal peace?" *Night Thoughts'* both/and logic of fame as the handmaiden of salvation is implicit in the life of Addison, a work that joins "the final approbation of angels to the previous applause of men" (46). To rephrase Pope, an honest man's the noblest work of an honest man; Addison's greatest work is not *Cato* but Addison himself. The *Conjectures* does not naively claim that virtue and genius are always found in direct proportion—Swift, who "laid [his] imagination in the mire" in *Gulliver's Travels,* is Young's whipping-boy counterexample (28). But genius without virtue is, for Young, not only demeaned but also diminished.

Throughout the *Conjectures,* Young takes it for granted that "a name immortal" is both the criterion for and the reward of literary greatness. Addison's death scene thus poses a theoretical problem: like all dramatic performances (Young calls Addison "a *Roscius* on the scene of life"), it has no enduring existence as an artifact (48–49). The self-conscious exemplarity of Addison's death "would have deserved immortality, tho' he had never written," but instead it threatens to "be dropped into oblivion" (44, 48). How is Addison to get his just reward? The answer, in the end, is the *Conjectures* itself, but Young does not claim this distinction for his essay immediately. Instead, he modestly notes that his "report is but a second edition" of what he previously called Addison's "grand work"; "it was published before, tho' obscurely, and with a cloud before it," in Thomas Tickell's "To the Earl of Warwick, on the Death of Mr. Addison," in which Addison's epigone mourns that the poem's subject "taught us how to live; and, oh! too high / A price for knowledge, taught us how to die" (Young quotes the lines on 47).

Tickell's poem is, however, an inadequate monument. Having read the *Conjectures* to this point, the reader might surmise that "On the Death of Mr. Addison" fails because it lacks originality or because its author lacks genius. In fact, Young gamely treats Tickell as his creative superior; the problem is that the lyric lacks circumstantial detail: "By what means *Addison taught us how to die,* the Poet left to be made known by a late, and less able hand; but one more zealous for his patron's glory" (47). Young, far from considering himself a "Poet" in memorializing Addison, describes his text as an "anecdote" and a "narrative" (46, 48). Poetry, the classical and early modern gold standard for preserving and memorializing heroes, here gives way to biographical anecdote. The *Conjectures,* culminating with this single deathbed, is as it were a prospectus for the comprehensive attempt to realize prose immortality for a subject in Boswell's *Life of Johnson.*

Boswell was a lifelong reader of Young, as allusions and quotations throughout his diaries and published essays indicate. The indices of the Yale Boswell editions point to references as early as December 1763 and as late as April 1784.[30] Young's privileging of intimate anecdote over lyric celebration as the means of literary immortality was not lost on Boswell, whose thoughts and conversation turned to Young in 1772, seven years after the poet's death, when he passed through Stevenage, six miles from Young's old parish of Welwyn: "I have for some time thought of writing an essay on the genius and writings of Dr. Young. . . . I may contrive to get some authentic information with regard to his private life."[31] In other words, Boswell imagines that an essay on Young's genius should include the same biographical detail that Young provides for Addison in the *Conjectures.* The barber who shaved Boswell in Stevenage informed him that the local celebrity had kept a mistress, and the idea that Young the sublime poet might coexist with Young the "whoremaster" troubled and fascinated Boswell. He sought information on the topic from the Rev. Thomas Percy and from Johnson, each of whom reassured him that the gossip was unlikely to be true.[32]

Boswell never wrote his projected essay, but he did visit Young's son Frederick in 1781 while traveling through Welwyn with Johnson and Charles Dilly. Boswell adroitly secured for his traveling party an invitation to Guessons, as the Young residence was called—Boswell knew that Johnson would refuse to call on Frederick Young unannounced and therefore went by himself to inform the heir that Johnson, an old friend of his father's, was passing through. The group then visited the house and garden, which contained "a gravel walk, on each side of which was a row of trees, planted by Dr. Young."[33] After discussing Young's "gloomy" character, Boswell and Johnson "went into the church, and looked at the monument erected by Mr. Young to his father."[34] The next paragraph finds them back "upon the road," their pilgrimage to Welwyn complete. The visit to Young's house thus follows the same arc as the *Conjectures*—from a pleasant garden to a monument, in this case Young's own burial tablet.[35] Young was a comparatively minor interest for Boswell, who in addition to his completed *Memoirs of Pascal Paoli* and *Life of Johnson* contemplated lives of Sir Alexander Dick, Lord Kames, Sir Joshua Reynolds, and others. But Young sketches out for Boswell a model, which the latter will more fully realize, for seeing an author's life as his true work, and biographical anecdote as the corresponding means of ensuring literary immortality.

The Afterlife of *Night Thoughts*

In his zeal to immortalize Addison, Young presents the *Conjectures* not merely as a monument but as a source of light that allows his readers to witness a resurrection: "This is the *sepulchral lamp,* the long-hidden lustre of our accomplished countryman, who now rises, as from his tomb, to receive the regard so greatly due to the dignity of his death" (3). In a passage quoted above, the eighth installment of *Night Thoughts* offers a far more pessimistic assessment of the relationship between text, audience, and immortality:

> But *Praise* she need not fear; I see my Fate;
>
> . . . .
>
> Since many an ample *Volume,* mighty *Tome,*
> Must die; and die Unwept; O Thou minute,
> Devoted *Page!* go forth among thy Foes;
> Go, nobly proud of Martyrdom for Truth,

Figure 1. Lucifer arraigns *Night Thoughts*, by William Blake.
(Copyright Trustees of the British Museum)

And die a double Death: Mankind, incens'd,
Denies thee long to live: Nor shalt thou rest,
When thou art Dead, in *Stygian* Shades arraign'd
By Lucifer, as Traitor to his Throne. (8.1392, 1394–401)

The metaphor of a literary work's "life" or "death" is ancient and conventional; Pope's "All but truth falls dead-born from the press" uses the metaphor to make the exact opposite of Young's claim (that truth triumphs rather than being martyred), and pious authors of the 1740s such as Aaron Hill and Patrick Delaney hope that their unpopular works will enjoy future "resurrection."[36] But Young's metaphor complicates the commonplace of literary death by adding an infernal afterlife. If the reader understands the death of a work to be indifference and oblivion, what is the meaning of the "double death" in which Lucifer "arraign[s]" *Night Thoughts* "in *Stygian* shades"?

It may simply be that Young's conflation of the language of personal and literary immortality has here enmeshed him in a mixed metaphor, one of the sort Samuel Johnson had in mind when he said that "there were very fine things in *Night Thoughts,* though you could not find twenty lines together without some extravagance."[37] If so, the rough point is that the poem, merely irritating to "incens'd" worldly readers, is properly seen as threatening by their more perceptive master. But the legal term "arraign'd" (from *ad + rationare,* to "reason at" someone) suggests a more complex reading, buttressed by the poem's statement seven lines later that "'The Mother of true Wisdom is the *Will;*' / The noblest *Intellect,* a fool without it" (8.1408–9). *Night Thoughts* explicitly and preemptively disavows all critical readings of itself—that is, all readings that treat it as an object for illumination, analysis, or aesthetic appreciation rather than a perlocutionary appeal to seek the Lord while he may yet be found. Blake, who completed a set of illustrations for *Night Thoughts,* glosses Young here. In his illustration, a phallic tongue of flame from Lucifer bears light (*lucem fert*) to the clearly titled book, which he reads with his upturned eyes while his hands tear it apart.

Even when a book is already dead, we can still murder to dissect. Modern scholars feel the need to excuse *Night Thoughts* when producing it as historical or literary evidence. But this is fitting: the poem, constantly appealing to the Judgment of an entirely different court, is a self-consciously hostile witness.

Part Two

THEOLOGY
AND
THE NOVEL

3
The Threat to the Soul in Butler and Warburton

To summarize the findings of the first section of this book: The reader who opens either the *Spectator* or *Night Thoughts* (and we would do well to remember that both were enormous best sellers in Britain and the subject of numerous Continental imitations and translations, respectively) is being asked to attend to and coordinate multiple schemes of time. Thematically, each work consists of moral exhortation rooted in the essential continuity between the quantifiable earthly time marked out by clocks and calendars and the endlessly succeeding posthumous time into which all human souls must eventually enter. Formally, each consists of discrete units whose cumulative force is a product of mere sequentiality, not narrative or argumentative progression. Historically, each was published in parts over a period of several years and then collected into a frequently republished monumental whole. Underlying the enormous difference in tone between Addison and Steele's chatty urbanity and Young's bombastic world-weariness is thus a shared framework that turns innovations in literary form and the material practices of publication into structures for reinforcing a new theology of time. Diurnality and nocturnality are two sides of the same road sign, and both point toward futurity.

In all the recipes that have been given in the last sixty years for the rise of the novel, this coordinated interest in daily time and endless futurity is a leaven that has hitherto escaped scholarly notice. Yet it is unmistakably in the air and lends, for the literary historian with the taste to discern it, a distinctive flavor to the finished product. This is particularly true in the case of Samuel Richardson, whose works avowedly combine "writing to the moment" with heavy-handed concern for the posthumous fate of characters and readers alike. Moreover, the texts that we now think of as the canon of the early British novel extend the themes and techniques of periodical immortality in a crucial new direction by combining them with the age-old literary effects of plot and character. *Clarissa* is, by Richardson's own account, a guidebook for readers on the way to heaven. In this respect it is no different from *Night Thoughts* (or many other devotional or homiletic works of the period with which it does not share the formal affinities that concern us here). But it is also a minutely particular account of Clarissa Harlowe's journey to her father's house. The same can be said, mutatis mutandis, of *Sir Charles Grandison:* it is both an exhaustive conduct book for the Christian gentleman and an interminably specific chronicle of two angels living happily ever after (a cliché whose dual applicability to marital bliss and posthumous beatification I will take up below). In neither case is it a coincidence that unprecedented anecdotal and chronometric specificity goes hand in hand with extensive and explicit thematic attention to the afterlife. On the contrary: Richardson's formal project is designed to impart distinct yet overlapping varieties of immortality to himself, his characters, and his implied reader.

This is not to say that *Clarissa* and *Sir Charles Grandison* articulate the theme of immortality in the same way. The two texts are profoundly different in design: *Clarissa* is tightly plotted and end-stopped by the irrevocability and finality of death; as E. Derek Taylor has so well put it, "It is perhaps the distinctive characteristic of [*Clarissa*] that from the outset the author knew how this one would end."[1] The effect is to force the reader to imagine its characters continuing beyond death. *Sir Charles Grandison,* by contrast, has no plot, or rather completes its plot and keeps on going. Richardson rejects the traditional logic of comedy and carries his narrative on past the marriage of Harriet and Sir Charles, with the result that the text has no obvious place to stop at all, and thus becomes an allegory of human infinitude. Each text is an experiment, a creation of Richardson's mind in the act of finding what will suffice to make the afterlife compelling to his skeptical or inattentive readers. Each develops new narratological possibilities that influence subsequent texts.

Richardson is not writing in a vacuum, and his interest in immortality is not idiosyncratic. Rather, his two final novels respond to an eighteenth-century moment in which the existence and nature of the afterlife is at once crucial and unsettled in the moderate Anglican worldview that is at the center of gravity for Hanoverian British culture. It is to that moment that I now turn in order to frame the readings of *Clarissa* and *Sir Charles Grandison* that follow.

Such Fools as Disbelieve a Futurity

Shortly before Lovelace rapes Clarissa, Jack Belford sends his friend a letter begging him to spare her. He reminds his fellow rake, "We neither of us are such fools, as to disbelieve a Futurity."[2] Belford's claim is prominently seconded by Richardson's preface, which makes a point of reassuring readers that not even the novel's archvillain would endorse so pernicious a doctrine as mortalism (1:6).[3] Disbelief in the afterlife, like blasphemous oaths, sodomy, and explicit bawdy, is beyond *Clarissa*'s representational pale.

In this respect *Clarissa* replicates in miniature a rigid convention of eighteenth-century British print culture: it contains no authors who are willing to deny belief in the afterlife. According to David Berman, the earliest published avowal of mortalism does not appear until 1801.[4] Indeed, given that the word "mortalism" could also refer to the doctrine that the soul was dissolved at death but miraculously re-created by God at the Last Judgment, there is not even a single *word* in the lexicon of eighteenth-century English that unambiguously denotes disbelief in the posthumous continuation of the human self. Belford's language in his letter to Lovelace does much to explain why. After identifying the disbeliever in futurity as a fool, he draws a sharp distinction in the following paragraph between what Lovelace must surely believe and what his actions imply: "If, Lovelace, thou laughest at me, thy ridicule will be more conformable to thy *actions,* than to thy *belief—Devils believe and tremble.* Canst thou be more abandoned than they?" (4:351). Belford follows an allusion to Psalm 14:1 ("The fool hath said in his heart, There is no God") with an explicit citation of James 2:19 ("Thou believest that there is one God; thou doest well: the devils also believe, and tremble"). Implicit in these references is a world picture that reaches Richardson virtually unchanged from Christian homiletics and apologetics of the sixteenth and seventeenth centuries: the elision of mortalism into atheism (Belford uses scripture passages that refer to belief in God in order to impute to Lovelace belief in futurity) and the identification of atheist/mortalist belief with immoral conduct. In this account so-called "speculative atheism" is a post hoc attempt, nearly always made in bad faith, to justify "practical atheism," or libertine conduct.[5] Indeed, the only occurrence of the word "atheist" or "atheism" in *Clarissa* is in a reprise on Belford's part of the argument to Lovelace just cited, that both men believe in God's posthumous judgment as a matter of fact even as they ignore its implications in practice: "God will judge us, in a great measure, by our benevolent or evil actions to one another. . . . And is this amiable Doctrine the sum of Religion? Upon my faith, I believe it is . . . we are not Atheists, except in *Practice*" (6:98). "Atheist" is here a negative moral quality rather than a philosophical position. Belief in God is unquestioningly associated with human immortality and posthumous judgment, and it is this connection that supplies the conceptual connection between the unbeliever and the rebel: atheists are bad livers who know they are going to be punished and pretend not to believe in the punisher.

Belford's axiomatic couplings of the existence of God with posthumous judgment and atheism with practical immorality are never explicitly questioned in *Clarissa*—the novel contains neither mortalists nor atheists. Indeed, the fact that villains such as Mrs. Sinclair lament that they have "no time to repent" on their deathbeds and scream in fear that "in a few hours . . . who can tell *where* [they] shall be" heightens the reader's pleasure in seeing evildoers punished, as well as reinforcing the lesson that moral formation cannot be the hasty work of a deathbed conversion (8:53). But it is also a diegetic version of the eighteenth-century apologetic and polemical topos that David Berman calls the "repressive denial of atheism": that is to say, the novel denies that atheism is even possible as a reasoned intellectual position while at the same time presenting arguments against it.[6] This incoherent position (Berman compares such anti-atheist writers to landlords who swear that there are no mice in the apartment and promise to set out traps and poison immediately) is the product of "the unconscious desire to discourage atheism and the conscious desire to deny it."[7] Thus Belford, who as we have seen repeatedly asseverates to Lovelace that they both believe in the afterlife, nevertheless adduces Clarissa's sufferings as an argument for it: "*Oh* LOVELACE! LOVELACE! *had I doubted it before, I should now be convinced, that there must be a* WORLD AFTER THIS, *to do justice to injured merit, and to punish such a barbarous perfidy!*" (5:293). Belford's "*had I doubted it before*" saves the logical coherence of his position, but the emotionally heightened typography of the passage reinforces the already obvious fact that he is not merely expressing a truism. Edward Young, reading the novel in manuscript, exhorted Richardson to ignore other coterie readers who pleaded for reconciliation and marriage between Clarissa and Lovelace by alleging that they doubted the existence of the afterlife and that *Clarissa* should prove it to them: "How came they then to give this advice? ... From such a degree of infidelity as suffers not their thoughts to accompany Clarissa any farther than her grave. Did they look farther ... they would find her to be an object of envy as well as pity."[8]

The print culture of eighteenth-century Britain, like the world of *Clarissa,* contains no avowed mortalists, yet both feel the need not only to deny that mortalism exists but also to offer arguments against it. In order to understand how *Clarissa* makes its argument, not only in its explicit statements but also in its form, we need to pin down its spectral adversary. What is the shape of this threat that is at once feared and denied, and why is it so menacing?

Mortalism, in the strong sense of complete disbelief in the continuation of human existence after death, is powerful both because the philosophical case for it becomes stronger and because the traditional assumption that it entails destructive moral and social implications becomes questionable. Both developments can be traced to the final two decades of the seventeenth century. John Locke's *Essay Concerning Human Understanding* (particularly in the second edition of 1694) offered an account of personal identity that undermined the traditional argument for the immortality of the soul by virtue of its being an indivisible and immaterial substance. By distinguishing between "man" and "person," making consciousness rather than continuity of spiritual substance the criterion of identity, and speculating that God could endow matter with the ability to think, Locke (though himself a firm believer in Christian revelation and the resurrection of the dead) challenged and exposed weaknesses in an account of the soul that was old as Plato's *Apology* and had achieved new currency in the seventeenth century through Descartes.[9] Meanwhile, Pierre Bayle's *Pensées diverses sur la comete* (1682) argued that belief in immortality of the soul was not indispensable as a guarantor of human conduct, and that the fear of earthly punishment or dishonor could be enough to deter vice.[10] In the generation that followed, Bayle's doubts about the minatory necessity of the afterlife were fortified by the Earl of Shaftesbury, who not only seconded Bayle's claim that atheists could be virtuous but argued that virtue practiced for the sake of posthumous reward was too mercenary and selfish to deserve the name.[11] Locke's challenges to the doctrine of the immaterial soul found a more radical exponent in Anthony Collins (a Locke protégé), and moreover remained current in their own right by virtue of the sheer weight of controversial energy brought to bear in order to refute them.[12]

These two late-seventeenth-century developments continued to structure the debate for the following fifty years. The defenders of immortality had the institutional advantages: no bishoprics were on offer for skeptics, and no one faced prosecution for defending Christian doctrine. But their opponents had less to defend, and could play a critical rather than constructive role. Eighteenth-century British moral philosophy can be divided into three broad streams: there were rationalists, who held that moral truth can be discovered by reason; fideists, who held that moral truth can be known only through direct revelation from God; and sentimentalists, who held moral truth to consist in conformity to a sense within human nature itself.[13] For moralists writing within the Anglican tradition at mid-century, these accounts were held to be mutually reinforcing, and the purpose of moral philosophy was to articulate their divinely ordained unity. Thus, William Warburton's *Divine Legation of Moses Demonstrated from the Principles of a Religious Deist* (1738–41) described "the moral Sense," "the reasoning Faculty," and "the Will of God" as a "threefold cord" and "triple Barrier, with which God has been graciously pleased to cover and secure Virtue."[14] Joseph Butler, whose *Analogy of Religion* (1736) became an influential school-text of Anglican apology, likewise sought to demonstrate the compatibility of human nature, the knowable structure of the universe, and the content and claims of Christian revelation. Their skeptical opponents, in contrast, sought to divorce moral sentiment from either divine will or the nature of creation, and to exalt it as the only tenable source of morality. This is the project, in particular, of David Hume, both in the *Treatise of Human Nature,* 1739–40, and in the more influential *Enquiries Concerning Human Understanding and the Principles of Morals,* 1748–51. (Although there are important differences among these three figures, this is the project not only of Hume but of Shaftesbury and Adam Smith as well.)

Logically, the strands of Warburton's threefold cord and the terms of Butler's analogy between natural and revealed religion each demand defense; like a complex machine, their systems break down if a single part goes wrong. Rhetorically, however, both Butler and Warburton make God's guarantee of immortality primary to their argument. Butler's *Analogy* begins with the chapter "Of a Future Life," and the entire first half of the text concerns itself with the indispensable role of the afterlife in the rationally discernible moral structure of the universe. In Warburton's *Divine Legation,* meanwhile, the doctrine of immortality as attested in the Bible structures the entire text; Warburton offers a daringly paradoxical argument from the absence of immortality in the Mosaic law to the credibility and therefore normativity of the Christian revelation of afterlife and judgment in the New Testament. Hume's system, in contrast, opens up a twofold attack on immortality, and in so doing it attacks the point on which Butler and Warburton lay the greatest argumentative weight. The first prong of Hume's attack is inherited from Bayle: Hume argues that the afterlife is superfluous, and that moral motivation is grounded in immanent human psychology, rather than in inferences about the nature of the universe or in the duties imposed by God. The second prong of attack is more direct: Hume implies that the afterlife almost certainly does not exist in any case.[15]

For the reasoner who accepts both parts of Hume's argument, there is no problem: having bid good riddance to bad dogmatic rubbish, he or she can go down the long slide to sociable and sentimental eighteenth-century happiness, as long as life permits.[16] The surviving evidence suggests that this is precisely what Hume and Smith did (and, as both opponents and sympathizers noticed at the time, living a sociable and moral life without believing in Christianity was itself a philosophically provocative and meaningful act).[17] But Hume himself recognized the possibility of being convinced by his arguments against the existence of the afterlife without a corresponding conversion to his arguments against its moral usefulness. The speaker who narrates "Of a Particular Providence and Of a Future State," the most radical attack on the afterlife that Hume published in his lifetime, though he clearly does not speak for Hume, does make precisely this point: "You conclude, that religious doctrines and reasonings *can* have no influence on life, because they *ought* to have no influence; never considering, that men reason not in the same manner you do."[18] And as a "natural historian"— something like what we might now call an anthropologist—Hume believed that hope and fear, rather than reason, were the source of popular religious practice.[19] Indeed, the cast of thought that made the existence of the afterlife a question of the fundamental fairness of the universe came naturally enough to Hume that he could use it as a source of wry humor. In a letter to Gilbert Eliot, he laments that his *History of England* has not sold as well as the competing offering of Tobias Smollett, and he "fanc[ies] there is a future State, to give Poets, Historians, & Philosophers their due Reward, and to distribute to them those Recompenses which are so strangely shar'd out in this Life. It is of little Consequence that Posterity does them Justice, if they are for ever to be ignorant of it, and are to remain in perpetual Slumber in their literary Paradise."[20] The wish-fulfilling power of a conscious afterlife draws Hume in here, if only in jest. But for eighteenth-century Britons who reasoned not in the manner of Hume but rather in the manner of Bishop Butler or Bishop Warburton, the Scotsman's jovial complacency was felt as an infuriating impertinence.

Both Butler and Warburton positioned themselves consciously as responding to the threat of mortalism and defending their respective Christian positions; in this sense, their two very different texts make common cause against what they took to be their most threatening opponent. With the whole system of ethics (rational, religious, and sentimental) to defend, both authors begin with the afterlife as the crux of the matter. The *Analogy* and the *Divine Legation* are thus representative of the way in which eighteenth-century theology felt itself to be newly vulnerable to objections from non-Christian positions, rather than intra-Christian heresies or unorthodoxies.[21] They assume the same rhetorical stance as the Boyle Lectures, which were begun in 1692 and were instituted as an annual series of sermons preached in London "for proving the Christian religion against notorious infidels, viz. Atheists, Deists, Pagans, Jews, and Mahometans; not descending to any controversies that are among Christians themselves."[22] Butler's treatise is representative of an Anglican culture eager to appeal to reason and adapt empiricist principles without abandoning special appeals to revelation, while Warburton testifies to the intense emotional and rhetorical energy unleashed by the perceived deist/skeptical threat. Both adumbrate sites of controversy and anxiety that will play out formally and thematically in the works of Richardson, Johnson, and Boswell.

Joseph Butler and the Constitution and Course of Nature

As the bishop of Bristol in the 1740s, it was the custom of Joseph Butler to "walk for Hours in his Garden in the darkest Night, which the Time of the Year could afford."[23] It is fitting that the nightly vigils of religious reflection narrated in *Night Thoughts* were the real-life practice of Edward Young's fellow clergyman during the years that Young was writing his long poem. Butler's *Analogy of Religion* (1736) gives philosophical expression to many of the themes whose nightly recurrence goes on to structure the form of *Night Thoughts* in the following decade: the agency of God in the daily time of human life, the relationship between earthly moral formation and eternity, and the necessity of looking beyond nature to the providence of God. Analogy is not the same thing as identity, and the *Analogy of Religion* is explicitly written against those deists who would collapse reason and Christian doctrine into one another, thereby rendering the latter superfluous. This gives the text's two-part division a curiously dialectical quality: in the first half of the *Analogy,* which discusses natural religion, Butler takes pains to vindicate the competence and authority of reason, and in particular reason's ability to infer with confidence from the structure of the created world that the human agent survives the death of the body and must live life on earth with a view to posthumous survival. In the second half, which vindicates Christianity, Butler instead emphasizes reason's limitations, and the necessity of borrowing light from religion.

Part of the critique of religious reason in the second half of the *Analogy* is the observation that natural religion may be a philosophical construct, but it is not an anthropological one: "It is impossible to say, who would have been able to have reasoned out That whole System, which we call natural Religion, in its genuine Simplicity, clear of Superstition; but there is certainly no Ground to affirm, that the Generality could."[24] Butler's natural religion, which can be reasoned out by philosophical elites but has never formed the basis for the religious practice of a whole society, is nothing other than the horizontal eternity of Addison's *Spectator* papers. Butler adduces a series of analogical arguments for this conception: prudence and care bring worldly happiness, while imprudence and folly produce unhappiness in life; we need not postulate a particular judgment on the part of God to assume that the same consequences will, in the natural order of things, continue to affect the part of us that survives death. Virtue and wisdom may suffer setbacks on earth, but they tend to win out in the long run; since in the long run we live forever, we may infer that virtue and wisdom will in the end be entirely triumphant. In life we regularly see challenges and difficulties leading to personal growth; there is thus reason to think that God has placed us in the world as a form of probation, to qualify us for the life to come: "Without determining, what will be the Employment and Happiness, the particular Life, of good Men hereafter, there must be some determinate Capacities, some necessary Character and Qualifications, without which, Persons cannot but be utterly incapable of it" (81). In life we see an immeasurable difference between the capabilities of infants or children and those of mature adults, while at the same time the discipline of childhood decisively shapes the character of the grown person; Butler proposes a like relationship between life and futurity. Following Addison, and implicitly arguing both against the competing Protestant conception of an austerely theocentric heaven and against the pantheism of John Toland, Butler imagines that individuality and character survive and flourish in the afterlife: "It is not impossible, that Mens shewing and making manifest, what is in their Heart, what their real Character is, may have Respect to a future Life, in Ways and Manners which we are not acquainted with. . . . The Manifestation of Persons Characters, contributes, very much in various Ways, to the carrying on a great Part of that general Course of Nature, respecting Mankind, which comes under our Observation at present" (103).[25] The afterlife may well be "social," just like this one (28). Yet, again like Addison, Butler does not imagine individuating self-formation as a good in itself, as Keats will do nearly a century later with his concept of the "vale of Soul-making." Butler locates personal development firmly within the moral purposes of God, postulating that "virtuous Self-government" brings us asymptotically ever closer to perfect coincidence with "the moral Principle" (94).

In the first half of the *Analogy*, that is, Butler looks into the book of nature and reads off the account of the universe proffered by his generation's preferred compendium of light but improving reading. The second half of the text retreats from the first half's confidence in the power of reason and the testimony of nature, counseling deference to revelation instead. Here Butler's guiding analogy is between the unpredictable and ex ante improbable nature of observable reality, and the corresponding probability that God's revelation will be equally obscure, incomplete, or difficult to understand:

> Since, upon Experience, the acknowledged Constitution and Course of Nature, is found to be greatly different from what, before Experience, would have been expected, and such as, Men fancy, there lie great Objections against; this renders it beforehand highly credible, that they may find the revealed Dispensation likewise, if they judge of it as they do of the Constitution of Nature, very different from Expectations formed beforehand, and liable, in Appearance, to great Objections. (171)

Among the particular doctrines of Christianity which nature does not reveal is the atonement; Butler devotes several pages and a braid of biblical quotations to make this point (217–20). Indeed, he inserts one more argument from nature: just as repentance and amendment of life cannot recover a squandered estate or a constitution destroyed by debauchery, without Christ we would have no prospect of avoiding the natural consequences of human peccability in the afterlife (199–200). Yet even in his discussion of revelation, Butler finds this turn to the conceptual framework of sinfulness and grace, which is so different from his earlier language of probation, moral formation, and self-improvement, hard to sustain. Like nearly all of the figures in this study, Butler represents an Anglican worldview that is mistrustful of both Calvinism, with its emphasis on human depravity, and Methodism, with its "enthusiastic" expressions of God's saving grace. The closing pages of the *Analogy* return to the language of religion as a regimen of moral improvement, preparatory to a distribution of reward and punishment commensurate with desert in the life to come. And in a revealing piece of analogical reasoning from part 2, chapter 6, of the *Analogy,* Butler suggests that the obligation to accept the evidence of Christianity although it is not intuitively obvious may itself be part of our probation: "The Evidence of Religion not appearing obvious, may constitute on particular Part of some Mens Trial in the religious Sense; as it gives Scope, for a virtuous Exercise, or vitious Neglect of their Understanding, in examining or not examining into That Evidence" (221). Faith itself becomes a meta-act of personal moral formation.

The *Analogy* is significant not only because it shows Addison's horizontal afterlife seated at the center of eighteenth-century Anglican theology, but because it shows that conception challenged by fragilizing contact with contemporary philosophical questions about personal identity. The word "soul" appears only twice in the *Analogy,* and both times in an explicitly non-theological context: Butler once begins a sentence with the conditional "If the soul be naturally immortal" and once refers to the "evidence of reason" for "the natural immortality of the soul" (29, 62). Elsewhere he refers to the "agent" or "person" who will enter into a different "state" upon death. By jettisoning the theological language of the God-created "soul" in favor of the philosophical language of the person, Butler places the *Analogy* in dialogue with contemporary debates about personal identity and the continuity of the self, and particularly with Locke. The *Analogy* concludes with two "Brief Dissertations," the first entitled "Of Personal Identity." An advertisement by Butler explains that he originally included this material in the first chapter of the *Analogy*, "Of a Future Life," but then decided to present it separately. "Of Personal Identity" is a critique of Locke's theory of personal identity, which Butler takes to consist in continuity of consciousness. Butler replies that consciousness may ascertain personal identity but cannot constitute it, just as knowledge cannot constitute truth, "which it presupposes" (302). The stakes of the question, as Butler understands them, relate to the afterlife: "Whether we are to live in a future State, as it is the most important Question which can possibly be asked, so it is the most intelligible one which can be expressed in Language. Yet strange Perplexities have been raised about the Meaning of That Identity or Sameness of Person, which is implied in the Notion of our living Now and Hereafter, or in any two successive Moments" (301). The problem of vindicating God's justice in assigning posthumous responsibility for actions performed while living was what had motivated Locke to take up the question of personal identity in the first place, and Butler believes that the problem has not been adequately solved.[26] As Butler continues the debate, "person" has replaced "soul" as the relevant concept for thinking about the afterlife. This means that, going forward, metaphysical debates about personhood will entail concrete moral and philosophical consequences, and it is in this context that the emotionally fraught relationship between Boswell and Hume, for instance, must be understood.

William Warburton: The Principles of a Religious Deist

If Joseph Butler is the philosophical superego of the mid-century Christian defense of the afterlife, William Warburton is its brawling theological id. A polemicist by temperament, he imagines himself in the preface to the second volume of the *Divine Legation of Moses Demonstrated* as a theological William III or Duke of Marlborough, waging offensive war against deists and infidels. Having "departed from the *old Posture of Defense*" and "projected a new Plan for the Support of *Revelation*," Warburton rebukes the pusillanimous clergy who "keep within [their] *strong Hold*" and do not, as he does, "sally out upon the Enemy, level his Trenches, destroy his Works, and turn his own Artillery upon him" (2:viii–ix).[27] Warburton believes that some outworks of the citadel that his clerical colleagues defend must be abandoned to the enemy, and he states frankly that in defending the fortress of revelation he will not hesitate "to dig away the Rubbish that hides its Beauty, or kick down an awkward Prop that discredits its Strength" (ibid.). In other words, Warburton acknowledges philosophical and theological challenges that make previous defenses of Christianity untenable, and he is willing to jettison them in order to strengthen the things which remain.

Warburton repeats one fundamental logical move again and again throughout the *Divine Legation:* he concedes an apparently damaging objection that a nonbeliever might offer against Christian orthodoxy, and then argues that this concession entails consequences that strengthen rather than weaken the Christian case. Though Warburton presents himself as bringing the fight to the enemy camp, the *Divine Legation* is a Parthian archer, enfilading the area it has vacated in retreat.

The full title of Warburton's work, *The Divine Legation of Moses Demonstrated, on the Principles of a Religious Deist, from the Omission of the Doctrine of a Future State of Reward and Punishment in the Jewish Dispensation,* adumbrates his most notable use of this tactic. Warburton takes the eighteenth-century freethinking critique of "priestcraft," the argument that priests and lawgivers cynically exploit human fear and superstition in the interest of personal gain and social control, and applies it specifically to the afterlife.[28] He argues that all successful lawgivers in the ancient world (including not only Pythagoras and Plato but also *"Zoroaster, Inachus, Orpheus, Melampus, Trophonius, Minos, Cinyras, Erectheus,* and the Druids") inculcated the belief in posthumous reward and punishment in their credulous subjects (1:177). Moreover, Warburton argues, no ancient philosopher who taught this doctrine could possibly have believed it, since it was inconsistent with the conceptions of the nature of God and of the soul held by all ancient schools (1:408). All philosophers and legislators—Warburton includes "the *Magi* of *Persia,* the *Druids* of *Gaul,* and the *Brachmans* of *India"*—have combined exoteric teaching of what Joe Hill would later call "pie in the sky" with esoteric unbelief (1:313).

Having conceded all of classical history to the priestcraft hypothesis, Warburton springs his trap: Moses, uniquely among lawgivers, does not promise rewards and punishments. Instead, he promises the people of Israel that under the theocratic rule of the true God, they will be governed by what Warburton calls *"temporal* Rewards and Punishments" and "an *equal Providence"* (2:437). This is to say that from Sinai to the Babylonian captivity, the Israelites were rewarded for righteousness and punished for wickedness by prosperity or suffering on earth, in this life, and that this miraculous deviation from what Warburton confesses to be the ordinary course of nature proves that Moses was not a cynical lawgiver but rather a true representative of God. Moses's divine commission established, Warburton takes as read the corresponding validity of Christ's new dispensation, in which an afterlife of rewards and punishments is at last revealed.

Warburton is giving up a great deal of terrain here. In particular, he abandons the seventh article of the Thirty-Nine Articles of the Anglican Church, which states in part that "the Old Testament is not contrary to the New; for both in the Old and New Testament everlasting life is offered to mankind by Christ, who is the only Mediator between God and man, being both God and man. Wherefore they are not to be heard which feign that the Old Fathers did look only for transitory promises," that is, merely this-worldly rewards for obedience to God.[29] In the century-long debate over whether Anglican clergy and English university students should be required to subscribe to the Thirty-Nine Articles, Warburton stood firmly in the pro-subscription camp.[30] It is revealing that he was willing to jettison an Anglican dogmatic shibboleth in order to salvage the more important doctrine of immortality.

Within this grand Parthian maneuver, Warburton executes numerous subordinate feints and volleys. Warburton enthusiastically agrees with his freethinking adversaries that religion is useful; but he argues that this makes it more likely to be true, rather than false: "If it should be said, that, supposing Religion true, it is of such Importance to Mankind, that we may well believe God would not suffer us to remain ignorant of it; I allow it. But then we are not to prescribe to the Almighty his Way of doing this. . . . Whether it be by *Revelation;* by the exercise of *Reason;* or by the accidental Imposition of it, for oblique Ends by the *Civil Magistrate*" (1:423). God, in his infinite wisdom, may choose to reveal his truth by directing it to be taught by cynical governors who do not believe it themselves. Indeed, the fact that people are so receptive to pretended revelations itself suggests that they feel an instinctive need for the guidance of revelation (2:3).

Similarly, Warburton admits that the ritual law of the Pentateuch contains demonstrable borrowings from the religious ritual of Egypt, at the cost of a lengthy refutation of the scripture chronology of Sir Isaac Newton (2:206–81). Rather than concluding, as "the ready Deist" might, that *"therefore the Establishment of the* Jewish *Policy was all Moses's own Contrivance,"* Warburton infers the opposite, that only divine wisdom would be so prudent as to allow some vestiges of the rituals adopted during their Egyptian captivity in the Hebrews' ritual practice, as a way of easing the tradition to theocratic monotheism (2:308). The fact that Moses was an Egyptian courtier and educated in Egyptian statecraft, rather than making him a more plausible imposter, merely vindicates God's ability to choose a well-qualified vice-regent (2:309). In general, the near indistinguishability of God's providence and the ordinary course of nature is no argument against the former, because "GOD, *in the moral Government of the World, never does that in an* EXTRAORDINARY *Way that can be equally effected in an* ORDINARY" (2:308). By the same token, the existence of so many false and pretended religious revelations furnishes a strong presumption that one of them is true, and Judaism, which is fulfilled in the revelation of immortality in Christianity, is Warburton's preferred candidate.

This strategy of drawing orthodox conclusions from what the title calls "the Principles of a *Religious Deist*" leads Warburton in several places to sail dangerously close to the wind. At the beginning of the second volume of the *Divine Legation,* he speculates that the devil may have inspired ancient paganism, a theory he attributes to "the ancient *Fathers*" (2:14). Yet he brackets this hypothesis by explaining that "as we have made it our business, all along, to enquire into the *natural* Causes of Paganism . . . we shall go on, in the same way" (2:15). Though this passage does not quite admit it, Warburton's argument assumes a worldview in which "Nature" is assumed to have basic explanatory force, except in the exceptional circumstances where the direct intervention of God is discernible. Thus his account of the development of language argues "from the Nature of the thing" in the manner of secular eighteenth-century conjectural history a la Rousseau or Herder, and relegates "the surer Instruction of Revelation" (Adam's naming of the animals) to a footnote (2:81). This reliance on secular-historical structures of argument, while it gives piquancy to Warburton's paradoxes, will supply infuriating (to Warburton) ammunition to secular historical accounts like Hume's "Natural History of Religion" (1757) and Gibbon's *Decline and Fall* that turn from the "*natural* Causes of Paganism" to their analogues in Christianity. In his argument that the book of Job dates to the post-exilic period, discussed in greater detail below, Warburton argues that an apparent allusion to God's publication of the law to Moses at Sinai is proof that the book was written after the Pentateuch, rejecting the theory of "the Rabbins" that "the Law of *Moses* is here spoken of by a kind of prophetic Anticipation" by an author of the patriarchal period (2:494). The principle that one man's prophecy is another man's anachronism, which could be quite damaging to Warburton's thesis elsewhere, is quarantined to this local argument. Perhaps most strikingly, he includes in his refutation of Newton's chronology of ancient Egypt a digression on legends current in the ancient world that imputed divine parents to mortals: "The first Cause of this *doubly spurious Offspring,* was the Contrivance of Wives to hide their Adultery, and of Virgins to excuse their Incontinence. The God bore the Blame, or rather the Mortal reaped the Glory: and Passion, as usual, was advanced into Piety" (2:251). If it crossed Warburton's mind that this explanation might be used by an anti-Christian skeptic to probe a very tender spot, he gives no sign.

Unlike Butler, Warburton has little interest in the questions that we now think of as philosophical; he fights the battle for Christian immortality on the field of biblical and historical criticism, rather than arguing for the metaphysical coherence or plausibility of the posthumous survival of the soul per se. His most sustained engagement with this kind of reasoning, the argument at the end of the first volume that the usefulness of a doctrine is evidence of its truth, is not exactly Kantian in sophistication (1:417). Hume, who admired Butler and sent him a copy of the *Treatise of Human Nature,* despised Warburton and thought that his arguments were below refutation.[31]

Indeed, the *Divine Legation* lacks a systematic exposition of Warburton's doctrine of the afterlife: in some places it emphasizes the immaterial soul, in others the resurrection of the body. Two emphases are constant throughout, however. First, Warburton insists that human beings will be accountable for the conduct of their mortal lives after death, and that for the majority of humankind that did not live under the Mosaic dispensation, posthumous reward and punishment at the hands of God will balance out any discrepancies between moral deserts and hedonic flourishing on earth. Warburton argues forcefully, contra Bayle, that without this belief only a few exceptional philosophers would have any reason to be virtuous, and that a civil society could never be built on an atheist or mortalist basis (1:33–78). Warburton was an Erastian; he held that the church was an indispensable yet subordinate prop to the state in preserving moral order, and believed that without heaven and hell, the moral appeal of Christianity was otiose.

Second, the *Divine Legation* is composed in a polemical tone that verges on the hysterical. While Warburton assumes various premises of his deist opponents throughout the work, sometimes with great fanfare and sometimes without appearing to notice that he is doing so, he never mentions them personally without vituperation.[32] Hume called Warburton "and all his gang, the most scurrilous, arrogant, and impudent Fellows in the world"; this description applies to a certain extent to Warburton's general affect as a man of letters, whether editing Shakespeare or defending the Anglican establishment.[33] But Warburton is particularly pugilistic in the *Divine Legation,* and its arguments suggest why; it is the work of a man who feels that his most fundamental convictions have been threatened and who is, despite his bluster, unsure of the ground on which he stands. Warburton's repeated boasts of the strength of his arguments are symptoms of insecurity and the anxiety that comes with it.

Warburton's dispensational account, which postulates a Mosaic period of theocratic rule and temporal providence and a subsequent Christian period in which reward and punishment are deferred, is an ingenious explanation of the near total silence of the Old Testament about the afterlife (albeit one that would satisfy neither a medieval hermeneut like Dante nor the higher critics of the nineteenth century and after). The rigidity of Warburton's scheme does, however, require him to explain away various refractory texts: apparent allusions to the afterlife in the Old Testament, particularly in the prophets, and passages in the New Testament that impute knowledge of immortality to Old Testament figures. Of particular interest is his extended discussion of the book of Job. Warburton's entrée into the text is Job's statement in 19:25–26: "For I know that my redeemer liveth, and that he shall stand at the latter day upon the earth: And though after my skin worms destroy this body, yet in my flesh shall I see God." In opposition to Christian readers who plausibly take this text to refer to the resurrection of the body, Warburton undertakes to prove that it refers only to Job's trust in God and faith in the restoration of his earthly health and prosperity (2:543). But Warburton goes on to offer a far more ambitious and daring reinterpretation of the book. Job is, after all, a dramatic debate about the nature of God's providence, precisely the question that interests Warburton and animates his account of the relationship between Moses and Christ. Does the book of Job depict a world of "equal providence" in which "God will not cast away a perfect man, neither will he help the evil doers"—the argument of Bildad the Shuhite in 8:20? Or does Job live under a "common providence," in which God "destroyeth the perfect and the wicked" (9:22)?

Warburton begins his answer by stating that there is only one place and time in all of human history where this is even a meaningful question: at the precise moment, which Warburton dates to the return from Babylonian exile, that God withdrew his special theocratic providence from the Jewish people. In all other time and places, the answer is too obvious:

This could never have been made *Matter of Dispute,* from the most early supposed Time of *Job's* Existence, even to ours, in any Place out of the Land of *Judea;* the Administration of Providence, which, throughout this Period, all Ages and Countries have experienced being visibly and confessedly *unequal.* . . . Nor *there* neither, in any Period of the *Jewish* Nation either before or after that in which we place it. Not *before,* because the Dispensation of Providence to this People was seen and owned by all to be equal: Not *after,* because by the total ceasing of GOD's extraordinary Administration the contrary was as evident. (2:501)

Warburton concludes that Job was written by Ezra during the period of the rebuilding of the temple, and not during the patriarchal period in which it is set.

Further, he concludes that the book is "dramatical," by which he means that it is not a chronicle of historical fact (2:487). Warburton nowhere uses the word "fiction," but his discussion of the book shows clearly that he means something very similar. This does not mean that Warburton doubts Job's historical reality; he just doubts that the book of Job contains any accurate record of it. To repurpose the old saw about Homer, Warburton argues that the book of Job is not about the proverbially patient patriarch but another man of the same name.

Job is thus an allegory, the purpose of which is "to reconcile the People by Degrees to an *unequal Providence*" (2:528). It is the record of a spiritual leader, the prophet Ezra, presenting his culture with a homiletic meditation on the nature and meaning of ongoing faithfulness to a God who is withdrawing himself from visible intervention in the affairs of the world, a God whose existence is becoming less tangible, more difficult to prove. Warburton's Job is a text that is forced to develop answers to questions that did not previously need to be asked, and to respond to arguments whose implications were previously unthinkable. In other words, by making Job a text of Ezra's time, Warburton makes it a text for his own time as well, a polemical theodicy on the model of the *Divine Legation* itself. The metaphors of battle and siegecraft with which Warburton begins his second volume cast him as a patriotic defender of established Anglicanism, but they also echo the bootstrapping military-religious ethos of post-exilic Judaism, when "every one with one of his hands wrought in the work [of building the second temple], and with the other hand held a weapon" (Nehemiah 4:16). Warburton aspires to build a constructive edifice of historical theology while at all times having weapons to hand against the sapping attacks of "deist" and "infidel" opponents. His citadel, which he comes closest to surrendering because it is the most precious to him, is of course the doctrine of the afterlife.

The literary careers of Warburton and Richardson intersect at several points in the 1740s and 1750s; Warburton wrote a prefatory note that Richardson inserted at the beginning of the fourth volume of *Clarissa* but omitted from subsequent editions. A perfectly representative sample of Warburtoniana, it combines fanciful historical speculation presented as incontestable fact (a history of the novel as a successively Spanish, French, and English form) with attention to the moral economy of providence (*Clarissa* is a "History of Life and Manners, where, as in the World itself, we find Vice, for a time, triumphant, and Virtue in Distress").[34] Richardson omitted the piece from subsequent editions, and relations between the two became frosty thereafter, not least because of Richardson's low estimation of the theology of Warburton's friend Pope and Warburton's petulant attacks on the editorial principles of Richardson's Shakespearean friend Thomas Edwards. It is unclear whether Richardson ever read the *Divine Legation* (Edwards makes a hostile reference to it in a letter to Richardson of February 1755).[35] But *Clarissa,* the novel that Richardson wrote after *Pamela* brought him to Warburton's notice but before their breach, can be read as updating the book of Job in precisely the terms suggested by Warburton's reading, as a religious fiction for an age coming to grips with the apparent retreat of God. *Clarissa,* in other words, is an apology for belief in the *deus absconditus* who allows vice to triumph and virtue to suffer in this world, with the paradoxical effect of diminishing the plausibility while increasing the necessity of a posthumous rebalancing of the providential scales. It is to this apology that we now turn.

4

The Beatified Clarissa

Is *Clarissa* a religious novel?[1] The critical tradition has generated formidable arguments for both sides. The inaugural "yes" belongs to Richardson himself; as he writes in a postscript to the novel, "The Author ... imagined ... he could *steal in,* as may be said, and investigate the great doctrines of Christianity under the fashionable guise of an amusement" (8:279). Meanwhile the origin of the naysaying tradition, as Florian Stuber has pointed out, lies with Smith and Diderot, deists who nevertheless "declared Richardson to be 'the greatest moralist of all time.'"[2] Subsequent secular readings have included the psychological (and in many twentieth-century incarnations, Freudian) approach that runs from Samuel Taylor Coleridge to mid-twentieth-century Richardsonians such as Ian Watt or the biographers T. C. Duncan Eaves and Ben D. Kimpel, as well as the Marxist reading of Terry Eagleton and poststructuralist interventions from William Warner and Terry Castle.[3] But the weight of recent scholarship has fallen overwhelmingly on the religious side of the scale, so much so that a better question now might be "What kind of religious novel is *Clarissa?*" As E. Derek Taylor observes, "Richardson has been claimed as a Puritan, a via media Anglican, [and] a Boehmian mystic"—and Taylor takes the view that this diversity of opinion is a result of Richardson's own syncretism, not modern scholarly fractiousness.[4]

The argument that follows claims a place for *Clarissa* in the tradition of eighteenth-century Anglican letters, an heir to Addison's *Spectator* and Young's *Night Thoughts,* and a novelistic exposition of the tenets of Butler and—despite his ambivalent personal relationship with Richardson—

Warburton. I also argue that Richardson cross-pollinates and vivifies this tradition with other theological influences. A recent study by E. Derek Taylor has "un-Locked" *Clarissa* in order to link it not with mainstream eighteenth-century empiricism but rather with the theology of the Anglican clergyman and Neoplatonic philosopher John Norris.[5] Equally important is Margaret Anne Doody and David Hensley's recovery of the novel's imaginative debt to the mysticism of Jakob Boehme and his English disciple, the nonjuror and mystic William Law. Without the influence of Norris, *Clarissa* would lack its reformatory appeal to the rational "attention" of its readers, who are presented with a noncoercive but unmistakable invitation to look beyond its welter of realistic detail for a supersensible Christian reality. Without Boehme and Law, the novel would lack both its "symbolic depth," in Doody's phrase, and what Hensley calls its "dialectical ambivalence," which resists both secularist reductionism and trite conduct-book morality.[6] *Clarissa* is capacious enough to contain many theological mansions.

And yet: the exemplary Clarissa Harlowe is a communicant of the established church, and her moral formation as a girl and young lady is attributed to correspondence with Anglican divines (8:203). She declines to leave London during her slow death because she wishes to benefit spiritually from attendance at its churches, and it is in an Anglican church that she is buried with her ancestors (6:420, 8:85–90). When outfitting Mrs. Sinclair's house with books that will win Clarissa's approval, Lovelace stocks it with Anglican devotional, exegetical, and liturgical works, as well as "lighter" works including "the Tatlers, Spectators, and Guardians."[7] This same tradition bulks large in Richardson's paratextual extensions of the work, from the preface by Warburton printed before the third and fourth volumes of the first edition to the extensive quotation of Addison in the postscript.[8] While *Clarissa* satirizes clerical pedantry and the irreligious classicism of university education, its proposed antidote to the contemptible Elias Brand is the pious Dr. Lewen, not a Bunyan, Boehme, or Wesley.

The status of *Clarissa* as a religious novel is not merely a matter of sociological detail. Like its near contemporaries *The Analogy of Religion* and *The Divine Legation*, *Clarissa* is a forceful argument for the reality and necessity of the afterlife, and like *Night Thoughts* it argues formally that personal and moral formation happen over time. In the teeth of notorious reader resistance, Richardson insists on a plot that sharpens the Butlerian argument from desire (human beings do not achieve full perfection in this life, so there must be something more) into a cri de couer of sympathetic anguish ("This cannot, surely, be All of my Clarissa's Story!" as Anna Howe puts it [8:79]). By the same token, Clarissa presents a vividly contemporary instance of Warburton's unequal providence, Job in 1740s London. Richardson reinterprets the mode of tragedy, and expands the representational possibilities of the novel, to supply each with a distinctly Christian purpose. Moreover, Richardson deploys the novel's length to show by precept and example that the afterlife is won through the gradual accumulation of practices, habits, and traits. Clarissa's perfection is the result of a demanding regimen of reading and writing; Belford's reformation is the work of years. The novel is vivid, minute, and immediate so that we will want to imagine Clarissa in heaven; it is long so that we will know how she gets there and how we can follow. Richardson emphasizes Clarissa's particularity in order to sharpen her exemplary power; the representational techniques of prose immortality, here developed to represent a fictional character, emerge from Richardson's theological commitments. Finally, the reception of *Clarissa* connects Richardson's own personal and literary immortality. Admiring readers saw the novel's moral-aesthetic power as a cause both for its author's enduring earthly fame and for his future heavenly happiness. To use Young's terminology, readers awarded *Clarissa* both the laurel and the palm. Indeed, I conclude this chapter with a brief episode from the reception of *Clarissa*—Goethe's account in *Dichtung und Wahrheit* of his ambition in young adulthood to write a Richardsonian novel in order to memorialize his beloved sister after her death—that illustrates Richardson's success in making the novel a forum for thinking about literary as well as personal immortality.

Her Last Scene

On the first of December 1748, five days before the publication of the fifth, sixth, and seventh volumes of *Clarissa*, Samuel Richardson presented his wife with a complete seven-volume set of the novel. He included a letter:

Dear Bett,
    Do you know, that the beatified CLARISSA was often very uneasy at the Time her Story cost the Man whom you favour with your Love; and that chiefly on your Account?
    She was.

And altho' she made not a posthumous Apology to you on that Account, as she did, on other Occasions, to several of those who far less deserved to be apologized to; I know so well her Mind, that she would greatly have approved of this Acknowledgement, and of the Compliment I now make you, in Her Name, of the Volumes which contain her History.

May you, my dear Bett, May I, and all Ours, benefit by the Warnings, and by the Examples given in them!—And may our last Scenes be closed as happily as Her last Scene is represented to have done!—Are the Prayers of

Yours most affectionate

Whilst

S. Richardson[9]

One could scarcely devise a more concentrated synecdoche of Richardson's temperament and his tragic novel's achievement than this 148-word domestic paratext. It is the composition of Richardson the graphomaniac, a self-described "sorry pruner" and "voluminous . . . Scribbler" for whom one letter, both in art and in life, must inevitably beget another.[10] Having written 537 letters in the first edition of *Clarissa,* Richardson cannot resist adding a 538th, though he acknowledges how much "Time" Clarissa's "Story" has already cost him. Clarissa does not apologize to Elizabeth Richardson in *Clarissa,* but Richardson imagines her approving of his own apology. At the same time, this letter juxtaposes the endless proliferation of text with the end-stopped finitude of Clarissa's earthly life. Richardson eschews the timeless present tense in which critics of our own time narrate the actions of fictional characters, deploying instead an emphatic past: "Clarissa was often uneasy," "she made not a posthumous Apology." Because Clarissa is now dead, her opinions cannot be known directly; for all of his authority, Richardson can only say that she "would greatly have approved" of his note. Both of these features are representative: the text of *Clarissa* was from the beginning a site of expansion, revision, and contestation, yet at the same time, structured around a non-negotiable, irrevocable, fatal end.

Clarissa works by forcing its readers to confront and fill the space between their own desires and the satisfactions provided by the text. The readerly desires in question are twofold. First of all, readers of eighteenth-century narrative longed for more story, more text. David Brewer has documented the prevalence of what he calls "imaginative expansion" in eighteenth-century reading communities, the practice of transposing characters such as Lemuel Gulliver or Pamela Andrews into new media, new settings, and new stories.[11] Richardson's *Pamela in Her Exalted Condition* is both a defensive response and a contribution to this tradition. *Clarissa* elicited several expansionary intertexts of this kind, including Richardson's above-cited letter of dedication to his wife, his own compilations of moral sentiments and scriptural meditations, the alternate ending written by Lady Echlin, and lyrics like Friedrich Gottlieb Klopstock's mourning elegy *Die todte Clarissa*.[12] Even greater than the desire to expand or contribute to a text, moreover, is the readerly longing for justice, satisfaction, for the good to end happily and the bad unhappily. As William Flesch puts it in *Comeuppance,* his study of the evolutionary roots of human interest in narrative, "We are constituted to take an intense emotional interest in the nonactual . . . and in the actors who involve themselves in adjusting the outcomes of nonactual events through strong reciprocation, that is, through rewarding those who are good . . . and punishing the cheaters."[13]

In the case of *Pamela,* the pleasures of imaginative expansion and of punishment and reward run in parallel: Richardson's sequel both gives his readers "more" of Pamela and shows her receiving further rewards for her virtue. In *Clarissa,* they pull in opposite directions. Richardson forecloses the possibility of a sequel depicting happy married life, channeling the expansive impulse into texts like Klopstock's ode or his own dedicatory letter to his wife. There can be no *Clarissa Lovelace in Her Exalted Condition,* and no alternate story that depicts such a condition can be compatible with his own. For this same reason, the novel also pointedly withholds from Clarissa the satisfying marital reward that crowns the earthly happiness of both her predecessor Pamela Andrews and her successor Harriet Byron. As Tom Keymer puts it, "The novel's denial of what Frank Kermode has called 'the sense of an ending,' that final gratifying resolution which lends a retrospective completeness and meaning to lives and texts, seemed intolerable; and most intolerable of all was the absence of visible justice."[14] The result is to leave the reader, however unwillingly, with a desire that can only be satisfied by imagining a heavenly afterlife for "the beatified Clarissa." The novel ends with Clarissa's death, and thus it invites the reader to realize that death cannot be the end of Clarissa. "I could not think of leaving my Heroine short of Heaven," Richardson tells Lady Bradshaigh in a letter written two weeks after he presented the completed novel to his wife.[15] Though Clarissa's thoughts and opinions must now be referred to in the past, as Richardson's letter to his wife suggests, she is herself "beatified." The adjectival participle is perfect in both the grammatical and theological sense—Clarissa is both done and without fault. *Clarissa* forces the reader to confront the space between Clarissa's fate on the one hand, and her moral deserts and their own desires on the other. In so doing, it channels the readers' desire for a happy ending into the morally formative project of positing an afterlife.

After visiting Clarissa at the glove shop whither she has fled from Lovelace and Sinclair, Belford writes a letter to Lovelace that mingles reproach with literary criticism: "What a fine Subject for Tragedy would the injuries of this Lady, and her behavior under them, both with regard to her implacable friends, and to her persecutor, make! With a grand objection as to the Moral, nevertheless (a); for here Virtue is punished! Except indeed we look forward to the Rewards of HEREAFTER, which, morally, *she* must be sure of, or who can?" (7:122–23).

Here Belford is doing what Lovelace does elsewhere in the novel: he is imagining Clarissa as a character in a play.[16] But he adds the reflection that such a play could only have a coherent moral were its heroine to have an afterlife. With almost Borgesian involution, that is, he imagines turning Clarissa into a literary artifact within the frame of the novel, only to perform on that artifact the same act of theological imaginative expansion, giving Clarissa the tragic heroine a heavenly afterlife, that Richardson and his readers do. Lovelace too turns Clarissa into a character, but when doing so he is unable to treat her as a "real" person: he prefers to think of her as "property"—in the word's implicit dramatic sense, that is, as an inanimate part of his drama rather than as a fellow actor (see, for example, 4:355, 5:17, 8:145). Despite his prowess as a creator of plots, Lovelace is thus a bad reader because he cannot open himself to the possibility that his creations might have life outside of his fiction. His obtuseness in the face of the father's house letter and his wish-fulfilling interpretation of his final dream are representative of a larger failure to read Clarissa herself correctly (7:175–79).[17]

In a footnote after the word "nevertheless," Richardson continues Belford's train of thought about tragedies and morals, extending it by imagining canonical characters finding their rewards in heaven: "Mr. Belford's objection that virtue ought not to suffer in a tragedy is not well considered. . . . Cordelia in Shakespeare's King Lear, Desdemona in Othello, Hamlet (to name no more) are instances, that a Tragedy could hardly be justly called a

Tragedy, if Virtue did not temporarily suffer, and Vice for a while triumph. But he recovers himself in the same paragraph; and leads us to look up to the FUTURE for the reward of virtue, and for the punishment of guilt" (7:123).

Horatio's flights of angels notwithstanding, we may find it odd to imagine Hamlet receiving a "well done, good and faithful servant" in the undiscovered country from whose bourn no traveler returns. According to Richardson, however, the reader must imagine just such an epilogue after the curtain comes down to understand the moral coherence of *Hamlet* (or *Othello* or *King Lear*). Where the plot of a play does not reward good and punish evil, the spectator is to imagine God's judgment doing so afterward. Imaginative expansion, imagining a life and indeed an afterlife for characters outside their texts, becomes Richardson's paradigm for reading not only his own characters, but Shakespeare's too.

Belford's reasoning, that Clarissa's sufferings on earth will be redressed in heaven, follows the eighteenth-century "moral argument" for the afterlife as a theodicean makeweight.[18] But the structure of *Clarissa* also connects it to the argument from desire. This is the idea, expressed by Addison, Young, Butler, and Johnson among others, that a benevolent creator would not limit the human soul, with its self-awareness and infinite potential, to the brief span of mortal life.[19] Two simple diagrams will explicate the connection to *Clarissa*. The following arc traces the plot of Nahum Tate's adaptation of *King Lear,* whose happy ending Richardson found inferior to the original.[20] The horizontal axis represents time and the vertical axis represents plot; that is, the arc marks the distance from the harmony and concord with which the play begins and ends:

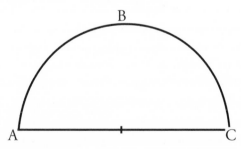

A marks the place where Edmund's plot and Lear's misguided division of his kingdom inaugurates the play's events; *B* marks the high-water mark of tragic chaos, say the putting out of Gloster's eyes. *C* marks the conclusion, where the good end happily, the bad unhappily, Edgar marries Cordelia,

"Peace spreads her balmy wings, and Plenty blooms."[21] Here we have a perfect realization of Thomas Rymer's concept of poetic justice.[22] Who could ask for more?

The following tragic arc, in contrast, plots *Clarissa:*

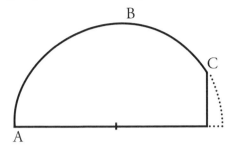

A marks Lovelace's entrance into the orbit of Harlowe Place, which sets in motion the disasters that follow. *B* marks the rape, and *C* marks Clarissa's death. This is not the end of the novel, of course, but it is the end of the hope, urgently expressed by so many early readers, that Richardson's narrative would close like Tate's. What is left is not only Lovelace's death but also an open space, outlined in dots above, where the reader is invited to close the circle herself, to take a leap of faith and imagine a Clarissa beyond the text, "divested of the shades of body . . . all light and all mind" (7:407).[23] If my plot diagrams recall *Tristram Shandy,* Richardson anticipates it, providing a tragic version of Sterne's comic invitation a decade later to "halve this matter amicably," leaving the reader "something to imagine, in his turn, as well as" the author himself.[24] The evidence demonstrates that early readers could not bear to limit Clarissa to Richardson's text, but instead extrapolated her into their own fictions and even their own lives. Yet through Clarissa's death, Richardson's novel directs this expansive energy toward the afterlife. Just as the argument from desire observes a space between human potential and mortal achievement and postulates a heaven for the gap, *Clarissa* leaves its heroine's posthumous existence unnarrated but encourages readers to feel the resulting absence and undertake to fill it.

It is important to register that the afterlife-shaped hole in the plot of *Clarissa* is radically empty; it cannot be filled by mere imaginative extrapolation, like an omitted letter whose contents the reader, with more than five hundred models to build on, can all too readily imagine. Clarissa speaks of foretastes and assurances of heaven in her final weeks, and Lovelace's dream in volume 7 includes a conventional vision of "golden Cherubs and glittering Seraphs," but the reader has no reason to believe that these are authoritative foreshadowings of heaven itself (7:147–48, 370, 424).[25] The reader is impelled to imagine a heaven that is unimaginable.

Richardson's deployment of the mysticism of William Law and Jakob Boehme is a substantial aesthetic and theological asset as he develops this theme. David Hensley, who uses the pious critic and man of letters Thomas Edwards as an exemplary mystical reader of *Clarissa* in the Law tradition, argues that the novel comprises

> first, an implicit demand on the reader to reconstruct or comprehend the whole story or truth to which the partial positions of Clarissa and Lovelace both lay claim: we are challenged to *totalize* the meaning of the book. Second, however, Edwards also recognizes the *untotalizability* of *Clarissa,* that its form remains indeterminate or open despite the incorporative priority of Clarissa's editorial framing and attempted control of the entire collection of letters. Edwards, the editorial scholar as passionately attentive reader, thus sees in *Clarissa* a paradoxical co-existence of formal demands for and claims to objective truth and the structural necessity of its unattainability. But this paradox itself, instead of being a weakness of the novel, constitutes for Edwards its "inexhaustible" beauty and sublimity.[26]

In Hensley's reading, Clarissa's death scene is a "structural and theological riddle," because as readers we witness "signs of Clarissa's absolute Neoplatonic return to unity," yet at the same time "we are made acutely aware that 'CLARISSA's Story' (8:79; 4:402) is an ongoing process in its effects both in the novel and on us."[27] To put this another way: we cannot follow Clarissa into heaven, or even know for certain that she is there. We can never, if we are Thomas Edwards or Lady Bradshaigh, stop crying at her tragic fate. As a result, we can never stop longing for heaven, either for Clarissa or for ourselves. Richardson ensures that the argument from desire can never be answered, because the desire for heaven can never be fulfilled.

Path Dependency in *Clarissa*

The metaphor of life as a journey that reaches its destination in death is both ancient and conventional. The concept of the *viaticum* (literally, "traveling money"), a final Eucharist administered before death, places the metaphor at the center of Catholic sacramental theology, while Bunyan's

Pilgrim's Progress makes it the governing allegory of a Calvinist narrative.[28] The action of *Clarissa* takes place overwhelmingly in enclosed domestic spaces: the closets and parlors of Harlowe Place, the dining room at Mrs. Sinclair's, the lodgings at Hampstead, the prison in High-Holborn, the apartments of Mrs. Smith, and finally the *"House"* that Clarissa orders from the undertaker (7:332). But its characters repeatedly describe their lives in terms of a journey taken along a path. Moreover, the major formal features of the text—its notorious length and its much-discussed realism—allow Richardson to model features of this metaphor that are merely asserted in previous literary articulations. A journey is gradual and cumulative; one cannot move instantly from the beginning to the end without covering the intermediate route. Traveling along a path takes time, and the longer one defers the journey the less time one has to complete it. *Clarissa* takes eight volumes to show these principles in action.

Thus Charlotte Montague exhorts her cousin Lovelace to marry Clarissa with a pitch-perfect pastiche of Addison: "O Cousin, what a vast, vast, journey have you take from the dreary Land of Libertinism, thro' the bright Province of Reformation, into the serene Kingdom of Happiness!—You had need to lose no time. You have many a weary step to tread, before you can overtake those travellers, who set out for it from a less remote quarter. But you have a charming Polestar to guide you; that's your advantage" (5:106–7). This vague and secularized allegory leaves unclear whether the "Kingdom of Happiness" is in this world (marriage with Clarissa) or in the next (efficacious repentance and salvation). Given that his family greeted the news of Lovelace's death with "apprehension with regard to his future happiness," the latter interpretation is not implausible (8:251). Other presentations of the idea place the emphasis more explicitly on the good death. Clarissa asks Belford for details of the death of his rakish friend Belton: "You must not wonder at my enquiries, Mr. Belford, said she; for who is it that is to undertake a journey into a country they never travelled to before, that enquires not into the difficulties of the road, and what accommodations are to be expected in the way?" (7:258).

In the first half of *Clarissa,* Clarissa Harlowe takes a "false step," down the faulty path out of Harlowe Place and into Lovelace's clutches.[29] While Clarissa goes astray, Lovelace prosecutes his plots against her with single-minded dedication, glorying in his power as an encroacher and contriver. In the second half of the novel, it is Clarissa's journey that takes on purpose and direction: she proceeds deliberately until she arrives at her Father's House.

Lovelace, in contrast, loses his way, meandering aimlessly first through the suburbs of London and then, after Clarissa's death, through the capitals of Europe. A letter from Lovelace to Belford from volume 7, with the miserable superscription "Uxbridge, Tuesday Morn. between 4 and 5," vividly shows this reversal:

> Forbidden to attend the dear creature . . . I ride towards London three or four times a day, resolving *pro* and *con* twenty times in two or three miles; and at last ride back; and, in view of Uxbridge, loathing even the kind friend and hospitable house, turn my horse's head again towards the town. . . . Yesterday, in particular, to give you an idea of the strength of that impatience . . . I had no sooner dispatched Will. than I took horse to meet him on his return.

> I order to give him time, I loitered about on the road, riding up *this* Lane to the one highway, down *that* to the other, just as my horse pointed; all the way cursing my very being. (7:362–63)

Lovelace has lost control of the plot, and is reduced to the status of a mere reader, waiting for news of Clarissa from Belford. At the same time, he has lost his way; with no path to follow, he merely "saunter[s]" through the streets (7:363). The starts and stops of his impatient ride symbolize the aimlessness that overtakes Lovelace after the rape. He repeatedly talks himself in and out of marrying Clarissa, expresses and then mocks at remorse, and flirts with the idea of repentance and amendment before changing his mind and rejecting it (see, for example, 6:27, 6:75, 7:85–86, 8:132).

Before the rape, Lovelace's protean changefulness is a source of power. Lovelace can keep Clarissa guessing about his intentions, penetrate her refuge at Hampstead in disguise, and deceive her with the brilliant dramatic duet he performs with "Captain Tomlinson." But even at the moment that his power seems to be greatest, Lovelace himself recognizes that mutability is not the same thing as freedom. In letter 21 of volume 5, Lovelace narrates strangling and stabbing his feminized "*Conscience*" as a preparative to his decisive assault on Clarissa two days later (224). As part of the struggle, the "intruding varletess" conscience steals his pen and writes the following words, "in a hand exactly like [Lovelace's] own": "As I hope to live, I am sorry (at the present writing) that I have been such a foolish plotter, as to put it, as I fear I have done, out of my *own power* to be honest. I hate compulsion in all forms; and cannot bear, even to be *compelled* to be the wretch my choice has made me!—So now, Belford, as thou hast said, I am a machine at last, and no free agent" (223).

Libertines, "Gentlemen of free lives," as Richardson calls them in his preface, are those who aspire to be free agents (1:v). Yet Lovelace's struggle with his conscience layers irony on top of gratuitous irony, showing just how unfree the freethinker and freeliver really is. His pen has been stolen by an automatic moral faculty within himself whose writing he cannot control. She in turn shows him how he has turned into a "machine" not merely morally (he is unfeeling, impervious to Clarissa's pleas for mercy) but even causally. He cannot not rape Clarissa: "Yet already have I not gone too far? Like a repentant thief, afraid of his gang, and obliged to go on, in fear of hanging till he comes to be hanged, I am afraid of the gang of my cursed contrivances" (5:223). At the moment that Lovelace's plots take on an anthropomorphized life of their own, forming a *Beggar's Opera*-esque criminal "gang," their author becomes a dehumanized "machine at last." The chiastic structure and ugly jangling rhyme of gang/hanging/hanged/gang underlines the force of this reversal, by which the momentum and inertia of his past actions deprive Lovelace of his freedom.[30] Lovelace has come along a path and cannot simply return to a previous place without retracing his steps. Yet this insight itself is intermittent, inefficacious, available only "at present writing." It is not in fact the first step in a new direction or the beginning of a cumulative process, like Clarissa's preparation for death or Belford's repentance.

Clarissa is a novel of inescapable path dependencies. As Clarissa puts it, rebuking Lovelace in Hampstead for the sham fire at Mrs. Sinclair's, "*Thou that hadst a plain path before thee,* after thou hadst betrayed me into thy power—At once my mind takes in the whole of they crooked behaviours" (5:130). Among other reasons, Richardson cannot end *Clarissa* with the happy marriage that so many readers wanted because this ending is explicitly closed off by earlier moments in the text, as a road not taken. Lovelace's murdered conscience returns from the dead after the rape and once more commandeers his pen to acknowledge the justice of Clarissa's formulation: "What force [Allow me a serious reflection, Jack: It *will* be put down! What force] have evil habits upon the human mind! When we enter upon a devious course, we think we shall have it in our power when we will to return to the right path. But it is not so, I plainly see" (5:351).[31] His conscience again in abeyance, Lovelace jokes about overtaking Belford on the road to repentance: "it is an up-hill work; and I shall see thee, at setting out, at a great distance; but as thou art a much heavier and clumsier fellow than myself, I hope that without much puffing and sweating, only keeping on a good round dog-trot, I shall be able to overtake thee" (7:196).[32] Instead, of course, Lovelace sets out on his aimless Grand Tour.

Preparation for death takes time: shortly before her own beatification, Clarissa administers a "charming lecture" to the penitent Belford "upon the happiness of a timely Preparation, and upon the hazards of a late Repentance" (7:420). The text has already made this point repeatedly with negative examples such as Mrs. Sinclair and Belton, the latter of whom wishes he could have a year to prepare "with the same sense of things" that he has on his deathbed (7:162). The length and minute detail of Richardson's text is thus part of its moral purpose. In an important recent article, Adam Budd has argued that in *Clarissa,* the "model for reformation" is not merely Clarissa but also Belford.[33] Belford's "editorial heroism" consists in a new course of life anchored in the attentive and time-consuming rereading of *Clarissa* itself: "Whenever I am in danger, I will read some of the admirable Lady's papers: Whenever I would abhor my former ways, I will read some of thine, and copies of my own" (8:139–40). As David Hensley has shown, this reader effect produced within the frame of the text is also well documented beyond it: "To die like Clarissa, what a full complement of felicity that would be!" the clergyman Thomas Edwards rhapsodizes to Richardson, while Friedrich Klopstock imagines molding himself into a "Clarissus."[34]

As Belford's resolution to reread Clarissa's writings suggests, part of Clarissa's exemplarity lies in the fact that she documents her life in such meticulous detail; part of the journey consists in leaving behind a map. For seventeenth-century Puritanism, self-documentation was a spiritual discipline because it allowed the writer to search out signs of regeneration, changes in the self that could be taken as signs of election.[35] For Clarissa, narrative writing plays a very different role: it is a record of gradual moral formation rather than sudden, inspired conversion. A recorded life and a good death, the two sides of Clarissa's exemplarity, are radically continuous. Sarah Fielding's *Remarks on Clarissa* (1749) is eloquent on this connection between a life lived in time and its end in eternity: "The gentle Clarissa's Death is the natural Consequence of her innocent Life; her calm and prepared Spirit, like a soft smooth Stream, flows gently on, till it slides from her Misfortunes, and she leaves the World free from Fear, and animated only by a lively Hope."[36] This connection is also embodied structurally in *Clarissa* through the doubling of Clarissa's death and the novel's genesis, by means of Belford's executorship. The novel is, as Richardson's alternate title would have it, *The Lady's Legacy,* a testament that doubles as a self-constructed and self-justifying Book of Life.[37]

In this way, theology enters into literary history. In order to show the difference between Belford's sincere repentance and Lovelace's fleeting, temporary remorse, Richardson must show time. In order for a text to be morally useful to the reader, it must be long enough that reading it takes time.

The Blessed Lord Jesus and King Philip's Skull

Clarissa's death asks the reader to take a leap of imaginative faith into emptiness, but only after the exhaustive archive of her life brings the reader to that point along a path paved by plenitude. Indeed, these two effects reinforce each other. Clarissa herself finds it easy to pass over into death precisely because she has spent so much time preparing for it: "What is dying but the common lot?—The mortal frame may *seem* to labour—But that is all!—It is not so hard to die, as I believed it to be!—The Preparation is the difficulty" (8:5).

This "Preparation" is, in large part, writing: Clarissa leaves behind posthumous letters, a series of meditations, her custom-ordered coffin, and of course the lengthy and discursive will that contains instructions for the editorial compilation of *Clarissa* itself.[38] Clarissa survives as text after she perishes as a human body.

Belford informs Lovelace of Clarissa's precise manner and time of death: Thursday, September 7, at 6:40 p.m., with the words "Blessed Lord— JESUS!" on her lips (8:7–8). But at the same time that his letter links this world and the next with chronometric specificity, it also slides over the instant of death: "And with these words, the last but half-pronounced, expired: Such a smile, such a charming serenity overspreading her sweet face at the instant, as seemed to manifest her eternal happiness already begun" (8:7). Belford records in full the word, "JESUS," that Clarissa lives to speak only in part. Even at the level of stenographic transcription, the text of *Clarissa* models the imaginative projection of the afterlife; Belford imagines Clarissa completing the word in the afterlife, just as she seems to have entered her reward before fully dying—her "eternal happiness" has "already begun."[39] For Clarissa, though not for her readers, death is just one moment in an unbroken trajectory.

Clarissa's death scene thus illustrates an eighteenth-century moral commonplace: individual moments are empty until they are aggregated into a cumulative, progressive whole. Lovelace's love of plotting furnishes a negative version of this same insight. What is true of *ars moriendi* applies to *cherchez la femme* as well: "What, as I have often contemplated, is the enjoyment of the finest woman in the world, to the contrivance, the bustle, the surprizes, and at last the happy conclusion, of a well-laid plot?—The charming *round-abouts,* to come the *nearest way home;*—the doubts, the apprehensions; the heart-akings; the meditated triumphs—These are the joys that make the blessing dear. For all the rest, what is it? What but to find an Angel in imagination dwindled down to a woman in fact?" (6:9–10).

The metaphor of the journey reappears in the "*round-abouts*" and bawdy "*nearest way home*" of a seduction. The moment of actual sexual conquest is always nugatory, characterized by the detumescent dwindling of the angelic fantasy object into mere reality. Thus at the moment of rape, Lovelace turns Clarissa from an angel into something less than a woman: "The affair is over. Clarissa lives" (5:291). Lovelace, for once at a loss for words, sees Clarissa as a bare life, a mere animal being. At the triumphant moment of her death, in contrast, the reader imagines the rape undone as Clarissa turns from a woman back into an angel.

Indeed, the parallel between the empty moment of sexual consummation and the transitory moment of death lies at the heart both of Richardson's text and Lovelace's worldview. Lovelace's first letter to Belford after the rape is the lapidary twenty-two-word note whose six crucial words have just been quoted, but his next letter, and first extended reflection on what he has done, contains the following:

> At times, I cannot help regretting, that I ever attempted her; since not *one power either of Body or Soul* could be moved in my favour; and since, to use the expression of the philosopher, on a much graver occasion, There is no difference to be found between the skull of king Philip, and that of another man.... When all's done, Miss Clarissa Harlowe has but run the fate of a thousand others of her Sex—Only that they did not set such a romantic value upon what they call their *Honour;* that's all. (5:295)[40]

Lovelace's train of thought concedes implicitly that raping a "senseless" woman, deprived of both her "strength" and "intellects," is a necrophilic act (6:174). But the explicit force of his conceit extends to all sexual consummations: in its plotless and universal physical immediacy, coitus is death.

Despite the "romantic value" she sets on it, the "*Honour*" of the peerless Clarissa is the same as that of "a thousand others," just as the skull of a king cannot be distinguished from that of any other man (5:295; see *OED*, s.v. "honour," definition 3b, for the anatomical use of the word to mean the female *pudenda/die Scham*). Lovelace compresses all the necrophilic frisson of Hamlet's graveyard scene, with the skull of Yorick, Alexander the Great's bunghole, and the corpse of Ophelia, into a single grotesque sentence.

Death is easy for Clarissa; preparation is all. Sex is empty for Lovelace; plots are what count. In both cases, the seemingly crucial moment is revealed as unimportant beside the gradual process that has led up to it. Not only is *Clarissa* a novel of path dependency, but it is also a novel in which the path is more important than the destination, because each individual must follow a unique path. That is to say, the novel's sexual and thanatic climaxes are empty in part because they represent experiences that are universal: we all die, and all "skulls" are the same. In an insightful recent article, Spencer Jackson has argued that Clarissa uses death "to assume divine independence . . . to pursue the life of the supremely detached and sovereign." Death is a form of resistance to patriarchy and a protest against the marriage plot. This reading cuts against earlier critics who have "interpreted [Clarissa's final weeks] according to a false dichotomy of divine transcendence and mortal particularity." I wish to appropriate Jackson's happy formulation, but repurpose it from his own interest in political theology and Clarissa's death to moral theology and Clarissa's preceding life. Clarissa is exemplary precisely because of her divine particularity. Richardson thus distinguishes his tragic allegory in prose from its medieval and Renaissance predecessors by insisting on the moral importance of the individual, as visible in the cumulative details of realistic narrative. Clarissa is not Pilgrim, or Everyman, or even Everywoman. Paradoxically, it is her individuality, the "character" that she wins within the conventions of the novel, that makes her exemplary. "Let me tell you, Sir," Lovelace addresses Hickman, "That you never saw, never knew, never heard of, such another woman as Miss Harlowe" (6:337). Conversely, it is the precise nature of Lovelace's particular plots, the specific unfreedom that overtakes him as he is hemmed in by his contrivances, that puts him on his own personal highway to hell.

The Afterlife of Clarissa

As noted above, the models of Clarissa and Belford invite readers to become writers, to work out their salvation with authorial diligence. Richardson's male coterie of fellow writers tend to express doubled hopes for the afterlife that recall this connection: mingling the metaphors of literary and personal immortality, Aaron Hill and Patrick Delaney, for instance, borrow the Christian language of resurrection to express the hope that their neglected works will find more appreciative audiences after their deaths.[41] A letter from Edward Young to Richardson shortly after the publication of *Clarissa* expresses this doubled conception of immortality yet more clearly: "And as I look on you as an instrument of Providence, I likewise look on you as a sure heir of a double immortality; when our language fails, one, indeed, may cease; but the failure of the Heavens' and the Earth will put no period to the other. . . . Happy is the man whose head has secured him one immortality, and whose heart entitles him to the other!"[42] In a poetics that assumes the ultimate purpose of literature is instruction, personal salvation and literary immortality are necessarily coextensive. Lengthy prose narratives are equipped to provide both.

But *Clarissa*, a fiction whose emotional force invited and elicited quixotic responses and imaginative expansions, also suggested to its readers new possibilities for documenting and preserving a real human life as a literary character. One such reader was Johann Wolfgang von Goethe, whose beloved sister Cornelia Friederike Christiane died at only twenty-seven after a deeply unhappy marriage.[43] In *Dichtung und Wahrheit*, Goethe records:

> Da ich dieses geliebte, unbegreifliche Wesen nur zu bald verlor, fühlte ich genugsamen Anlaß, mir ihren Wert zu vergegenwärtigen, und so entstand bei mir der Begriff eines dichterischen Ganzen, in welchem es möglich gewesen wäre, ihre Individualität darzustellen; allein es ließ sich dazu keine andere Form denken als die der Richardsonschen Romane. Nur durch das genauste Detail, durch unendliche Einzelheiten, die lebendig alle den Charakter des Ganzen tragen und, indem sie aus einer wundersamen Tiefe hervorspringen, eine Ahnung von dieser Tiefe geben, nur auf solche Weise hätte es einigermaßen gelingen können, eine Vorstellung dieser merkwürdigen Persönlichkeit mitzuteilen: denn die Quelle kann nur gedacht werden, insofern sie fließt. Aber von diesem schönen und frommen Vorsatz zog mich, wie von so vielen

anderen, der Tumult der Welt zurück, und nun blieb mich nichts übrig, als den Schatten jenes seligen Geistes nur, wie durch Hilfe eines magischen Spiegels, auf einen Augenblick heranzurufen.

Since I lost this beloved, incomprehensible being all too soon, I felt sufficient inducement to represent her worth to myself, and so there arose in me the idea of a poetic whole, in which it would have been possible to exhibit her individuality, but I could think of no other form but that of the Richardsonian novels. Only by the minutest detail, by endless particular points which all bear vividly the character of the whole, and while springing from a wonderful depth give some feeling of that depth—only in such a way could one in some measure succeed in communicating a representation of this remarkable personality, for the spring can only be understood while it is flowing. But from this beautiful and pious resolve, as from so many things, I was drawn away by the tumult of the world, and now nothing remains for me but to call up for a moment the shadow of that blessed spirit, as though by the help of a magic mirror.[44]

Richardsonian realism is a generic road that Goethe does not, in the end, take. But this passage recognizes what such a treatment is capable of doing: by representing "minutest detail," a *Clarissa*-like novel of Cornelia's life could represent her personality to those who did not know her. The metaphor of a spring combines the idea of depth—interior complexity of personality and character—with dynamism, the flow of "endless particular points." Because the details of a Richardson novel flow endlessly, they mimic a living being; after the spring of life has been stilled by death, the spring of narration and description provides it with a moving afterlife. The English language forces the translation I have cited here to close off several meanings in the German original that underline this point. Goethe imagines a novel whose "particular points" (*Einzelheiten*) are *lebendig,* not merely "vivid" but literally alive. Conversely, the spring that can only be "understood while it is flowing" (really "insofar as" or "in that" it is flowing) is a *Quelle,* not only a literal spring but also a (literary) source.

The paragraph closes with Goethe reflecting on what of his sister remains to him, given that the novel *Cornelia* was never written: fleeting shadowy visions in a magic mirror. An affirming irony runs beneath this apparently rueful conclusion. Faust first sees the vision of feminine beauty that leads him to Gretchen in a magic mirror in *Faust I;* the liaison that results will lead Gretchen to pregnancy, infanticide, and execution.[45] Goethe may thus be signaling that the common thread of Clarissa Harlowe and Cornelia Friederike Christiane Goethe's lives—unwanted sexual and romantic attention leading to unhappiness and premature death—has in fact been masterfully embroidered in his hands. As this study turns to Johnson and particularly Boswell, however, it is worth noting that, by Goethe's own account, when inspired in the late 1770s to compose a work of memorial biography that would preserve the "minutest detail" and "endless particular points" of his beloved sister's life, the only formal model that seemed adequate was the anecdotal technique of Richardson.

5

Happy Ever After in
Sir Charles Grandison

Sir Charles Grandison is a rebel with a cause; Richardson's good man lives his life in open and principled protest against the aristocratic mores of his day. He refuses to duel, drink, or drab, and he will not squander his money in country sports, London amusements, or the temptations found on the Grand Tour. As a narrative, *Sir Charles Grandison* is in equally frank rebellion against the comic conventions and expectations that its readers, in both Richardson's time and our own, bring to the text. It refuses to end with marriage.

The reader of Shakespeare's comedies and Jane Austen's novels will search those canonical heavyweights in vain for a depiction of its heroes' and heroines' married lives—no Mrs. Darcy, no Hermia and Lysander household. Furthermore, neither author depicts a happily married couple whose courtship might conceivably itself have furnished narratable plot material. Elizabeth Bennett has no models on which to base her performance of the new role she takes at novel's end. For Austen, married couples are mismatched (Mr. and Mrs. Bennet, Sir Thomas and Lady Bertram) or they are both so awful/limited/inconsequential that they deserve each other (Mr. and Mrs. Elton, John and Fanny Dashwood, Sir William and Lady Lucas, Lieutenant and Mrs. Price). Shakespeare's couples tend to be wranglers (Titania and Oberon, the Capulets), and he often resorts to widows and widowers (Egeus, Prospero, the Countess of Rousillon) when filling in the blocking or enabling figures of the older generation. In Austen, the few examples of marital felicity tend to be a star below the sphere of the novel's protagonists (the Gardiners are in trade, Admiral and Mrs. Croft are by no means rich), and in Shakespeare the only pair that might fit the bill of happily married couple are Margaret and George Page, who get along well but nevertheless bet on different horses in the race to marry off their daughter Anne in *The Merry Wives of Windsor.* (Incidentally, marriage fares little better in the plays that the First Folio identifies as tragedies or histories.)

I insist on this seven-league booted march across two summits of the undergraduate syllabus not primarily because Richardson was a careful reader of Shakespeare and Austen was a careful reader of Richardson (though both statements are true), but rather because Shakespeare and Austen exemplify a tradition that is as old as New Comedy and continues today, according to which marriage brings down the curtain on young lovers and married life is ridiculous, or unhappy, or exclusively concerned in meddling in the affairs of the young.[1] The eighteenth-century sentimental comedies of Richard Steele that Lady G and Harriet Byron love to cite to each other in *Sir Charles Grandison* fall squarely into this tradition, as do *Joseph Andrews* and *Tom Jones* (in the latter of which Fielding makes Squire Allworthy a widower, unlike his stated real-life analogue Ralph Allen, whose wife outlived him by two years). Richardson's first novel does not follow this pattern; nearly half of *Pamela* narrates the first two and a half weeks of its heroine's married life, to say nothing of his continuation *Pamela in Her Exalted Condition.* Richardson's final novel builds the representation of happy married life into the foundation of its narrative structure. Like its hero's conscientious objection to the dueling code, this generic protest on the part of *Sir Charles Grandison* is conscious and purposeful.[2] *Clarissa* is more direct than its successor about the relationship between narrative and immortality, because its heroine lives and dies in a way that at once impels the reader to postulate an afterlife for her and to regard her textual legacy as a road map for getting there. *Sir Charles Grandison* moves death from center stage to the wings, where it preys on minor characters such as Sir Charles's father, Mr. Danby, and the penitent Sir Hargrave Pollexfen. But it considers the theme of immortality structurally, by breaking open the traditional courtship plot. To put the argument in a nutshell: life does not end with marriage for Richardson because life does not end, period. And telling the story of a life with no imagined end—a life lived in view of Christian immortality— requires a fundamental shift in the concepts of plot and narrative closure.

Changing One's State: Marriage and Immortality

Samuel Johnson famously argued that *Samson Agonistes* has a beginning and an end but no middle.[3] Similarly, one might say that *Sir Charles Grandison* has a beginning and a middle, but no end. Richardson does not close with the Grandisons' marriage, or even with a less traditional milestone such as the birth of a Grandison heir or Clementina's final choice between married and monastic life. Rather, he simply stops, and when Julia Bere, an admiring reader, asks him to continue, he replies that the events narrated in the seven published volumes "bring it down pretty near to the present time," rendering further narration impossible.[4] As it happens, this is a slightly disingenuous protest: Richardson's letter to Bere was written in May 1754 and the day/date alignments in the novel, and the fact that it takes place after the '45 and before the calendar reform of 1752, establish without doubt that he used a calendar to set the action from January 1749 to May 1750. Thus, Richardson did in fact leave a practicable if not overgenerous temporal margin for further updates from his cast of characters, and he certainly might have decided Clementina's fate without encroaching on the time of composition. It is nevertheless highly significant, and appropriate, that when Richardson is asked to extend the narrative, his demurral appeals first to obstacles in the chronology and then only secondarily to the state of the plot.

To a greater extent even than *Clarissa,* whose earthly plot is after all end-stopped by the finality of death, *Sir Charles Grandison* imports into narrative fiction the diurnal, sequential, almost plotless nature of the *Spectator* or *Night Thoughts.* Moreover, it imports into such plot as it does have the structural principle of morally formative repetition, with both reader and character reaping improvement from the same things happening over and over again. *Sir Charles Grandison* depicts a world in which human life is not a unidirectional sequence of crises and inflection points, leading to a tightly plotted denouement. Rather, it is iterative and incremental, circling back to places it has been before. From an aesthetic standpoint, one might call this formal realism. Richardson called it instruction.

Harriet Byron disposes of suitor after suitor, and acquires surrogate parent after surrogate parent, each according to his or her deserts. Wherever he goes, Sir Charles is inevitably called upon to defuse duels, execute wills, and intervene in scenes of attempted violence on the public roads. (His repeated refusals to fight, though indisputably admirable, have the side effect of making Sir Charles's endless peregrinations through England and continental Europe into a parody of chivalric shaggy dog stories like *Le Morte D'Arthur;* by the time he conciliates Mr. Greville in the sixth volume, Sir Charles has become a cautionary illustration to authors of the tedium that can result when knights errant undergo Norbert Elias's civilizing process and begin to refuse to fight each other.) Marriage negotiations between the Catholic Porretta family and Sir Charles have the same rhythm, with the moral polarity reversed, of the narrator's endlessly repeated appeals to Lorenzo in *Night Thoughts;* they exhort him again and again to convert, but he never does. Clementina makes a nonaggression pact with her family on the topic of marriage on 3:374–75, only to break it on 3:426 with a renewed request to be allowed to enter a nunnery. The wounds of Jeronymo della Porretta, into which Mr. Lowther and his Italian surgical colleagues introduce "hollow tents" of lint in order to promote the discharge of "matter," are a synecdoche for the various plots of *Sir Charles Grandison* itself: they are never quite allowed to close (2:452).

This is not to say that nothing happens in the novel: on the contrary, everything does, from the birth of Lady L and Lady G's squalling "marmousets" to the cheerful senectitude of Grandmother Shirley and the pious death of Sir Harry Beauchamp (3:261). The reader sees every aspect of eighteenth-century bourgeois and aristocratic private life; in particular, as I have argued above, Richardson devotes exceptional narrative energy to depicting not only the single but also the married state. Moreover, his characters spend much of their time talking about these two states, and the transition from the one to the other. In *Sir Charles Grandison,* the "married state," particularly for women, is an abstraction that need not have reference to any particular spouse. Hence Sir Charles wants his sister Charlotte to marry on the principle that he "is a great friend to the married state; especially with regard to our sex," and the married Charlotte, Mrs. Shirley, Lady Gertrude, and the girls of Selby-House can reason casuistically on the merits of singleness and marriage in various economic and family situations (1:290, 3:408).[5] As Harriet's various proposals demonstrate, marriage is not so much a passionate meeting of souls, or even a bilateral contract, as it is an initiation into a new set of kinship and friendship networks. Harriet has far more interaction with Sir Rowland Meredith and the Countess of D. than with either Mr. Fowler or the Earl of D., her nominal suitors. Sir Charles, writing to Dr. Bartlett from Bologna with his offer to Clementina yet pending, hopes that Harriet Byron will be happy in life: "The Countess

D. is a worthy woman: The Earl, her son, is a good young man: Miss Byron merits such a mother; the Countess such a daughter" (2:455). One need not have recourse to the psychologizing hypothesis that Sir Charles is reluctant to think directly about Harriet and the earl as a pair to explain this bizarre placing of emphasis. Harriet would in fact be marrying her mother-in-law as much as she would be marrying the earl, who unlike his resourceful and articulate mother is a narrative nonentity.[6] Only downright villains such as Sir Hargrave woo with reference to their personal merits and the intensity of their love (see 1:112–15) rather than by appealing to their place in a larger social context. The Grandisons, of course, ally themselves to Harriet as an extended family group (with Lord L and even Lord G into the bargain).

Harriet's suitors, Sir Charles not excepted, assume that the primary function of marriage is not the creation of a new emotional or erotic dyad; rather, marriage transposes the bride into a new social space. Sir Charles's youngest sister shows marriage in a different but equally non-dyadic light: as a crucible of personal transformation. While retaining the essential features of her individuality, Charlotte Grandison becomes Lady G by changing her habits and manners, and smoothing out the impertinent or improper aspects of her personality.

Marriage, for Richardson, is an allegorical type of immortality: just as human existence is divided between a terrestrial "state of trial" and a posthumous "happier state," the former comprises, in the preferred course of things, a "single state" or "maiden state" followed by the "happy state" of matrimony.[7] In each case, individual selfhood persists, though it is irreversibly transformed and irrevocably transposed into a new milieu. (Strikingly, this analogy makes the woman's experience of marriage, which involves greater alteration, paradigmatic for the universal experience of transformed posthumous survival; like the related New Testament image of Christ as the bridegroom and the church as the bride, Richardson's typology of marriage and immortality makes women of us all.) In *Clarissa,* Richardson invites his reader to sublate human tragedy into divine comedy, drawing the reader from earth to heaven. *Sir Charles Grandison* continues on beyond the traditional end of human comedy, and in so doing depicts, typologically speaking, heaven on earth. This formulation echoes Jocelyn Harris's claim that Richardson's works express his hope for "a temperate, very English paradise here on earth," but I wish to emphasize that this paradise figures the literal immortality of the human soul, not just the possibilities of moral and political reform.[8] Hence Sir Charles offers a prophecy in volume 4 that he will go on to fulfill himself in volumes 6 and 7: "May the man, said he, who shall have the honour to call Miss Byron his, be, if *possible*, as deserving as *she* is! Then they will live together the life of angels" (2:339). Richardson never uses the phrase "happy ever after" (the *OED* gives no example before 1853), but it perfectly describes what *Sir Charles Grandison* is about.

The conceptual and lexical resonances between changing one's state from singleness to marriage and changing one's state from life to immortality echo throughout the text of *Sir Charles Grandison*, as thinking about marriage invariably sets Richardson's characters thinking about the afterlife. This thinking tends to be causal in nature: marriage has this or that implication for one's posthumous fate. But underlying this metonymic relationship is the metaphoric one in which marriage provides an earthly model for how the afterlife works. Most famously, Clementina refuses to marry Sir Charles because she fears that marriage to a Protestant would endanger her salvation. Sir Charles reasons as follows with Jeronymo when persuading him to renounce his mistress and marry:

> Virtuous love, my dear Jeronymo, looks beyond this temporary scene; while guilty attachments usually find a much earlier period than that of human life. Inconstancy, on one side or the other, seldom fails to put a disgraceful end to them. But were they to endure for *life,* what can the reflexions upon them do towards softening the agonies of the inevitable hour?
>
> Remember, my Jeronymo, that you are a MAN, a rational and immortal agent; and act up to the dignity of your nature. Can sensual pleasure be the great end of an immortal spirit in this life? (2:140–41)

Sir Charles's argument here mingles causal/metonymic and analogical co-ordinations of marriage and immortality. On the one hand, "virtuous love ... looks beyond this temporary scene" in the sense that it gives us nothing to regret on our deathbed (unlike "guilty attachments," which bring no comfort in the "inevitable hour" of death). Marriage is virtuous and thus a causal factor in a happy afterlife. But it is also an unbreakable lifelong commitment, and as such an appropriate end for "a rational and immortal agent" (unlike "guilty attachments," which virtually always end with "inconstancy"). Marriage is virtuous precisely because its long duration is analogical to immortality and as such has a dignity worthy of an immortal such as man. In this appeal to Jeronymo's dignified manly nature, Sir

Charles offers the weight and seriousness of marriage as an inducement; in a prenuptial catechizing that he gives to Charlotte on the morning that she becomes Lady G, this same weight takes on a more forbidding aspect: "Her brother had been talking to her," Harriet reports to Lucy Selby, "and had laid down the duties of the state she was about to enter into, in such a serious manner, and made the performance of them of so much importance to her happiness both here and hereafter, that she was terrified at the thoughts of what she was about to undertake" (2:338). Thoughts of the "here" of marriage bring thoughts of the "hereafter" in their train.[9]

Later in Lord G and Charlotte's wedding day, Sir Charles turns the topic of conversation to marriage again, wishing the couple happiness. Lord W (a case study in the unhappiness of keeping a mistress like Mrs. Giffard rather than marrying a wife like Miss Mansfield) expresses his gratitude for the match Sir Charles made for him: "All the joys of my present prospects, all the comforts of my future life, are and will be owing to you" (2:239). Here "future life" refers both to Lord W's remaining years on earth (which will be comforted by Lady W's solicitude for his gout rather than embittered by Mrs. Giffard's termagancy) and to his fate thereafter (which will be formed by his years spent as a married man rather than the keeper of a mistress, as per Sir Charles's argument to Jeronymo). This ambiguity is reinforced by Lord W's awkward next remark, which imputes to marriage a status traditionally given to the afterlife, to wit that of being a reward: "Here had he stopt, it would have been well: But turning to me [writes Harriet], he unexpectedly said, Would to God, madam, that YOU could reward him! I cannot; and nobody *else* can" (2:339). This is even more of a faux pas than Lord W knows: after all, Clementina was offered to Sir Charles with the intention of rewarding him, and the consequences were not as the would-be rewarders hoped. In covering the awkwardness and blushes that follow Lord W's plainspoken words, Sir Charles continues and develops their implication, for he replies with the remark quoted above that Harriet and her eventual husband would "live together the life of angels."

Examples of the marriage/afterlife analogy in *Sir Charles Grandison* might be multiplied—after all, this is the book that is never content to teach a given lesson only once. One further example, too striking to omit, occurs at the beginning of volume 6. Harriet describes to Lady G her sensations when she realizes that she is the woman whom Sir Charles wishes to marry:

I know not how to describe what I felt in my now fluttering, now rejoicing, now dejected heart—

Dejected?—Yes, my dear Lady G. Dejection was a strong ingredient in my sensibilities. I know not why. Yet may there not be a fullness in joy, that will mingle dissatisfaction with it? If there may, shall I be excused for my solemnity, if I deduce from thence an argument, that the human Soul is not to be fully satisfied by worldly enjoyments; and that therefore the completion of its happiness must be in another, a more perfect state. You, Lady G. are a very good woman, tho' a lively one; and I will not excuse *you*, if on an occasion that bids me look forward to a very solemn event, you will not forgive my *seriousness*. (3:18–19)

Harriet is repeating an argument for immortality that she might well have read in the *Spectator* or in Butler's *Analogy of Religion:* that the perfectibility of the soul and the imperfect state of the world suggest that the former survives the latter, to find hereafter happiness and improvement that were not available on earth. Indeed, Harriet's reasoning might imply that even marriage to Sir Charles cannot be "the completion of . . . happiness" for her soul.[10] But this is not the primary force of her response, in which marriage and death are fixed and portentous future events that contrast with her current fluttering state. The prospect of a wedding, "a very solemn event," renews her awareness of the afterlife; the married state points beyond itself to the "more perfect state" that follows.

Indeed, the fixity of marriage vows makes an imprudent choice a type of hell. Thus the "proud, affected, and conceited" Miss Cantillon's elopement with a penniless "nominal captain" and Laurana Sforza's suicide are in a sense parallel cases of making a premature but irrevocable choice. "Her punishment was of her own choosing," Harriet says of the former, while Sir Charles reflects soberly in the latter case that an "immortal Being [has fixed] its eternal state by an act dreadful and irreversible; by a crime that admits not of repentance; and shall we not be concerned?" (1:42, 3:13, 3:14, 3:448). In the *Analogy of Religion*, Butler had argued that we can infer posthumous divine justice from the fact that crimes in general find their punishment in this world.[11] Sir Charles applies this general argument to the case of a marriage between a greedy yet beautiful young woman and a rich and lustful old man, pointing out that when the woman, no longer young, inherits the money and marries a young rake in her turn, she will now very probably be the despised mate to the young second husband that her old first husband was to her: "The violators of the social duties are frequently punished by the success of their own wishes. Don't you think, my Lord, that it is suitable to the divine benignity, as well as justice, to lend its sanctions and punishments in aid of those duties which bind man to man?" (1:430). In the continuous moral fabric of the Butlerian universe, marriage is once more both metonymy and metaphor for divine justice as a whole.[12]

Presented with the central eighteenth-century vindication of the afterlife—that its rewards and punishments would complete the work of God's justice left manifestly unfinished on earth—skeptics such as Hume could reply that humans certainly did not live their lives as though they were particularly concerned with futurity: "The whole scope or intention of man's creation . . . is limited to the present life. With how weak a concern, from the original, inherent structure of the mind and passions, does he ever look farther?"[13] The essay from which this quotation is taken, "Of the Immortality of the Soul," could not have been known to Richardson, and it was in any case not printed until 1755 (in a small run that Hume himself quickly suppressed), a year after the conclusion of *Sir Charles Grandison*. But it represents a broader challenge to which both *Clarissa* and *Sir Charles Grandison* respond. The characters whom Richardson holds up as examples invariably live their lives with simultaneous reference to this life and the next. This is not to say that Sir Charles, or Harriet, or Grandmother Shirley emulate the otherworldly melancholy of *Night Thoughts* (although Harriet does call Young her "favorite author" and quotes seven heavenly minded lines from *Night the Eighth,* which is much further into *Night Thoughts* than most of Young's readers got [1:298]). On the contrary, Mrs. Shirley, who, in Lucy Selby's account, "has already one foot among the stars," and thus serves as an emblem of the continuity between earth and heaven, is avowedly a friend to innocent amusements and pleasures (3:264; in the index that Richardson included at the end of the seventh volume, repeated reference is made to her being a promoter of the innocent pleasures of youth). In the center of a cluster of references to heaven and the afterlife around the marriage of Harriet and Sir Charles, the following verses, which the latter sings while accompanying himself on his "noble organ," sum up their shared attitude:

> *My soul, with gratitude profound*
> *Receive a Form so bright!*
> *And yet, I boast a bliss* beyond
> *This angel to the* sight.

When charms of mind and person meet,
How rich our raptures rise!
The Fair that renders earth so sweet,
Prepares me for the skies!

"I thought at the time, I had a foretaste of the joys of heaven," reports Harriet on hearing the performance (2:274–75). Carol Houlihan Flynn's wickedly funny line, that "*Sir Charles Grandison* is a classic saint's life" in which "unfortunately, the corpse walks among his admiring mourners, complacently accepting their choruses of praise," works because it assumes what Richardson's novel attempts to disprove: that death is a static end, and that heaven and earth are radically discontinuous.[14]

Of course, this angelic duet between Harriet and Sir Charles is counterpointed by a minor third. If the married state is heaven on earth, is God not doing an injustice to the deserving Clementina? For Sir Charles, Harriet's beauty and mind make life sweet and preparation for the afterlife easy; these two forces interfere rather than harmonize for Clementina, who sees in her love for Sir Charles the possible perdition of her immortal soul. Clementina presents the reader with a softened and less crucial version of the imaginative challenge posed by Clarissa; Clarissa does not belong on earth, and so we must imagine her in heaven.[15] Clementina, with her unsettled fate, is a similar reminder that even the happiest lives on earth are not fully perfected, fully synthesized with divine goodness. *Sir Charles Grandison* presents the marriage of Harriet and Sir Charles as an allegory of heaven, but at points where the characters reach toward a more literal imagination of what heaven will be like, they are faced with the vagueness and even inconsistency that is characteristic of the era. Harriet imagines a continuing relationship with Sir Charles, and Clementina imagines that all three will be in heaven together. Sir Charles, meanwhile, points out that in heaven there will be no sex (a proleptic argument, by the way, against Hume's skeptical reasoning in "Of the Immortality of the Soul" that the mental inferiority of women is an argument for mortalism) and imagines his resurrected body being drawn out of sleep in the ground.

Heaven, unknowable in its sensory particularity, functions for *Sir Charles Grandison* as a synthesis of theses that cannot be harmonized on earth; it is the place where the marriage relationship that unites Harriet and Sir Charles will be capacious enough to contain Clementina as well. But it will do so, the novel implies, in terms that continue and develop those of earthly life. Refused by Clementina for the final time, and leaving Naples for England and Harriet, Sir Charles promises to correspond with the woman who will not be his wife. In typical Grandisonian fashion, her first letter to him chews over yet once more the courtship she has broken off: "Nothing but the due consideration of the brevity as well as vanity of this life, in which we are but probationers, and of the eternity of the next, could have influenced me to act against my heart" (2:612). In the reply that follows immediately, Sir Charles quotes his correspondent's words back to her virtually verbatim: " 'Nothing', says the most generous and pious of her Sex, 'but the due consideration of the brevity as well as vanity of this life, and of the *duration* of the next, could have influenced me to act against my heart' " (2:614, emphasis added). Sir Charles has silently changed "eternity," with its connotations of stasis and timelessness, to "duration," which in contrast carries Addisonian suggestions of continuation and the endless extension of time. Resolved to be silent on matters of confessional controversy, Sir Charles nevertheless signals his commitment to the Addisonian/Anglican picture of a horizontal afterlife.

Lifespan and Plot

To articulate why Richardson's thematic preoccupation with immortality has deep formal implications, it is necessary to return to the roots of the most fundamental constitutive feature of narrative: that it has a plot. Aristotle's *Poetics,* which Richardson encountered through the *Spectator* and through the English translation of René Rapin's *Reflections* on it, will stand in here for the incumbent Western tradition.[16] Aristotle distinguishes between narrative poetry and history in two ways in chapter 23 of the *Poetics:* first, the historian "describes the thing that has been," whereas the poet describes "a kind of thing that might be."[17] Second, narrative poetry should have a plot, like tragedy: that is to say, "based on a single action, one that is a complete whole in itself, with a beginning, middle, and end, so as to enable the work to produce its own proper pleasure with all the organic unity of a living creature" (1459a18–21; compare Rapin 2:186–87). History, by contrast, is structured by time rather than plot: "A history has to deal not with one action, but with one period and all that happened in that to one or more persons, however disconnected the several events may have been" (1459a22–24). As such, history presumably lacks "the organic unity of a living creature" (this is less of a mouthful in Greek: history is merely not like *zoon holon*, "a complete organism") and the pleasure that comes with it. Aristotle is aware that his rule here can be broken, that there is no necessary connection between his ontological criterion (poetry is probable, narrative is factual) and his formal criterion (poetry has a single action, history covers a given period of time). Poems such as "the *Cypria* and *Little Iliad*" (post-Homeric epics describing incidents from the Trojan War, now lost) have the narrative form of histories, and thus are inferior to the works of Homer (1459b2; compare Rapin 2:187–88). Though the notorious non-survival of Aristotle's treatise on comedy leaves us on uncertain ground, we can nevertheless imagine that he would be equally unhappy with *Sir Charles Grandison* and would prefer Fielding's *Joseph Andrews,* which, as a "comic epic poem in prose," was consciously tailored to fit within the approved Aristotelian taxonomy as a fiction with a beginning, middle, and end.

Aristotle's comparison of narrative poetry and history occurs near the end of the *Poetics,* as part of his discussion of epic. His concept of plot points back to a fuller discussion earlier in the treatise, in which he considers tragedy. In Aristotle's view, plot is "the first and the most important thing in tragedy," and it is required to have "beginning, middle, and end" (1450a26). In explaining why this is the case, Aristotle offers an extended comparison (which, as we have seen, remains in his mind throughout the *Poetics*) of a tragic plot with a living organism:

> To be beautiful, a living creature, and every whole made up of parts, must not only present a certain order in its arrangement of parts, but also be of a certain definite magnitude. . . . Just in the same way, then, as a beautiful whole made up of parts, or a beautiful living creature, must be of some size, but a size to be taken in by the eye, so a story or plot must be of some length, but of a length to be taken in by the memory. . . . As a rough general formula, a length which allows of the hero passing by a series of probable or necessary stages from bad fortune to good, or from good to bad, may suffice as a limit for the magnitude of the story. (1450a34–36, 1451a2–6, 11–15)

This comparison of a plot (*muthos*) to a living being (*zoon*) appears to be a considerable conceptual reach; as the twentieth-century commentator Gerald F. Else tartly points out, it "involves a change of medium from sight to sound and from space to time. Aristotle seems unaware of any difficulties, such as a modern aesthetician might raise, about the validity of the transfer from one sense to the other."[18] But we would do well to remember that Aristotle is not only a founder of Western aesthetics, but also the founder of biology and zoology. Plots and animals are two things he has thought carefully about. What does it mean that he sees the former as a simile for the latter?

The connection is that for Aristotle the beautiful order of a complete organism is the result of a process of development. A "beautiful living creature" (*kalon zoon*) and "the organic unity of a living creature" (*zoon holon*) are both the culmination of nutrition and growth, the teleological process of a creature reaching its appropriate size and shape.[19] A finished plot looks like a mature animal because each has passed through a necessary sequence of stages: infancy, youth, maturity; beginning, middle, end. Animal life and narrative plot are both bound to follow a course that is inherent in their nature, and as such each is finite.

This comparison comes naturally to Aristotle because it is thematized in the Athenian tragedies that exemplify his aesthetics. Consider the parable of the lion from the chorus of Aeschylus's *Agamemnon*:

> A man raised as his own
> a lion cub, not weaned
> yet, robbed of the breast
> gentle in the beginning. . . .
> And often in his arms
> he rocked it like a baby. . . .
> But as time passed it showed
> the color of its bloodlines
> and in return for all
> the kindness it received
> from those who fostered it,
> it made a bleak, forbidden
> feast, cruel slaughter of all.[20]

The eighteenth-century scholar will, of course, recognize the source of Clarissa's third "mad paper," which tells the story of "a lady" who "took a great fancy to a young Lion, or a Bear, I forget which."[21] Both the chorus and Clarissa draw the same moral: that the lion "showed the color of its bloodlines," or, as Clarissa puts it, "what *it* did, was *in* its own nature" (5:304–5). We may note something different: that the lion grows from being a cub (or, in Clarissa's version, a "whelp") into maturity and thus its own treacherous nature. The chorus anticipates Aristotle's metaphor of the plot as a complete organism insofar as its lion may be read as an allegory of tragedy itself: it grows up over time to its full proportions and ends with "a chaos of strewn / corpses."[22]

Equally striking in its coordination of plot and the span of animal life is the case of Sophocles's *Oedipus the King,* Aristotle's touchstone of a perfect plot. The play nowhere recites the famous riddle of the Sphinx. But it assumes that the audience has the riddle in mind throughout: the identity of the creature walks on four feet, on two feet, and on three feet is an inescapable subtext of the play. As Diskin Clay puts it in his commentary, "Oedipus is revealed as an infant on Kathairon, a man standing steady at the height of his power, and a blind exile who must walk upon the earth with a staff to support him and direct his way."[23] The course of a man's life is like a day, which in turn is like the plot of a tragedy: each has a beginning, a middle, and an irrevocable end. (Indeed, this was particularly true of tragedies like those of Sophocles that were performed in Athens: in the ordinary course of things, each play was only performed a single time). The riddle of the Sphinx is thus a progenitor of Aristotle's conception of plot. *Oedipus the King* does not depict the death of Oedipus (that is reserved for Sophocles's final play, *Oedipus at Colonus*). But the final words of the chorus describe the inevitability and finality of death:

> Keep your eyes on that last day, on your dying.
> Happiness and peace, they were not yours
> unless at death you can look back on your life and say
> I lived, I did not suffer.[24]

But what if death is not the end? For Sophocles, Oedipus has a certain numinous afterlife, insofar as his corpse, buried on the outskirts of Athens, exerts a tutelary power.[25] But what if, to undertake a wrenchingly anachronistic thought experiment, Oedipus were to live on instead in eighteenth-century heaven? The finality of death would be suspended, and with it, analogically, the aesthetic logic of an end-stopped plot. For the Addisonian eighteenth-century Christian, man is the organism that never stops improving, a *kalon zoon* that becomes ever more beautiful in the afterlife and a *zoon holon* whose full perfection is only partially realized on earth. To return from ancient Greece to Samuel Richardson: what walks on four, then on two, then on three, then "with one foot among the stars," then, presumably, with both feet among the stars? Why, Grandmother Shirley, who narrates her early education and is only taken lame when she is leading out her granddaughters at a ball. What has a beginning and a middle but no end? *Sir Charles Grandison.*

Part Three

AFTERLIFE
WRITING

6

Laetitia Pilkington
in Sheets

Thus far, this study has concentrated on literary figures whose concern about uniting text and person in the life to come has been unencumbered by worries about keeping body and soul together from day to day. As Whig politicians, well-connected clergy, and London men of business, Addison, Steele, Young, Butler, Warburton, and Richardson did not engage in literary composition and theological speculation from positions of leisured *otium*, but they did sit securely within sight of the pinnacle of the Hanoverian rank and class hierarchy. Laetitia Pilkington—penniless, divorced, female, Irish—has a different story to tell. Her *Memoirs*, published in three volumes (the first and second in 1748, the third posthumously in 1754) chart the downward trajectory of a gentlewoman's daughter who marries a brute and is reduced to living by her pen and her wits in the London demimonde.[1] Pilkington is Pamela Andrews in reverse. Nevertheless, she keeps her gaze firmly fixed on the prospect of literary immortality. Even while narrating the ignominious and faintly salacious details of her divorce, Pilkington predicts that she *"like the Classics, shall be read / When Time, and all the World are dead"* (87).

So far, so good; Pilkington is (occasionally) read today, by eighteenth-century scholars who can rely on an authoritative and sympathetic edition of her *Memoirs* published in 1997 by A. C. Elias. She has been the beneficiary of some recuperative feminist scholarship (particularly in Felicity Nussbaum's *The Autobiographical Subject*) and a fine recent biography by Norma

Clarke.[2] But she remains a comparatively little-known figure. Pilkington was born c. 1709 into Dublin's Protestant elite as Laetitia van Lewen, the daughter of a fashionable physician. She was married young to a clergyman, Matthew Pilkington, and spent the early 1730s as part of Jonathan Swift's Dublin circle of male and female poets. In the mid-1730s her life took a pronounced downward turn; her father died, and his disappointing estate turned her husband against her. Pilkington passed the 1730s and '40s in circumstances that ranged from precarious to desperate, moving between Dublin and London in pursuit of a literary livelihood. She died in 1750.

Pilkington's reputation rests on her *Memoirs*. This work, though written in a very different set of circumstances than any of the texts considered thus far, shares with the writings of Addison, Young, and Richardson an explicit aspiration toward literary immortality, as well as an awareness that documentary prose provides new possibilities for achieving this goal. Yet the *Memoirs* also show that to a woman writing in a garret, prose immortality looks rather different than it does to an incumbent in his parsonage or a publisher in his printing house. First, Pilkington preserves herself in insistently bodily terms: her body was an object of male interest and desire, and this fact influences her literary self-presentation. Second, Pilkington weaves personal and theological immortality into a darker fabric than her predecessors. She had ample experience of clerical hypocrisy in her life, from abuse at the hands of her adulterous husband to propositions from lecherous bishops. The *Memoirs* are thus written in part to settle scores and to punish enemies with lasting literary infamy. Instead of ushering the virtuous into coffeehouse heaven, Pilkington condemns the secretly vicious to Grub Street hell.

Gender and Genre

The *Memoirs* are a hybrid text, at once an anthology of poetry and autobiographical narrative chronicling Pilkington's life in Dublin and London. Numerous poems and a substantial dramatic fragment by Pilkington are interspersed through her narrative, and her prose style is shot through with innumerable poetic quotations from Shakespeare, Swift, Pope, and other English poets. This form makes *Memoirs* a transitional text in the eighteenth century's reconceptualization of literary immortality. Traditional lyric immortality, the tradition of *exegi monumentum,* is predicated on one of the most fundamental metonymies in language: that authors are their works.[3] Horace's poem lives and therefore so does Horace; Dryden's poems are his own best monument. In Addison and particularly Richardson, we have seen the emergence of a new kind of metonymy of immortality, that characters are their texts. This is why Mr. Spectator can be said to live on in the republication and rereading of the *Spectator,* and why it is so fitting, given the way Richardson wrote about it/her, that Richardson gave the name "Clarissa" to *Clarissa.* Pilkington's bid for immortality in the *Memoirs* stands between the old and the emerging tradition. On the one hand, she has so deeply internalized the English poetic pantheon that it is only natural to express the desire to be located within it by printing her poems.[4] On the other hand, Pilkington's text is unwilling to present her poems without locating them in biographical context, explaining the circumstances and audience for which they were written and assuring the reader that they met with the approval of previous readers such as Swift. Pilkington's poetry pulls toward immortality-as-poet; her prose, toward immortality-as-character.

Pilkington's gender, which plays such a marked role in determining the course of her life, likewise determines the form that this immortality-as-character will take. The *Memoirs* contain virtually no physical description of Pilkington, besides noting that she had very fair skin. But they acknowledge and exploit the fact that her body was a site of erotic interest for men, both those who knew her and those who read her. The *Memoirs* are far from being a bawdy book, by the standards of either the eighteenth century or our own. But they are filled with ambiguities, in both language and plot, that keep Pilkington's body in the reader's view. Going beyond quibbles on words, the *Memoirs* takes the comic verbal device of the double entendre and replicates it on a deeper, structural level. Pornography is perlocutionary—like the sentimental novel, whose ability to elicit tears is so well documented from Richardson on, the book that can be read "only with one hand" takes the shortest possible route to a reader's physical response.[5] The essence of the double entendre, in contrast, is that it turns language into sex without negating its status and properties as language. As a divorcée and poetess, who claims equivocally in the *Memoirs* that she sold her poetry but not herself, Pilkington makes the double entendre the master figure of her life story.

It is also through the double entendre that Pilkington makes her most original claim for literary immortality. Pilkington knew Richardson during her eight-year London sojourn in the 1740s, and she was one of the earliest advance readers of *Clarissa*.[6] Her own *Memoirs* lack the temporal and circumstantial precision that Richardson perfected. But Pilkington's text shares *Clarissa*'s preoccupation with the preservation of the female body. If sexual double meaning is the word made flesh, it also carries the possibility of the flesh being made word, carnality becoming incarnation. Indeed, immortality and the sexualized body form an uncanny couplet throughout the *Memoirs*. Pilkington is an aspiring poet, but living by her pen in 1740s London, she realizes that stories about her body may appeal more than the products of her mind to male patrons and customers. Yet the *Memoirs* contain not scandalous confessions but instead the image of Pilkington's body as a palimpsest inscribed with the British literary canon; as such, they represent Pilkington, as both poet and autobiographer, making a sophisticated bid to win fame and posthumous immortality on her own terms.

Black and Blue Favors, or Body Writing

The "fatal hour" in which Matthew Pilkington ambushes his wife in compromising circumstances with the dashing surgeon Robin Adair is the climax of the first volume of the *Memoirs* (88). In the pages leading up to this denouement, Pilkington makes it clear that she has been the victim of a setup; after her father died without leaving her the legacy her mercenary husband had been counting on, he had tried every possible means to drive her from him or trap her into an affair that would give him grounds for divorce. Pilkington is clear about her husband's motivations and actions but circumspect about her own, inviting the reader to speculate on whether she was really guilty. Claiming that she was merely reading a book that Adair would not lend out to her, she offers equivocation and undecidability rather than a robust defense: "And here, gentle Reader, give me leave to drop the Curtain. To avouch mine own Innocence in a Point where Appearances were strong against me, would perhaps little avail me: The supreme Judge of Hearts alone will at the last great Day clear or condemn me; to whose unerring Justice and boundless Goodness I submit my Cause" (84). Like Clarissa, Pilkington reposes her faith in God's judgment, but her language conspicuously leaves the content of that judgment open: acceptance by a God capable of both "unerring Justice" to the innocent and merciful "boundless Goodness" to the guilty clarifies nothing about earthly events. This is because the possibility of multiple interpretations is for Pilkington the engine that creates immortality, both for herself and for her villainous husband:

And so if my *Quondam* Husband arrives at Fame, or ever goes to Heaven, either of which I very much doubt, I think he must still rest my Debtor.

> For Fame *has but two Doors, a white and a black one,*
> *The worst you say, he's stole in at the back one.*

And that Cuckolds go to Heaven, no body ever yet disputed. Were he one, he ought to that me that help'd send him thither. If I have bestow'd on him Fame in this World, and Salvation in the next, what could a reasonable man desire more from his Wife? . . . But whether he is entitled to the Horn, or not, must always be a Secret: I hope some curious Commentator will hereafter endeavour to find out the Truth of it, for my Mind gives me,

> *That I, like the Classics, shall be read*
> *When Time, and all the World are dead.* (87)

Pilkington's sexual status, here as for the greater part of the *Memoirs,* is a structural double entendre, ambiguously suspended between fidelity and adultery. Analogously, the *"I"* of Pilkington's last-cited couplet hovers between book and person, text and character: just as a carnal meaning lurks behind a literally unexceptionable phrase, Pilkington's body is imagined to linger immortally behind the text that we future "Commentators" read.

"I . . . shall be read": Pilkington's body is both read and written on throughout the *Memoirs,* and nearly always with concepts of sexuality and immortality in play. This does not mean that Pilkington exposes her body to the reader's voyeuristic pleasure. As Elias points out in his introduction, the memoirs "give us no help in imagining the author's body, whether it was full-figured or wispy, sedentary or athletic." She goes out of her way to deny that she "ever was handsome, farther than being very fair" (l–li, 14). Her light complexion, however, makes her body legible in a different way, as the paper on which her "Tutor," Jonathan Swift, brutally writes when teaching her:

And if I have any Merit, as a Writer, I must gratefully acknowledge it due to the Pains he took to teach me to think and speak with Propriety; tho', to tell the Truth, he was a very rough sort of Tutor for one of my Years and Sex; for whenever I made use of an inelegant Phrase, I was sure of a deadly Pinch. . . . Had he thought me incorrigibly dull, I should have escap'd without Correction, and the black and blue Favours I receiv'd at his Hands, were meant for Merit, tho' bestow'd on me. (45)

Pilkington imagines her body as the poetic manuscript upon which Swift records "Correction" in black and blue ink—her word "Favours" carries both the ironic meaning of "bruise" and the punning meaning of "epistle," with the sexual connotation of a "favour" (usually bestowed by a woman on a man) hovering in the background as well.[7] The *Memoirs* contain many further plays on words that link the lexicon of text to the female body, especially when that body is suffering or a victim of violence. "I . . . am weary of the World," the narrator complains halfway through the third volume: "but what of that, I gave not Life to myself, nor dare I attempt to abridge it" (290). Seven pages later she describes a woman whose imprudent marriage has brought unhappy results: "But I believe she is sufficiently punish'd, for I was well assured the Groom took the Liberty of correcting her, and nobody pitied her" (297). Pilkington describes herself as "an Heteroclite, or irregular Verb," and her final paragraph uses a similar effect: "And here, gentle Reader, my Story and my Life draw to a Period" (273, 334).[8] A few dozen pages before, among a miscellany of Swift anecdotes near the end of the final volume of the *Memoirs*, Pilkington reports her witty reply when Swift "daubed [her] face all over" with melted pitch and resin that had been used to seal the corks of wine bottles: "Instead of being vexed, as he expected I would, I told him he did me great Honour in sealing me for his own. Plague on her, said he, I can't put her out of Temper" (309).

These images of Pilkington's body as the site of Swift's sadistic inscription and sigillation supply a further connection between the gendered body, text, and immortality. The *Memoirs* are written through with poetic quotations; Katherine Berens counts "two hundred and fifty quotations culled mostly from 'the British verse Masters,'" and Pilkington's language is so suffused with Shakespeare at the level of individual words and phrases that this figure is if anything an undercount.[9] Just as her literal body has been written on by Swift, her text is palimpsestically overwritten by the poets who have come before. Because Pilkington wrote the *Memoirs* with only the most limited access to books, every quotation that is written on the page has been engraved on her memory first, a process that Pilkington links with immortality. This alignment of poetry, memory, and fame connects Pilkington to seventeenth-century predecessors; Harold Weber describes the authorial aspirations of Margaret Cavendish, the Duchess of Newcastle, in terms that apply almost verbatim to Pilkington: "For Cavendish, fame depends on the relationship between a collective memory that shapes the dreams individuals share, and the power of poetry to transform the merely mortal into the stuff of dreams. In such a world creation depends on 'the God-head Wit,' for poets preside over memorial processes that represent the second life we might live."[10]

Volume 1 contains a set-piece between Pilkington and Swift that testifies to the power of her memory. The latter allows her to take home his own "Poem on the Death of Dr. Swift"—his willingness to lend the poem out anticipates the complications in which Robin Adair's refusal to be equally generous with his book will involve Pilkington several dozen pages later—on the condition that she not copy it: "But the Dean did not know what sort of memory I had, when he entrusted me with his Verse: I had no occasion for any other Copy, than what I had registred in the *Book and Volume of my brain*" (55). When accused of taking a copy against Swift's orders, Pilkington exonerates herself by reciting Shakespeare until Swift is convinced of the power of her memory. The "Poem on the Death of Dr. Swift" and *Hamlet* 1.5 are both appropriate intertexts: each is concerned with life after death, how a person, whether the Dean or the Ghost of Old Hamlet, endures in the minds of the living. Unlike Hamlet, however, Pilkington does not "wipe away all trivial fond records" so that Swift's words live "Unmix'd with baser matter" (*Hamlet* 1.5.99, 104). Rather, Swift is the latest of a succession of male English poets, including Spenser, Shakespeare, and Milton, who are preserved by being written on Pilkington's brain. The connection between writing and immortality is made explicit in the poem "Memory," which Pilkington wrote following her recitation for Swift, and which follows immediately in the *Memoirs*:

> And when at length we quit this mortal Scene,
> Thou still shalt with our tender Friends remain,
> And Time, and Death shall strike at thee in vain.

> Lord, let me so this wond'rous Gift employ;
> It may a Fountain be of endless Joy,
> Which Time, nor Accident, may ne'er destroy.

Still let my faithful Memory impart,
And deep engrave it on my grateful Heart,
How just, and good, and excellent thou art." (56)

Of course it is God, not Swift, who writes on Pilkington's "grateful Heart" in her poem.[11] But the role of memory as a guarantor of continued existence on earth, invulnerable to "Time, and Death," is continuous with *Hamlet* and "On the Death of Dr. Swift." The latter, though too cynical to imagine that his friends will be particularly "tender," indeed imagines Swift's character being preserved by the testimony of survivors:

> Suppose me dead; and then suppose
> A Club assembled at the *Rose;*
> Where from Discourse of this and that,
> I grow the Subject of their Chat:
> And while they toss my Name about,
> With Favour some, and some without;
> One quite indiff'rent in the Cause,
> My character impartial draws.[12]

Pilkington has internalized Swift's poem, exactly as she claims.

But Pilkington's bid for fame does not rest only on the twin pillars of poetry and memory that she shares with Swift (and, though she never cites her, Margaret Cavendish). Pilkington's book is also a narrative, specifically a memoir. Admittedly, its truth-claims have been contested: early- to mid-twentieth-century commentators have been troubled by Pilkington's cavalier treatment of dates, places, and names, as well as their lack of reference to important events (particularly the '45) in the wider world that occurred during the period narrated.[13] Subsequent scholars have offered two lines of defense: Elias, whose edition presents a cornucopia of primary sources both confirming and discrediting Pilkington's account, concludes that she is no less reliable on the "facts" than other (male) memoirists and anecdotists of her era—and certainly more reliable than her own son, Jack—while Diana Relke simply argues that such readings miss the point: "A shift of critical emphasis from 'factual' to psychological truth is in order."[14] These defenses are in tension with each other; there's no point in saying Pilkington got "the facts" right if it does not matter, and little is gained by saying that it does not matter if she got things right after all. But the tension is productive: in fact, Elias and Relke are describing what the linguist Roman Jakobson called the metaphoric and metonymic poles. Factual truth, linking the right dates to the right people and places, is metonymic, associated by Jakobson with "realism" and prose. "Psychological truth," the identification of similarity and symbolism, is metaphoric, associated by Jakobson with "romanticism" and poetry.[15] The structure of the double entendre also illuminates the relationship of the *Memoirs* to historical fact.

This twofold defense of the historical veracity of the *Memoirs* therefore emerges from the text's generic doubleness. The *Memoirs* are a blend of poetry and prose. As discussed above, the rhythm of Pilkington's prose is shot through with tags and phrases from Shakespeare, Pope, Swift, and others. She prints many of her own poems (including an unfinished play in verse in the second volume) as well as whole couplets or quatrains from others. There is a biographical reason that her poems figure so prominently: Pilkington originally intended to publish a volume of *Poems* by subscription, and decided only in the mid-1740s that an autobiographical narrative would likely sell better.

An untitled poem near the beginning of volume 1 of the *Memoirs* compresses all of these themes—the double entendre and immortality, writing and the ambiguously sexualized female body—into a lapidary set of eight tetrameter couplets. The poem has a complicated publication history, but in the *Memoirs* it immediately follows the account of Swift's "black and blue Favours," to which it serves as a verse commentary:

> O spotless Paper, fair and white!
> On whom, by Force, constrain'd I write,
> How cruel am I to destroy
> Thy purity to please a Boy?
> Ungrateful I, thus to abuse
> The fairest Servant of the Muse.
> Dear Friend, to whom I oft impart
> The choicest Secrets of my Heart;
> Ah, what Attonement can be made
> For spotless Innocence betray'd?
> How fair, how lovely didn't thou show,
> Like lilly'd Banks, or falling Snow!
> But now, alas, become my Prey;
> No Floods can wash thy Stains away.

Yet this small Comfort I can give,
That which destroy'd, shall make thee live. (45–46)

The poem's pervasive sexual subtext is scarcely a subtext at all, especially if any of the three uses of the word "fair" reminds the reader that the author describes herself as "very fair" in the preceding pages. Pilkington, who has had Swift's "Favours" on her skin, whose heart is a palimpsest engraved by a succession of poets, is clearly, by the time the *Memoirs* are written, in a position to empathize with the stained paper. With this in view, the "small Comfort" of the poem's final couplet is striking: it is by being "betray'd," covered with "Stains," even "destroy'd," that the paper can "live." Writing, for the feminized paper, is not only a sexual contamination but also a vitalizing intervention. After her husband, Matthew, divorces her, Pilkington too is stained. Nevertheless, as volume 2 of the *Memoirs* narrates, she makes a life for herself in London selling her poetry—but not, she claims, her body—to aristocratic men. Her livelihood is thus written as taking place in the space between body and text, the space of the double entendre.

A Noun Substantive: Mrs. Meade and Mr. Savage

The first volume of Pilkington's *Memoirs* follows an anti-comic arc, offering a chronological narration of the memoirist's youth, marriage to Matthew Pilkington, ascent into intimacy with Swift, mistreatment at the hands of her husband, ignominious divorce as a confessed adulteress, and impecunious flight from Ireland. The second and third volumes feature a more digressive narrative style and a more relaxed chronology. Interpolated with further reminiscences of Swift and substantial quantities of verse, they tell the story of nearly a decade of hand-to-mouth existence in London, in which Pilkington ekes out a living writing praise poems, running a pamphlet shop, and ghostwriting verse for the painter James Worsdale, before finally returning to Dublin in 1747. Like *Sir Charles Grandison*, the *Memoirs* seek a narrative structure that can carry a female protagonist beyond courtship and marriage. But Richardson's uxorial paragon is far from providing a satisfactory pattern for Pilkington's memoiristic self-construction. Felicity Nussbaum's reading of Pilkington and other "scandalous" female memoirists of the eighteenth century underlines this point, emphasizing the lack of models available to them for the construction of female character: "No existing model fully or consistently satisfies them—not seduced maiden, remorseful convert, lusty lass, or prodigal son."[16] Samuel Johnson's *Life of Savage* (1744), however, provides a close analogue. Both the *Life of Savage* and the *Memoirs* are about how to make a living as a writer in the first half of the eighteenth century—with a particular emphasis on how to relate to patrons. In the politically charged literary climate of the Walpole era, the lexical fields surrounding "patronage" and "prostitution" stood in close proximity.[17] For a male writer, the charge of prostituting one's pen was almost always strictly metaphor. In the *Memoirs*, the connection threatens at all times to become unmistakably literal.

The historical parallels between Richard Savage and Pilkington throw their gendered differences into sharp relief. Savage claimed to be the illegitimate son of the Countess of Macclesfield; Pilkington, similarly though less spectacularly, opens her *Memoirs* by asserting that she is "by my Mother's Side descended of an ancient, and honourable Family, who were frequently intermarried with the Nobility," and underlines this connection by assuming the name of "Mrs. Meade," a surname held by her most genteel Irish relatives, for the entirety of her London sojourn (10). Defrauded, he believed, of his aristocratic inheritance, Savage spent his adult life writing for the stage and the reading public (his most successful poem, an apologia entitled *The Bastard*, went through six editions in its first year) as well as cultivating and alienating a long succession of patrons. Savage collected subscriptions and pensions from a range of figures that included his alleged first cousin, Lord Tyrconnel; Queen Caroline; and Alexander Pope, before eventually dying in a Birmingham jail where he had been detained for a debt of £8.[18] Both Pilkington and Savage thus lived by their pens in an era when this meant writing for patrons and potential subscribers—often offering highly focused poems of praise or petition—as much as writing works that would sell widely in the popular book or pamphlet market.[19] Both had a difficult time of it. Savage had a somewhat better run than Pilkington—he drew a pension of £200 a year from Lord Tyrconnel for the first half of the 1730s—but each poet died indigent within a few years of turning forty. The biographical *Life of Savage* and the autobiographical *Memoirs* are thus structured around the poet's quest to stay alive in a wintry market.

The memoirs provide no direct evidence that Pilkington was familiar with Johnson's *Savage*, but she certainly knew the history and works of Savage; volume 3 contains a couplet adapted from *The Bastard*, deployed, unsurprisingly, in the context of thanking the *Memoirs'* dedicatee, Lord Kingsborough, for his financial support (306). Elias draws attention to Pilkington's conscious use of Colley Cibber's *Apology* as a formal and stylistic model for her own autobiography, but in the actual course of her life, which was spent at the margins of genteel and aristocratic society in a succession of precarious patronage relationships, she resembles Savage far more than the politically astute and economically secure Cibber (xxv–xxvi).

The opening pages of the second volume of the *Memoirs* inaugurate a pattern of economic subsistence that recalls Savage's and characterizes the remainder of the text; until she returns to Ireland and publishes the *Memoirs* themselves, Pilkington will live off of subscriptions and monetary gifts from male patrons, usually ranging from one guinea to ten or twenty. Reduced from time to time to indigence and imprisonment, she never accumulates enough capital to become independent: "I have observed, if my Life had any Sunshine, it was but a faint and watery Gleam, too soon overcast" (174).

From the beginning, Pilkington's text is ambiguous, in a way that Johnson's *Life of Savage* need not be, about what exactly her male patrons are buying. A begging poem addressed to the Lt. Col. John Duncombe, who, Pilkington says, "used to hire [her] to write Love Letters to him," puts two different products on offer: "Now, pray, Sir, consider the Case of your Mistress, / Who neither can kiss, nor write Verses, in Distress" (138).[20] On the following page, Pilkington protests elaborately that not even a £50 gift received during a tête-à-tête with the charismatic Duke of Marlborough (the grandson of the famous general) was received with any "hard Conditions," but the gift inspires her to write a poem to Duncombe threatening that "with Antlers [she'll] adorn [his] Brow" if he does not offer her more attention (139). Written after she has supposedly resisted great financial and sexual temptation, in other words, Pilkington's poem implies that she's already given herself on far less flattering terms. An equally ambiguous interview ensues the following morning with the Duke's brother-in-law: "Mr. *Trevor* assured me, he was at my Service, and would hornify the Colonel whenever I pleas'd. I told him, I was oblig'd to him for his kind Offer, and would certainly apply to him, if I found myself in any Distress; and in the mean Time, I hop'd, as an earnest of his future Favour, he would be so kind as to subscribe to my Poems, which accordingly he did" (140). In this bantering bait-and-switch, the promise of sex becomes the promise of text.

Again and again, this double entendre repeats itself. Nowhere in the

Memoirs does Pilkington confess directly to making herself sexually available to the men who subscribe to her poems or give her guineas when she is in financial straits. Indeed, she offers several vignettes in which her poetic talents distinguish her sharply from a common prostitute. For instance, she describes a time when her coarse landlady and a sailor "were gone to Bed together, both dead drunk," while Pilkington and a gentleman caller passed a rational evening in which they "talked of History, Poetry, and every Muse-like Theme; called all the mighty Dead before us, rejudged their Acts, commented on the Works of *Milton, Shakespear, Spencer,* and all the *British* classics."[21] In this case, sex and text are sealed off from each other in separate bedrooms: the landlady's "Talk became so offensive, that, as I had left the Door open, in Point of Decency, I was now on the same account obliged to shut it" (179).

But the implication that more than talk was at stake echoes through Pilkington's narrative of her London years. She describes months spent in semi-captivity at the house of James Worsdale, who gave her "a Shilling a Day to live on" in return for her ghostwriting services (274). A shilling a day is eighteen pounds a year—starvation wages, even by Grub Street standards. While composing ballad operas for Worsdale, which he seizes, "Sheet by Sheet," she also writes "Love-Letters" on behalf of a young woman to "a Gentleman, who had, it seems, kept her until he married, and then forsook her" (276–77). The parallel between the two women, the one kept as a hack and the other as a mistress, is hard to miss. Elsewhere, Pilkington forestalls insinuations linking her to other men with the witty protest that the price of a book subscription should not be able to buy anything more: "You told a Nobleman here, I had been quite compliant to your Desire: Why then you prove yourself a generous Lover, in sending me Five British Shillings for a Book" (303). Part of the joke here is that Pilkington claims in her first volume that she collects subscriptions as a form of protection racket. Reversing the usual practice of printing subscribers' names in a book, Pilkington promises to leave married men who have propositioned her *out* of her *Memoirs* in return for hush money: "If every married Man, who has ever attack'd me, does not subscribe to my *Memoirs,* I will . . . insert their Names, be their Rank ever so high, or their Profession ever so holy" (93). Pilkington offers economic necessity as an excuse for a woman in her situation who becomes sexually active, though she frames this excuse in noncommittally hypothetical terms: "Had I stray'd from the Paths of Virtue, when turn'd out desolate to the wide World, forsaken by all my once dear seeming Friends, and tender relatives, I might at least have hoped for Pity, and given Necessity as a Plea for Error" (290).

The point of this argument is not to open an investigation into whether sex with her male patrons was one of the means, along with begging-poems, ballad operas, and pamphlet selling, by which Pilkington eked out an existence as an Irish divorcée in 1740s London. The *Memoirs* certainly raise the reader's prurient curiosity on this point, but they consciously refuse to satisfy it. Rather, I wish to argue that Pilkington rewrites the Richardsonian trope of textual preservation of the body through her own ambiguous incarnation in the *Memoirs*. Pilkington turns the Christian tragedy of *Clarissa* into something that combines pious satire and secular picaresque. Within Richardson's novel, as I have argued above, *Clarissa* is Clarissa's legacy, the corpus that John Belford will assemble to exonerate Clarissa to the world's readers, just as her physical corpse will be reanimated on the Day of Judgment, when she will be exonerated based on the evidence in the heavenly Book of Life. The *Memoirs* are Pilkington's legacy (her literal legacy to her son, Jack, who received the profits of the posthumously published volume 3, as well as her figurative legacy to posterity), and like *Clarissa* they represent an attempt to preserve a body in the text. But Pilkington cannot, as Clarissa can, preserve herself through near-exhaustive documentation of her physical existence. The precision of Clarissa's endless, accurately dated letters is not available in the *Memoirs*. Rather, the reader of the *Memoirs* senses Pilkington's body hovering behind her book. In the first volume, this is because her body, like a book, has been written on. In the second and third volumes, Pilkington accustoms the reader to an endlessly repeated substitution of text for sex, book for body. The men who solicit her "favours" end up subscribing to her book instead. This should make them, of course, the first readers of the *Memoirs* as they were eventually published. It is significant that until about 1741–42, Pilkington collected subscriptions for a collection of poems, only thereafter soliciting money for copies of her autobiographical narrative instead. Pilkington recalibrates her literary project to accommodate the recognition that it was not just her words but herself whom her patrons desired to possess. The role of the implied reader, in the *Memoirs*, is thus that of a man who has reached out, attracted by her literary wit and poetic talent, to embrace the famous Mrs. Pilkington, and found himself reading a book instead.

"The Fate of All Things Mortal": Satire and Damnation

Laetitia Pilkington was an unconventional parson's wife, and the cleric who bulks most largely in the *Memoirs,* Jonathan Swift, was no ordinary priest. Yet Pilkington's text is a product of eighteenth-century clerical culture, and it endorses the orthodox and highly conventional Anglican alignment of pious literary fame with a happy Christian afterlife in terms that Edward Young, for instance, might have used. Thus, the dedication to the first volume celebrates the name and virtues of its dedicatee, Sir Robert King, while at the same time commending his soul to heaven: "These, Sir, are unfading Honours! these shall embalm and sanctify your Name on Earth; and, when this transient Scene is past, be a sweet and acceptable Sacrifice to God" (5).

On the other hand, Pilkington pairs encomiums on Christian piety and generosity with an acerbic and at times vituperative vein of anti-clerical satire. Though she has kind words for Swift and for Patrick Delany, the hospitable and generous Dean of Down and what Pilkington calls "a *real* Divine," the work as a whole abounds in what Pilkington calls "general reflections . . . against the clergy" (86, 51). These include not only ad hominem comminations against hypocrites such as her husband, Matthew, and the lascivious bishop Robert Clayton, but also more philosophical attacks on "Priest-craft" attributed to the "admirable Lord *Shaftesbury*" (103). Yet Pilkington cannot go all the way with Shaftesbury, who argued that posthumous rewards and punishments demean both God and his creatures by turning virtue into a self-interested strategy. Pilkington prefers to take Anglican orthodoxy at face value, arguing that its clergy rather than its doctrines are corrupt.

As a result, the *Memoirs* combine satiric denunciation with the threat of posthumous punishment. Where Aaron Hill wishes Richardson lasting literary fame in this world and eternal life hereafter, Pilkington wants to wound the reputations of hypocrites as well as prophesy their reprobation. Thus she paints a doubly damning portrait of Clayton, quoting verses from Swift's similarly minded "On the Irish Bishops" for the purpose:

> I was once acquainted with a Prelate, who had certain stated Prices for all his Sins . . .
> And
> > *Yet he was a Bishop, and he wore a Mitre,*
> Which, all in good Time, may be

Surrounded with Jewels of Sulphur and Nitre. . . .
As I do not chuse to be guilty of *Scandalum magnatum,* if nobody can guess who I mean, I will fairly acknowledge myself to be as arrant a Dunce as any Bishop or Parson in the world, and really that is speaking largely. (94)

A passage already quoted from Pilkington's many complaints against her husband shows a similar logic: "And if my *Quondam* Husband arrives at Fame, or ever goes to Heaven, either of which I very much doubt, I think he must still rest my Debtor" (87). In this passage Pilkington considers oblivion rather than satiric infamy to be the earthly equivalent of posthumous damnation, but in this case too she sharpens the often-complacent eighteenth-century association of literary and personal immortality into a satiric weapon.

The Afterlife of Laetitia Pilkington, or Autobiography in Sheets

Given that the *Memoirs* show Pilkington again and again deflecting a male interlocutor's desire for sex into the consumption of text, it is entirely fitting that at the climax of the first volume, the scene in which Pilkington's husband catches her alone in a bedroom with another man, she claims that the only thing going on was reading. As Pilkington tells it: "I own myself very indiscreet in permitting any Man to be at an unseasonable Hour in my Bed-Chamber; but Lovers of Learning will, I am sure, pardon me, as I solemnly declare, it was the attractive Charms of a new Book, which the Gentleman would not lend me, but consented to stay till I read it through, that was the sole Motive of my detaining him" (88). Elias's edition supplies the following note:

> L[aetitia] P[ilkington] anticipated that many would doubt her story, and a *bon mot* ascribed to Samuel Foote, seemingly her ally at the time this volume of the *Memoirs* appeared, bears this out. Somewhat garbling the story, William Cooke reports Foote commenting on an "intrigue" between "Surgeon-general A[dai]r," then a young Army surgeon, and an unnamed "married woman of high fashion," whose friends maintained that when he was caught in her bedroom he was reading to her from a rare book she had to return the next day. Foote strenuously defended the lady and said he could even specify which book it was, "namely, *The Christian's Daily Practice, in sheets.*" (475–76)

There is plenty to laugh at in Foote's remark, whose pun on "sheets" perfectly straddles the printing house and the bedroom. The fact that Pilkington's husband was a priest sharpens the juxtaposition of sacred and profane. Moreover, *The Christian's Daily Practice* could not have been "in sheets"; it was a single-sheet or even half-sheet pamphlet, scarcely of a length to keep a young man in one's bedroom to an "unseasonable Hour" unless something other than reading were in question.[22] Though Pilkington does not mention Foote's witticism in her book, it perfectly encapsulates the traffic between the erotic and the literary around which her work is structured.[23]

Foote was not the only eighteenth-century wag for whom "sheets" provided an opportunity for wordplay. In the Anacreontic poem "Reason," published in his 1772 *Songs, Comic, and Satyrical* (24), George Alexander Stevens (not to be confused with his homonymous contemporary George Steevens the Shakespeare editor) asks rhetorically, "Can all the clasp'd volumes of learned mens feats / Be equal to clasping one Beauty in sheets," and then reprises the quibble in the bawdier "Sentiment Song" a hundred pages later (126). A fitter successor to Foote's bon mot about Pilkington and Robin Adair appears in the pseudonymous *Ode to the Hero of Finsbury Square* (1795), a satiric epithalamium that targets the prosperous discount bookseller and pioneering autobiographer James Lackington: "Great 'HERO,' list! whilst thy sly Muse repeats / Thy Nuptial Ode—thy Prowess great, IN SHEETS." Lackington was nearly fifty, this was his third marriage, and the broadside goes on to cast some broad hints that its subject was impotent, with no heir for what the poem emphatically calls his "NINE HUNDRED THOUSAND VOLUMES" (10). "Peregrine Pindar," as the author of the *Ode* signs himself (the name rides the coattails of "Peter Pindar," the nom de plume of the satirist John Wolcot), is thus making what Christopher Ricks calls an "anti-pun." He sharpens his derision of Lackington's *Memoirs of the First Forty-Five Years of My Life* (1791), and of the staggering scale of Lackington's trade in remaindered and other inexpensive books, by implying not that his target's "Prowess" is distributed across textual and thoral sheets, but that is strictly confined to the former.[24]

Unlike Pilkington's better poems, *Ode to the Hero of Finsbury Square* is not a minor classic awaiting rediscovery; it got bad reviews on publication and has not improved with age.[25] But Peregrine Pindar chose a significant target. Lackington's *Memoirs* were a successful early example of a word that had been used for the first time in English only six years before: autobiography.[26] Michael Mascuch argues that autobiography is a late-eighteenth-century development and the generic correlative of a cultural development he calls "the individualist self"; Lackington's *Memoirs* are Mascuch's preferred candidate for the first autobiography in English, the first "work deliberately composed to represent to the public the authoritative ethos of its subject."[27]

For Mascuch, Lackington represents a watershed in the development of modern subjectivity; for Peregrine Pindar, Lackington is a laughable narcissist whose penchant for self-advertisement deserves scorn. The poem is punctuated by footnotes directing the reader to outrageous passages of Lackington's memoir, where "OUR HERO," as the poem derisively calls Lackington, documents his youthful poverty or writes his own epitaph. Here Peregrine follows the lead of his better-known namesake Peter Pindar, who a decade before attacked "Bozzy and Piozzi" (James Boswell and Hester Piozzi) for recording indecorous and minute "anecdotic scraps" about Samuel Johnson.[28] Like Johnson's biographers, Lackington's "prowess in sheets" includes airing his and others' dirty linen in public.

Though satirically, even scurrilously topical, Peter Pindar's *Bozzy and Piozzi* and Peregrine Pindar's *Ode to the Hero of Finsbury Square* are, in their fashion, Pindaric. They fight a rearguard action against a world in which biographical and autobiographical anecdote preserves everyday bodies—Johnson eating peas with Piozzi, Lackington's first wife subsisting on water gruel—not beatified Olympic paragons. This is the world that Pilkington's *Memoirs,* which presents its readers with both a mind overwritten with British poetry and a body tattooed black and white by Jonathan Swift's "favours," helped bring into being a generation before. As the target shifts from an attractive young woman to an aging man, the joke about "sheets" shifts its subtext from promiscuity to impotence, but Samuel Foote in 1748 and Peregrine Pindar in 1795 are at bottom reacting to the same development: bodies preserved in text.

7

Johnson's Eternal Silences

This study opened with the claim that when eighteenth-century understandings and representations of time changed, understandings of immortality changed as well. I have argued that Addison and Steele's diurnal,
periodical eternity appears transformed in Young's nocturnal epic and in
Richardson's heaven-directed writing to the moment. In my final chapter, I
describe the new expression that this dialectic of time and eternity takes in
the *Life of Johnson*. Boswell's biography is a thoroughly Johnsonian work,
not only because Johnson tacitly countenanced its creation and provided
theoretical and practical models for its form, but because it is a powerful
response to concerns that both Johnson and Boswell share about the nature
of the self and soul, and about the redemption of time.[1]

In this chapter, however, I consider Johnson as he himself wrote—and
did not write. Johnson's works confront the moral challenge of writing daily
life in view of both posterity and eternity. But his published writings do not
fit straightforwardly into the narrative of generic, intellectual, and theological innovation that structures this study. Where other writers see literature
as a technology for creating epistemological and soteriological confidence,
Johnson raises problems, expresses skepticism, or fights shy of the issues.
This chapter will therefore make arguments from absence, checking the
works to which he attached his name against his personal and anonymous
writings and the biographical record, attending to what is discrepant or silent. After an overview of Johnson's anxieties about time and eternity, and
how they shape his published writing, I revisit the very beginnings of his
career as an author, when a poetry competition about heaven and hell was

the catalyst of his long years of collaboration with Edward Cave. I turn then to Johnson's conflicted conception of literary fame, which he both valorizes and mistrusts. Finally, I locate the intersection of fame and eternity in the *Rambler*'s submerged fear of the unrecorded life. While Addison, Richardson, and Boswell wholeheartedly embrace the possibilities of diurnal genres such as the periodical paper and the diary, and their potential to record life with unprecedented fullness, Johnson experiences self-documentation as one more demand that it is impossible for him to fulfill. Johnson repeatedly resolved to keep a diary but was unable to do so for more than brief periods. The phantom of an unwritten journal lies behind Johnson's published discussions of the vacuity of life. Johnson asks questions about immortality, fame, and life writing that Boswell will undertake to answer in the *Life of Johnson*.

Johnson Out of Time

For a man who has an age named after him, Johnson had a very difficult relationship with time.[2] He was born late, when his mother was forty and his father over ten years older.[3] His May-December marriage to Elizabeth Porter, a widow twenty years his senior, seems like time's joke until we read his mournful prayers after her untimely death. Johnson jarred with time in small things as well as great—he couldn't keep it well enough to dance, or even to appreciate music. John Hawkins reports that the inscription on Johnson's pocket watch was misspelled.[4] Like his too-small wig and too-big body, the hours of the day didn't fit on Johnson—his extant *Diaries, Prayers, and Annals* record thirty-five resolutions to rise earlier in the morning, the last written only a few months before his death, none of them successful.[5] Numerous witnesses record his irregular hours.[6] Johnson resolves again and again to keep a journal, but can never persist. A diary or journal (both words, as already noted, derived from the Latin *dies,* or day) requires a harmony with time's ebb and flow that Johnson cannot master. Therefore, with rare exceptions, we read the passage of time in Johnson's personal writing not in a continual record, but only in the sporadic prayers and resolutions that, already acknowledging the inevitability of failure and the futility of petition, record his desire to document himself over time.[7] In Johnson's history as a professional writer, similarly, short but intense bursts of concentrated creativity balance periods of lassitude and depressive stasis.

Johnson was a Christian, and he saw immortality as a crucial doctrine uniquely revealed in Christian scripture.[8] But Johnson's discomfort within time produced intense anxiety about eternity. At times he feared that he was misusing the God-given gift of time, and thus incurring damnation. Hell was real for Johnson, as it never was for the complacent Addison or the triumphant Richardson.[9] At other times, Johnson feared that the vicissitudes of time left no enduring self, and that death therefore meant annihilation. He found this prospect every bit as terrifying as that of eternal punishment.[10]

We know a great deal about Johnson's religious life and thought from his written prayers, his sermons, and the conversations recorded by Boswell and others. Each of these genres at once offers and withholds intimacy: his prayers record deep suffering in the formal, ritual diction of the Book of Common Prayer; he gave his sermons to others to preach, including a heartfelt funeral sermon for his wife which John Taylor refused to give; and though Boswell frequently cajoled him to speak about religion, in the writings that appeared under his own name or were widely connected with him in his own lifetime, Johnson's statements on both Christianity and the afterlife are tentative and indirect.[11] W. J. Bate and Albrecht B. Strauss point out that the Bible is cited only seven times in the *Rambler,* compared to 103 quotations from Horace and 37 from Juvenal (*Works* 3:xxxii). Besought by Boswell to write, like Addison, more explicitly about religion, Johnson only answered, "I hope I shall."[12]

Johnson can only hope to hope. He is reluctant to use his authorial persona to represent Christian doctrines of the afterlife in detail, in either the allegorical, evangelistic mode of Bunyan or the scholarly mode of Warburton. There are exceptions, such as *Idler* 41, in which a letter on grieving reflects on the inadequacy of Stoic or Epicurean consolation and states that "surely there is no man who, thus afflicted, does not seek succour in the Gospel, which has brought 'life and immortality to light'" (*Works* 2:130). Written in the weeks immediately following his mother's death, *Idler* 41 finds Johnson writing for the periodical press in a voice that shares affinities with the private prayer he wrote a few days before (*Works* 1:66). But more typical is his *Vision of Theodore, the Hermit of Teneriffe,* which follows a mountain-climbing course that recalls *The Pilgrim's Progress,* but substitutes the generic allegorical figures of "Religion" and "the temple of Happiness" (which is shrouded in mist and described as being located in "the regions of obscurity") for Bunyan's frequent appeals to scripture, Calvinist soteriology, and vivid description of heaven (*Works* 16:203–9).[13] Similarly, as Adam Potkay has observed, *Rasselas* ends with Nekayah vowing to attend for the future to the "choice of eternity," only to undercut that choice with an ironizing "Conclusion in Which Nothing is Concluded," where the seasonal rhythms of earthly life (the inundation of the Nile) wash away the characters' pious resolutions.[14]

Scholars have attempted to explain Johnson's public reticence. For Potkay it is an expression of Johnson's wish "to be read as the polished [author] of 'an enlightened age.'" For Bate, in contrast, it was the consequence of an "inner censorship imposed by his conscience." Blanford Parker takes this second line of thought further, arguing that Johnson saw all literature and art as "a bauble to distract us from common miseries," both inferior to and incommensurable with "the one true lasting good" of Christian faith.[15] Without deciding between these accounts, I wish to emphasize that Johnson nearly always leaves an empty space for theology in his writings, even if he declines to fill it. When Rasselas says that he "is not ignorant of the motive" that draws pilgrims to Palestine, or the Rambler expresses satisfaction that his papers are "exactly conformable to the precepts of Christianity," Johnson explicitly points his readers elsewhere, asking them to attend to sources of authority beyond his text (*Works* 16:48, 5:320).

Reading and Writing the Last Things in
The Vanity of Human Wishes

In the *Rambler* and *Rasselas,* Christian doctrine is clearly discernible, though only as a subtext. Elsewhere in Johnson's writings, the gap left by Johnson's omission or suppression of religious content is harder to discern. Johnson's 1754 letter to Lord Chesterfield marks his coming of age as an author; indeed, for Alvin Kernan, writing in the tradition of Thomas Carlyle, the figure of the modern author is itself born with Johnson's epistle.[16] But Johnson's career as a *writer* may be said to begin two decades earlier, in November 1734, with a rather different letter, offering a "Literary Article" of "short literary Dissertations . . . Critical Remarks . . . forgotten Poems that deserve revival, or loose pieces . . . worth preserving" to Edward Cave, the editor of the recently founded *Gentleman's Magazine.*[17] This letter bore little immediate fruit, but it inaugurates the relationship that allowed Johnson to establish himself as a professional writer when he moved to London in 1738. We need not be surprised that Cave did not take immediate advantage of an unsolicited business proposition submitted by an unknown, pseudonymous provincial. Indeed, one might wonder why Johnson thought that Cave might be interested. At the time he wrote the letter, Johnson's only visit to London had been in his mother's arms, to be touched for scrofula by Queen Anne. Why Cave and the *Gentleman's Magazine*? Why 1734?

"Your late offer," Johnson explains to Cave in the letter, "gives me no reason to distrust your generosity." The previous July, Cave had opened the poetry section of the *Gentleman's Magazine* with an advertisement offering a £50 prize to "the person, who shall make the best Poem, Latin or English, on Life, Death, Judgment, Heaven, and Hell," giving candidates until May 1735, the better part of a year, to submit entries. Advertisements in August and October provided further publicity and clarified the terms of the competition. After several further announcements, a selection of the thirty-some poems submitted appeared in a special issue of the magazine, printed between the July and August issues. Predominant were serious treatments that considered the five topics sequentially, drawing on traditional depictions of resurrection and judgment. After various delays, the awarding of the prize formed the subject of the lead article in the February 1736 issue.[18]

This was the third of eight poetry prizes offered by Cave in the early years of the *Gentleman's Magazine,* and there is no question that it captured Johnson's imagination; in the short life of Cave that Johnson wrote for the magazine in 1754 following Cave's death, nearly a third of his analysis of the *Gentleman's Magazine* focuses on this competition—an astonishing proportion.[19] The 1754 account emphasizes Cave's disappointment that the £50 prize was insufficient to lure contributions from the foremost poets of the era, but as his 1734 letter makes clear, what struck Johnson at the time was the largeness of the prize. When Cave printed Johnson's poem *London* for Robert Dodsley four years later, Johnson received only ten guineas.

When Johnson decided in his twenties to seek his fortune as a London professional writer, an invitation to write about life, death, judgment, heaven, and hell was one compelling inducement. The invitation drew Johnson's attention and remained in his memory. Although the competition was part of what led Johnson to contact Cave, there is no evidence that he submitted a poem. But it seems likely that he read the "Extraordinary" issue of the *Gentleman's Magazine* in which the contenders were printed, and quite possible that the first poem printed (the eventual third-prize winner) stuck in his famously retentive mind:

What is this life we strive with anxious care
So much to keep? so much to lose we fear?
Let us thro' all its winding mazes stray
And from the cradle, to the grave survey.[20]

These first four lines anticipate the more sophisticated opening of *The Vanity of Human Wishes,* written a dozen years later:

Let observation with extensive view,
Survey mankind, from China to Peru,
Remark each anxious toil, each eager strife,
And watch the busy scenes of crouded life
Then say how hope and fear, desire and hate,
O'erspread with snares the clouded maze of fate. (*Works* 6:91–92)

The lexical and grammatical elements that the two poems share ("let [us/observation] . . . survey," "anxious," "maze," "strive/strife") are absent from Johnson's Juvenalian model.[21] *The Vanity of Human Wishes* is, in fact, one fifth of the poem Cave requested, a portrait of life that truncates and blurs death, judgment, heaven, and hell together into its final two dozen lines. Given that the poem explicitly advertises itself as an imitation, perhaps it is not surprising that it imitates not only Juvenal but a magazine poem from a decade before. Lawrence Lipking has observed that *The Vanity of Human Wishes* "pauses on the brink of Christian mystery, and refuses to profane the truth of revelation by translating it into the visions of poetry."[22] Robert DeMaria Jr. has argued that the tentative turn to Christian consolation at the conclusion of the poem is carefully designed for a mid-century audience of readers interested both in acquiring classical wisdom in English and in seeing the limitations of that wisdom exhibited.[23] But if Cave's prize poem exists as a second, hidden intertext behind Johnson's avowed imitation of Juvenal, the reticence of *The Vanity of Human Wishes* about heaven and hell is as noteworthy as its refusal to locate ultimate human happiness on earth as the Stoic Juvenal does. The pseudo-classical reference to a "happier seat" in the poem's final lines does not obscure the fact that Johnson has, in his own mind if not that of his readers, written a poem with an afterlife-shaped hole in it.

Johnson uses the word "immortality" to refer to literary lastingness as well as to the human afterlife, but the term he uses most frequently for the endurance of texts across time is "fame." It is a key theme throughout his moral and critical writings. Yet if Johnson's attitude toward personal immortality is one of reticence, his attitude toward literary fame is one of ambivalence.[24] Johnson's wary but constant interest in literary fame produces a worldview in which time is forever eroding human achievement, but in which aspirants to textual lastingness must continue to struggle against it.

Johnson sees time as the most valuable empirical test of excellence; the *Preface to Shakespeare* adopts the Horatian standard of a century as "the term commonly fixed as the test of literary merit" (*Works* 7:61). In one of the first *Ramblers,* Johnson preemptively parries critical attacks with an allegory in which Criticism, empowered by Justice with a scepter that can convey both "immortality" and "oblivion," deputizes her authority to Time (*Works* 3:16–18). The passage of time, in Johnson's view, allows a *public* consensus to develop. In his history of fame from the classical world to the twentieth century, Leo Braudy describes the seventeenth and eighteenth centuries as the era of "the democratization of fame."[25] H. J. Jackson, focusing on the *Lives of the Poets,* has argued that Johnson's concept of fame privileges broad popular appeal, derived from treatment of general subjects.[26] When Johnson wrote to Edward Cave in the letter discussed above with an offer to submit "loose pieces . . . worth preserving," he was offering to participate in the creation of this popular fame (*Letters* 1:5–6). As Johnson puts it in the *Rambler,* it is works that "come home to mens business and bosoms"—a quotation from Francis Bacon—that "will live as long as books last" (*Rambler* 106, *Works* 4:204).

Like the *Spectator,* the *Rambler* sees the human desire for fame as evidence for the immortality of the soul: "The soul of man, formed for eternal life, naturally springs forward beyond the limits of corporeal existence, and rejoices to consider herself as co-operating with future ages." Johnson argues further that departed authors may be able to trace the progress of their works from above: "Since we suppose the powers of the soul to be enlarged by its separation, why should we conclude that its knowledge of sublunary transactions is contracted or extinguished?" (*Rambler* 49, *Works* 3:266). Johnson's openness to the possibility of meaningful communion between the worlds of the living and the dead in his writings and unpublished prayers resembles the salvation economy of high medieval Catholicism, in which saints intercede for the living and the living assist the dead in purgatory: "Let hope therefore dictate, what revelation does not confute . . . that we who are struggling with sin, sorrow, and infirmities, may have our part in the attention and kindness of those who have finished their course and are now receiving their reward" (*Idler* 41, *Works* 2:130).[27]

In a letter of condolence he wrote to James Elphinston following the death of the latter's mother in 1750, Johnson expresses this idea in a form that follows Addison and Richardson in privileging the diurnal and anecdotal:

> You have, as I find by every kind of evidence, lost an excellent mother; and I hope you will not think me incapable of partaking of your grief. . . . The greatest benefit which one friend can confer upon another, is to guard, and excite, and elevate his virtues. This your mother will still perform, if you diligently preserve the memory of her life, and of her death. . . . I cannot forbear to mention, that neither reason nor revelation denies you to hope, that you may increase her happiness by obeying her precepts; and that she may, in her present state, look with pleasure upon every act of virtue to which her instruction or example have contributed. . . . There is one expedient by which you may, in some degree, continue her presence. If you write down minutely what you remember of her from your earliest years, you will read it with great pleasure, and receive from it many hints of soothing recollection, when time shall remove her yet farther from you, and your grief shall be matured to veneration.[28]

Johnson at once encourages Elphinston to imagine his mother's soul watching over him from heaven and to "continue her presence" on earth through the minutiae of biographical documentation. These two afterlives have the identical dual purpose of softening Elphinston's grief and encouraging him to live virtuously. By preserving his mother's life in writing, he can transmute his grief to veneration and become a son in whom she takes pride from the perspective of her current state. Johnson's word "diligently," with its etymological root of *deligere*, to delight in, and its English evocation of ongoing effort, perfectly unites these two purposes. The empirical data of her life are likewise the source of Johnson's confidence that Elphinston's mother is now in a better place; even pious consolation, for Johnson, must refer to "every kind of evidence" to establish that the deceased was "an excellent mother." A dozen years before Johnson was to meet his own surrogate son and biographer in Thomas Davies's bookshop, he imagines filial piety as biographical diligence in terms that strikingly anticipate Boswell's description of his own project.

In fact, Johnson's positive evaluations of fame imagine it as providing the same intercession through cultural memory that he imputes to biographical anecdote in his letter to Elphinston: "The true satisfaction which is to be drawn from the consciousness that we shall share the attention of future times, must arise from the hope, that, with our name, our virtues will be propagated; and that those whom we cannot benefit in our lives, may receive instruction from our examples, and incitement from our renown" (*Rambler* 49, *Works* 3:268). His *Essay on Epitaphs* makes a similar claim for the lyric immortality provided by sepulchral inscriptions: "Honours are paid to the Dead in order to incite others to the Imitation of their Excellencies."[29]

But Johnson does not always coordinate personal immortality and posthumous fame; elsewhere, he places the two in tension or outright opposition. The oft-quoted final paper of the *Idler*, with its claim that "there are few things not purely evil, of which we can say, without some emotion of uneasiness, *this is the last*," repeatedly uses the word "last" but eschews the dynamic word "lasting" (which is used in *Spectator* 553 in a metaphor for that paper's value for rereading and might well be applied to the final *Idler* itself). Instead, it evokes the forbidding prospect of "ever*last*ing futurity . . . determined by the past"—a veiled but clear reference to divine judgment (*Works* 2:316).[30] As Blanford Parker puts it, for Johnson "the end of writing was not immortality, but death."[31] Devaluation of earthly fame can also be found throughout the *Rambler*, where Johnson draws on the authority of Cicero to subordinate fame to goods either more immediate or more permanent, or offers those ambitious for reputation the prescient admonition that "names which hoped to range over kingdoms and continents shrink at last into cloisters or colleges" (*Works* 4:269, 5:16). Johnson frequently discourages aspiring authors from seeking fame, and he does not lay claim to or even express interest in posthumous reputation for himself. *Spectator* 101 imagines a "Historian" reading the periodical in 2011 and lavishing it with praise so effusive that Mr. Spectator's modesty forces him to redact it. Taking the long view of his periodical's future audience in *Idler* 40, Johnson assumes that copies will survive only because of the hoarding propensities of collectors, and that future readers will mostly be struck by the hyperbolic self-praise of advertisers: "There are men of diligence and curiosity who treasure up the papers of the day merely because others neglect them, and in time they will be scarce. When these collections shall be read in another century, how will numberless contradictions be reconciled, and how shall fame be possibly distributed among the tailors and boddice-makers of the present age" (*Works* 2:127–28).[32] Far from being a conduit for the transmission of virtues, fame is here clogged by ephemera and detritus.[33] Where the *Spectator* concludes its series by confidently imagining an afterlife of rereading, the *Rambler* approaches its final papers by reflecting that "reputation is ... a meteor which blazes awhile and disappears forever" before ending with the shrugging claim that the reader and writer have gotten tired of each other and should part ways (*Works* 5:295).

This ambivalence about fame is synecdochic of a larger ambivalence about history. Johnson draws moral authority from the past and projects it into the future by postulating a uniform and unchanging human nature which philosophers have always sought, and will ever seek, to correct: "Writers of all ages have had the same sentiments, because they have in all ages had the same objects of speculation; the interests and passions, the virtues and vices of mankind, have been diversified in different times, only by unessential and casual varieties." (*Adventurer* 95, *Works* 2:425).[34] This is why essays that "come home to men's business and bosoms" retain enduring relevance (*Rambler* 106, *Works* 4:204). In Phillip Smallwood's phrase, Johnson's writing shows a deep "commitment to the human common ground."[35] This faith in the essential continuity of human moral life enables the allusive range of Johnson's periodical essays, which can cite, for instance, Plato, Horace, Virgil, Cicero, Ovid, Boethius, Pope, Waller, and Prior, assuming that the experience of each is equally relevant to the condition of the reader (*Rambler* 143, *Works* 4:393–401).[36] Johnson must also postulate the uniformity of human nature through history to imagine the possibility of enduring posthumous fame.

But there is a darker side to this continuity. If society is without a progressive vector, lacking the "central, ongoing stress on the process and the principle of continuous, directed self-improvement, with no end point currently imagined," which Eric Rothstein defines as the essence of modern self-understanding, then time brings both gains and losses.[37] Stuart Sherman has argued that Johnson's conception of time is itself untimely, a "retrograde" holdover from the Renaissance: "Where the culture increasingly construes time as sheer *chronos,* newly powerful and enabling, Johnson insistently reinstates the long-standing (classical, medieval, and Renaissance) paradigm of *tempus edax,* debilitating and destructive."[38] When describing the history of criticism in the *Preface to Shakespeare,* Johnson's paradigm is not progress but entropy: "The tide of seeming knowledge which is poured over one generation, retires and leaves another naked and barren," just as the inundation of the Nile concludes *Rasselas* while concluding nothing (*Works* 7:99).[39] Johnson does make some local claims for cultural progress, as when he lauds eighteenth-century advances in women's education in *Rambler* 173.[40] But the elegiac tone with which Johnson describes ruined churches in the *Journey to the Western Isles of Scotland,* for instance, makes clear that he does not share the unqualified belief in progress widely current among eighteenth-century British men of letters.[41] "The present age," he remarks in an early *Idler,* is "not likely to shine hereafter, among the most splendid periods of history" (*Idler* 4, *Works* 2:14). Even languages die, particularly modern languages, as Johnson ruefully acknowledges when he describes the *Dictionary* as written "in hope of giving longevity to that which its own nature forbids to be immortal" (*Preface to the Dictionary, Works* 18:109).[42] It is only within these limitations that the past can supply momentum toward the future. Yet the present must attend to the past as much as it can: "If the wits of the present age expect the regard of posterity . . . surely they may allow themselves to be instructed by the reason of former generations" (*Adventurer* 85, *Works* 2:412–13).

Johnson practices what he preaches. With their explicit appeals to a long literary tradition and implicit appropriation of the conventions and techniques of the previous generation of periodical writers, the *Rambler, Adventurer,* and *Idler* show little interest in laying claim to originality. Johnson's periodical essays are heavily influenced by Addison and Steele. Of particular importance is the way in which Johnson adapts their technique of cumulative instruction and valorization of habit and repetition as the building blocks of moral formation, reiterating emphasized themes ("the deceitfulness of hope, the fugacity of pleasure, the fragility of beauty, and the frequency of calamity") with suitable variations (*Rambler* 143, *Works* 4:395). As all Johnsonians have read many times, "Men more frequently require to be reminded than informed" (*Rambler* 2, *Works* 3:14). The need for frequent reminders is particularly urgent for Johnson because bad habits can be powerfully debilitating, as in *The Vision of Theodore, Hermit of Teneriffe,* where they enchain numerous climbers on the Mountain of Existence (*Works* 16:195–212). A comparison with the *Vision of Theodore*'s most important classical precedents, the "Choice of Hercules" of Prodicus and

"The Picture of Human Life," attributed to Cebes, makes this point clear. Both depict life as a choice between virtue and its false alternatives, and the "Picture of Life" anticipates the *Vision* by depicting life as a journey. But neither places the strong emphasis on habits, and the gradual exertion over time needed to overcome them, which characterizes Johnson's allegory.[43] Even if moral regeneration is an impossible ideal (here we see the shadow of Johnson's resolutions and prayers fall over his periodical essays), we must strive for it: "It is, however, reasonable, to have perfection in our eye; that we may always advance towards it, though we know it can never be reached" (*Adventurer* 85, *Works* 2:416–17).

The movement of human society through time is, in other words, a macrocosm of the individual project of moral formation that Johnson, continuing the program of Addison and Steele, writes out in his periodical essays. When *Rambler* 129 imagines that individual authors are able to add, albeit in a modest way, "to the hereditary aggregate of knowledge and happiness," it draws an implicit analogy between an individual author in a wider literary history and an individual paper in a periodical series (*Works* 4:325). Just as each *Rambler* adds to the efficacy of its predecessors, each writer contributes to the stock of learning left by those who have come before. Fame is Johnson's concept for a culture (re)forming itself through time.

Of course, the analogy between an individual life and the course of the wider world has important limits, as Johnson reflects in a translation of Horace's *Ode* 4.7:

> Her losses soon the moon supplies,
> But wretched man, when once he lies
> Where Priam and his sons are laid,
> Is naught but ashes and a shade. (*Works* 6:343)

If nature and history are cyclical, human life is linear. The fact that Johnson translated Horace's poem a month before his own death underlines this fact. Moreover, although Johnson does not say so in this classical translation, he believed the individual to be headed to something beyond time—judgment—in a way that human culture is not. Johnson's eschatology is personal, not millenarian.

Johnson discusses fame frequently, but his view of it shifts with the context. When fame doubles, promotes, or harmonizes with personal immortality, Johnson values it highly. When it is opposed to immortality, or merely overwhelmed by the passage of time, he is far less laudatory.

Johnson and the Vacuity of Time

In my discussion of Addison and Steele in chapter 1, I identify the periodical paper as a harbinger of Walter Benjamin's "homogeneous, empty time," albeit one with a plan to fill that time en route to eternity. It is worth remembering that the *Tatler* and the *Spectator* offered a particular appeal to readers whose time was empty in a less metaphysical sense. Addison's programmatic *Spectator* 10 commends the paper to those "whom I cannot but consider as my good Brothers and Allies, I mean the Fraternity of Spectators who live in the World without having any thing to do in it," as well as "the Blanks of Society, as being altogether unfurnish'd with Ideas, till the Business and Conversation of the Day has supplied them."[44] The periodical paper is written for those who have nothing better to do and nothing else to think about. In *Spectator* 10, Mr. Spectator makes common cause with those who have nothing to do, but elsewhere he is less charitable, as in 317, where he reprints the diary of a man who did absolutely nothing with his life (example entry: "Nap as usual") and asks readers to think about whether their own ways appear "Graceful in this Life, or will turn to Advantage in the next."[45]

For Johnson, the "Blanks of Society" epitomize the universal human condition. As Arieh Sachs puts it, "Johnson's basic metaphor for human experience is the empty receptacle that cannot tolerate its own emptiness."[46] Sachs cites Hester Lynch Piozzi, who describes "the vacuity of Life" as an idée fixe of Johnson's: "it became by repeated impression his favorite hypothesis . . . all was done to fill up the time."[47] Piozzi draws on the imagery of emptiness and fullness, and the high view of the power of repetition, which have structured my own discussion of time and the periodical essay.

If filling up time is the most basic human motivation for Johnson, filling it well is the most basic ethical imperative. The proper use of time is an ancient topic for moral writers, with dual roots in the Virgilian observation that *tempus fugit* and New Testament warnings such as the parable of the talents—an obsession of Johnson's—or of the virgins and the bridegroom. Novel in the late seventeenth and early eighteenth century is the idea that self-documentation is a worthy use of time in its own right and a means to a more virtuous life more generally. Addison makes this argument explicitly, recommending to readers that they "keep a Journal of their Lives for one Week" because "this Kind of Self-Examination would give them a true State of themselves, and incline them to consider seriously what they are about."[48] As I have argued, the idea of writing one's life to work out one's salvation is also deeply embedded in the structure and fictional world of *Clarissa,* not only in the form of the novel but also in set-pieces such as Anna Howe's description of the "accounts" Clarissa kept of all twenty-four hours of each day.[49]

Johnson's preoccupation with the stewardship of time was deep and life-long, and anxiety about its misuse was often a heavy psychic burden to him. Clocks and other techniques for quantifying and measuring time obsessed Johnson and made him uneasy; when describing a severe bout of youthful depression to his friend John Paradise at a remove of some decades, Johnson chose as a representative detail "that he was sometimes so languid and inefficient, that he could not distinguish the hour upon the town-clock" (*Life* 1:64). His pocket watch, according to Hawkins and Boswell, was inscribed with the words Νὺξ γὰρ ἔρχεται (*nux gar erchetai*), derived from the words of Jesus in John 9:4: "The night is coming, [when no man can work.]"[50] The original scripture reads merely ἔρχεται νὺξ (*erchetai nux*). In reversing the word order and adding the emphatic postpositive particle *gar,* Johnson replaces Jesus's words with a literal retranslation from the Book of Common Prayer's "Commination, or Denouncing of God's Anger and Judgments against Sinners," a litany of curses and warnings read in Anglican Ash Wednesday services: "Therefore, brethren, take we heed betime, while the day of salvation lasteth; for the night cometh, when none can work."[51] Johnson's manuscript prayers witness his immersion in the Anglican ritual year, and particularly Holy Week, as a structure for self-examination and repentance. His watch inscription connects Christian ritual to the latest developments in chronometry; its maker, Thomas Mudge, competed for the Longitude Prize and received £2,500 for improvements on John Harrison's winning design.[52]

The quantification of time exerted an imaginative pull on Johnson that extended well beyond literal attention to the clock. Among his earliest personal records is a chart of various daily reading regimes, with a daily *pensum* of lines extrapolated out to weekly, monthly, and annual totals (*Works* 1:27). Records coordinating reading regimes with time survive from throughout Johnson's life.[53] A similar cast of thought is evident in chapter 4 of *Rasselas,* when the prince calculates with precision that the twenty months he has daydreamed away are "the four and twentieth part" of his rational life (*Works* 16:19). Here Johnson has clearly manipulated both Rasselas's estimate of his lifespan (forty years for "the true period of human existence" rather than the biblical threescore and ten) and the duration of his inactivity to yield a proportion that recalls the hours of a day.

Through the mechanism of Belford's executorship, *Clarissa* comes into being when Clarissa dies. Three years after Richardson published the final volumes of his novel, Johnson's wife, Tetty, died in the seventeenth year of their marriage. His grief-filled response was to write, recording resolutions for the reformation of his own life with her dead body in view (*Works* 1:46). As I noted at the beginning of this chapter, one of these was to keep a journal—and Johnson resolved to do so at least nine further times between 1753 and 1781, listing this resolution with others to read scripture and attend church (*Works* 1:50, 71, 73, 439). Beginning with their earliest meetings, moreover, he advised Boswell to do the same.[54] Although it is likely that the papers burned in the final days of Johnson's life included some diary material, the frequency of these resolutions suggests, that like Johnson's vows to rise early, they were honored largely in the breach. From at least the middle of his life, the time of his wife's death, Johnson held daily self-documentation to be a crucial spiritual discipline. But it was one that he could not bring himself to practice.

Johnson's private resolutions to keep a journal have no explicit analogue in his published writings. Imlac never tells Rasselas to keep a diary (in fact, books are seldom mentioned in *Rasselas*). And although the introductions to two fictional journals published in Johnson's periodicals acknowledge the *Spectator*'s mastery of the form, and he cites the *Tatler* when defining both "diary" and "diurnally" in the *Dictionary,* Johnson's periodical personae do not echo Addison's advice that readers keep journals themselves (*Idlers* 33 and 67, *Works* 2:102, 208). But this may simply be a sign of the enormous spiritual importance that Johnson imputed to the diary as a discipline, the spiritual reticence noted above asserting itself. The close connection in Johnson's mind between journaling and his own salvation may make him less, rather than more, likely to write explicitly on the subject in, for example, the *Idler.*

Nevertheless, the idea of diaristic self-recording casts its shadow in Johnson's published writings, particularly his periodical essays. The periodical genre itself has close affinities with the diary in the way it transforms time into text.[55] And Johnson's periodicals turn again and again to the small-scale texture of daily life, as in the observation of *Rambler* 68 that "the main of life is, indeed, composed of small incidents, and petty occurrences" (*Works* 3:359). The oft-cited *Rambler* 60 praises biographical writing, and claims that it should "lead the thoughts into domestick privacies, and display the minute details of daily life," while *Idler* 84, though it antedates the invention of the word "autobiography" by half a century, argues that the best biographer is the subject him- or herself (*Works* 2:262, 3:321).

Even more important than these positive traces of diaristic discourse, however, is the negative space opened up by the existence of diaries and journals. The invention of the diary makes it possible that one's life *may not* be documented. The power of a diary to preserve daily life gives rise to the fantasy that writing can preserve everything, which in turn creates the fear that what once was merely life lived is now, through not being recorded, life lost. I have already cited Boswell's definitive statement of this attitude: "I should live no more than I can record, as one should not have more corn growing than one can get in. There is a waste of good if it be not preserved."[56] *Tristram Shandy,* published over the same decade as Johnson's periodicals, both shows the acute cultural currency of this fantasy of complete self-documentation and serves as its reductio ad absurdum. Sterne shares Johnson's intuition that writing is fundamentally a response to death, but Sterne (like Henry Fielding in *Journal of a Voyage to Lisbon*) sees writing as a means to flee death, while Johnson (like Richardson in *Clarissa*) sees writing as a means to prepare for it. The *Rambler* and *Idler* do not, as *Tristram Shandy* does, burlesque the idea that life could be fully preserved in writing; they never express the idea explicitly. Instead, self-documentation becomes one more demand which human fallibility (including Johnson's own tendency to depressive lassitude) renders unrealizable. Lurking behind Johnson's discussions of the vacuity of life is the diary that he should have written but did not.

Idler 24, for instance, takes up Locke's question of "whether the soul always thinks." The essay is not a serious philosophical treatise à la Butler's *Analogy* (among human beings who do not think it numbers "younger brothers who live upon annuities" and "the sportsman in a rainy month"), but it does articulate the idea that undocumented time simply disappears: "We every day do something which we forget when it is done, and know to have been done only by consequence. The waking hours are not denied to have been passed in thought, yet he that shall endeavour to recollect on one day the ideas of the former, will only turn the eye of reflection upon vacancy; he will find, that the greater part is irrevocably vanished, and wonder how the moments could come and go, and leave so little behind them"

(*Works* 2:75–77).⁵⁷ *Rambler* 108 shows this effect at work still more clearly. The paper begins with the words of Horace that will three decades later become, in the mouth of Kant, a motto for the Enlightenment project as a whole: *sapere aude* (*Works* 4:210–14). But Johnson exhorts his readers not to the independent use of reason, but to the scrupulous use of time. He opens with Lucretius's observation that the vast majority of the earth's surface is both barren and uninhabitable, pointing out that the Epicurean's "system of opinions obliged him to represent" the world "in its worst form." Johnson's second paragraph transposes Lucretius's claim from space to time, and from Epicureanism to a philosophical framework that postulates an afterlife: "The same observation may be transferred to the time allotted us in our present state." The space that Lucretius assigns to oceans, mountains, and deserts becomes the time we must dedicate to sleep, custom, and the daily tasks of provision and survival. His metaphor in place, Johnson delivers the essay's moral thrust: that just as diligent cultivation enables us to nourish ourselves from the small arable proportion of the earth's surface, so careful husbanding of our time "would yet afford us a large space vacant to the exercise of reason and virtue." This is accomplished by the careful division of time into manageable portions; the cultivator of time "must learn to know the present value of single minutes, and endeavour to let no particle of time fall useless to the ground." Johnson closes with the anecdote of Erasmus writing *The Praise of Folly* on horseback and a motto from a sixteenth-century Italian humanist that "time was his estate."

The counsel that many a little makes a mickle in minutes as well as pennies, while characteristic of Johnson, is also an eighteenth-century commonplace; Lord Chesterfield, for instance, advises his son to "not neglect half hours and quarters of hours, which, at the year's end, amount to a great sum," and John Wesley advises readers of his journal to "redeem every fragment of time" by sharing the Gospel during chance social and economic transactions.⁵⁸ Of greater interest is where and how Johnson surveys the border between desert and arable time. *Rambler* 108 is structured around the dichotomy of labor and work, which Hannah Arendt traces to the philosophy of the ancient world and through the modern European languages.⁵⁹ Labor is the human exertion dictated by necessity, serving "the needs for the maintenance of life"—Johnson's sleeping, eating, providing food for the following day.⁶⁰ Arendt's labor is equivalent, in other words, to Johnson's deserts of time. Work, in contrast, creates a durable "human artifice" with "stability and solidity"; it is the output of those like Erasmus who, in Johnson's analysis, "have contributed to the advancement of learning."[61] Work is Johnson's arable land.[62]

Arendt supplements the labor/work dyad with a third, valorized term, "action," that is, human political activity and agency in community more generally. And in the preface to the *Praise of Folly* that Johnson cites, Erasmus praises its dedicatee, Thomas More, for the way he makes his time available to others socially: "The incredible sweetness and gentleness of your character makes you able and willing to be a man for all seasons with all men."[63] But Johnson excludes the social from the arable territory of his temporal world, deducting "all that passes in regulating the superficial decorations of life, or is given up in the reciprocations of civility to the disposal of others" (*Works* 4:210). Indeed, almost nothing counts for Johnson as the fertile use of time: "Whether the time of intermission is spent in company, or in solitude, in necessary business, or in voluntary levities, the understanding is equally abstracted from the object of inquiry" (4:213). In contrast to Arendt and Erasmus (and Chesterfield), Johnson subtracts from productive life the things that we think of as living.[64] What Descartes and Hume do with the faculties of consciousness, Johnson does with the hours of the day; he pares them away until the reader doubts whether anything is left.

Yet Johnson's conclusion in *Rambler* 108 is neither skeptical nor predominantly pessimistic. When biological and social commitments have been removed from life, reading, writing, study, and learning remain. Cultivated in the correct rhythm of application and rest, the subject's slivers of working time can yield abundant fruit. Moreover, the proper use of writing time redeems, that is retrieves (in Proust's sense of "retrouver"), the time that was lost: Erasmus was "so much versed in common life, that he has transmitted to us the most perfect delineation of the manners of the age, [joining] to his knowledge of the world, such application to books, that he will stand for ever in the first rank of literary heroes" (*Works* 4:214). This is the fate that Johnson calls "fame" and Arendt calls "immortality." Written down, the table talk that would otherwise have been waste becomes something enduring. Labor becomes work.

Without mentioning journals or diaries explicitly, *Rambler* 108 is thus written in a diurnal world. The ordinary activities of human life are threatened by meaninglessness, dissociated from the subject who supposedly performs and experiences them. Yet a few minutes of writing a day, inserted into the interstices of ordinary life, can preserve and give meaning to the rest of lived existence. In the crypto-religious register of the *Rambler*, this enables the writer at best to enter "the first rank of literary heroes." But given the connection between virtuous fame and the afterlife proposed elsewhere in Johnson's periodicals, the analogy between literary heroism and the spiritual discipline inherent in Johnson's private resolutions to keep a diary is clear.

Conclusion

Johnson's career as a writer opens with an invitation to write about death, judgment, heaven, and hell. Cave's poetry competition attracts him, but he does not enter it. In the ensuing decades, this pattern is repeated: Johnson leaves a Christian afterlife–shaped space in his narrative and periodical writings, while his unpublished personal records, sermons, and documented table talk testify to his deep investment in the topic. His reticence about the four last things intersects with an ambivalence about fame; Johnson values it as a transmitter of virtues and commends the pursuit of good fame as both evidence for and progress toward the afterlife. But his nonprogressive view of the larger course of human history makes him skeptical of fame's ultimate power and value. Johnson is obsessed with the emptiness of life in an era when the rise of the diary creates the idea that life can be permanently preserved if it is recorded in a sufficiently copious textual record. Though Johnson frequently advised friends to keep diaries, he does not offer this advice in his published writings. Yet his periodical essays imagine a world in which only writing can make fruitful the desert wastes of lost time.

In my final chapter, I turn to the *Life of Johnson*, reading it not only as a response to Boswell's own fascination with death, immortality, and writing, but as a complement to Johnson's thought. In the record that Johnson provided to Boswell, the presence that he knowingly created in Boswell's biographical record, Johnson is at last able to fill the lacunae discernible in his own published writings.

8

James Boswell, Also, Enters into Heaven

Boswell was a more serious philosopher than Hume. Not a better philosopher, obviously, but a more serious one. For Hume, philosophy was an intellectual exercise and professional vocation; it was academic, in something like our modern sense. Despite the immensity of the mature Hume's philosophical ambitions and achievement, philosophy never seems to have given him any dark nights of the soul. He admired the ancients for whom it was an elite hobby: "Let us revive the happy times, when Atticus and Cassius the Epicureans, Cicero the Academic, and Brutus the Stoic, could, all of them, live in unreserved friendship together, and were insensible to all those distinctions, except so far as they furnished agreeable matter to discourse and conversation."[1]

For Boswell, in contrast, philosophy was urgent, obsessing, existentially important. A philosophical treatise could catalyze an intense emotional reaction:

> I went to Bothwell Castle in very good spirits. But unluckily, I believe
> the very day after my arrival there, I read in Lord Monboddo's *Ancient*
> *Metaphysics* that there *could be no such thing as contingency,* and that
> every action of man was absolutely fixed. . . . I then looked into Lord
> Kames's *Sketches,* where . . . he maintains the necessity of human reso-
> lutions and actions in the most positive manner. I was shocked by such
> a notion and sunk into dreadful melancholy, so that I went out to the
> wood and groaned. I had with me Volusenus *De Anima Tranquillitate,*

passages of which were a comfort to me, and I read some of Montesquieu's *Persian Letters,* one of which is in favour of human liberty....
But still the arguments for necessity were heavy upon me.[2]

The conceptual world of this passage belongs to the Enlightenment: unlike
his Scottish Presbyterian ancestors, Boswell is concerned with necessity and
free will rather than predestination and election. But his attitude to philosophy is the opposite of Hume's pose of *dix-huitième* detachment. Boswell
reads Monboddo and Kames, his father's colleagues in the Court of Session
and lesser lights of the Scottish Enlightenment behind Smith and Hume,
with the affective earnestness of the Puritan encounter with scripture. The
battle between Montesquieu and Monboddo in Boswell's mind recalls not
Cicero's leisured *Tusculan Disputations* but rather John Bunyan's record of
how two Bible passages, one offering condemnation and the other redemption, "boulted both upon me at a time, and did work and struggle strangely
in me for a while" until "at last, that about *Esaus* birthright began to wax
weak, and withdraw, and vanish; and this about the sufficiency of Grace
prevailed, with peace and joy."[3]

Boswell responds to his philosophical perplexities and religious fears
through writing. The paradigm of prose immortality, which Boswell fully
realizes in the *Life of Johnson,* emerges, formally speaking, from the daily
moral formation and being-toward-heaven of the *Spectator* and *Night
Thoughts,* Richardson's writing to the moment, and Johnson's ethical-
religious preoccupation with the proper cultivation of time and practice of
biography as literary mode. Indeed, the chapters that precede this one in my
study might serve as a résumé of Boswell's major influences: he consciously
modeled his life after Mr. Spectator during his year in London 1762–3,
quoted Young frequently and saw Welwyn as a site of pilgrimage, and, of
course, worshipped Johnson.[4] Oddly, given their stylistic affinities, Boswell
nowhere records reading Richardson, although the twentieth-century Boswellian Frederick Pottle believes that he must have done so. (Incidentally,
the 1825 sale catalogue of James Boswell, Jr.'s library includes a 1749 Dublin
edition of Laetitia Pilkington's *Memoirs,* although it is not known whether
it belonged previously to his father.[5])

Although Boswell's predecessors supply formal models, however, the im-
petus for the *Life of Johnson* can be found in Boswell's own mental world:
not only in his well-understood yearning for a father figure to replace
the distant and icy Lord Auchinleck, but also in his preoccupations with

heaven, ghosts, fame, inheritance, feudal continuity, and reanimating the dead. Contemplating death and what lies beyond elicited the same visceral emotions in Boswell as the treatises on human freedom and determinism cited above, and he grasped at every available means of preserving life. Illustrative is the case of John Reid, a petty criminal whom Boswell successfully defended against a charge of sheep-stealing before the Lords of Justiciary in 1766, but was unable to save from a death sentence for a similar crime in 1774. In addition to a passionate and imaginative courtroom defense of Reid, undertaken pro bono, Boswell drafted a petition for royal clemency on Reid's behalf, made him promise "to write his life very fully," commissioned a portrait of him from an Edinburgh painter, exhorted him with Bible in hand to full confession and repentance, enlisted a medical doctor in a scheme to reanimate Reid after hanging, and finally wrote up his client's life and death for the newspapers. Like the man in Freud's *Interpretation of Dreams* who answers the charge that he returned a borrowed kettle in bad condition by protesting that "in the first place the kettle wasn't damaged at all, in the second it already had a hole in it when he borrowed it, and in the third he had never borrowed a kettle from his neighbor," Boswell responds to the shadow of the gallows by simultaneously seeking to prove Reid's innocence and convince him to confess; keep him from execution and prepare him for heaven; memorialize his death and bring him back to life.[6] The accomplishment of the *Life of Johnson* lies in Boswell's synthesis of his disparate protests against mortality into a harmonious whole. As Gordon Turnbull points out, "character" is what kills John Reid, as his conviction is based in part on his being in "habit and repute" a thief.[7] In the *Life of Johnson,* character preserves, as Boswell's forensic legal skills are turned to biographical research, which at once preserves Johnson's earthly *haeccitas* and makes the case for his posthumous salvation.

In his lifelong quest to defeat finitude, the *Life of Johnson* is Boswell's most successful gambit. The first task of this chapter will be to read the *Life* as a definitive instantiation of the prose immortality paradigm, both in its narrative techniques and in its conscious reflections about the purpose and nature of biography. The sections that follow trace Boswell's varied uses of writing as an instrument not only of self-creation but also of self-preservation, through his diaries and memoranda, *Account of Corsica,* periodical essays, and other writings. As the John Reid case illustrates, Boswell is inconsistent and even self-contradicting in the uses to which he put writing and publication; but as the mental fight between Kames and Montesquieu at Bothwell Castle suggests, he treated literature as a matter of life and death. The chapter then concludes with a brief look at the nineteenth-century reception of the *Life of Johnson,* and how prose immortality provides a framework for understanding the book's achievement.

"An Honourable Monument to His Memory"

Much of the *Life of Johnson* consists of Boswell's diary entries from the years of his friendship with Johnson, edited and in some cases expanded for publication. When Boswell revised his 1763 journal to tell the story of his first meeting with Johnson in the *Life,* he gave Thomas Davies, the bookseller whose shop Johnson "unexpectedly came into" while Boswell and Davies were visiting, a new and crucial five-word speech: "Look, my Lord, it comes."[8] This Shakespearean quotation turns Boswell into Hamlet, Davies into Horatio and Johnson into Old Hamlet. Thus Boswell makes his biographical subject at once a ghost, a literary character, and his own father, at the moment that the two meet for the first time. There is a fitness to reading these words as an unconscious invention of the late 1780s when Boswell, his English legal career stillborn and his political ambitions in shambles, indeed had no choice but to "wipe away all trivial fond records" and remember Johnson "within the book and volume of [his] brain / Unmixed with baser matter" (*Hamlet* 1.5.99, 103–4). Whether "Look, my Lord, it comes," was spoken by Davies in 1763 or imagined by Boswell over twenty-five years later, it is of a piece with the latter's earliest recorded ambitions to undertake the *Life of Johnson.* In September 1764, Boswell was entering the second year of his continental studies and travels; in the year since Johnson had seen him to Harwich and on to the packet boat for Holland, Boswell had written Johnson several letters and received a single long one in reply. On the last day of the month, Boswell arrived at Wittenberg, where he visited the tombs of Luther and Melanchthon. The simple inscriptions on the reformers' adjacent tombs record that they died at the same age, fourteen years apart. "In a true solemn humour" at the sight of Luther and his disciple undivided in death, Boswell records in his diary that "a most curious and agreeable idea presented itself, which was to write to Mr. Samuel Johnson from the tomb of Melanchthon."[9] Boswell lay down on the church floor in order that his pen and paper might literally rest on the monument as he wrote: "I vow to thee an eternal attachment. It shall be my study to do what I can to render your life happy: and, if you die before me, *I shall endeavour to do honour to your memory;* and, elevated by the remembrance of you, persist in noble piety" (*Life* 3:122, emphasis added).

This prostration reenacts Boswell and Johnson's visit to the church at Harwich before Boswell embarked for his year of studies at Utrecht; the *Life* records that Johnson "sent [Boswell] to his knees, saying 'Now that you are going to leave your native country, recommend yourself to the protection of your CREATOR and REDEEMER'" (*Life* 1:471).[10] In Wittenberg (young Hamlet's university, in addition to Luther's) praying becomes writing, and Johnson's remembered and recorded example becomes an intercessory medium between Boswell and God. Boswell did not send the Melanchthon letter to Johnson until 1777, when he explained that he did not send it before lest he "should appear at once too superstitious and too enthusiastick" (*Life* 3:118).[11] In the intervening thirteen years Boswell's vow had taken the form of a biographical project of which both Boswell and Johnson were conscious, as Boswell's diary from his trip to the Hebrides with Johnson in 1773 makes clear: "I shall lay up authentic materials for *The Life of Samuel Johnson, LL.D.,* and if I survive him, I shall be one who shall most faithfully do honour to his memory." Boswell perpends a footnote to his journal MS: "It is no small satisfaction to me to reflect that Dr. Johnson read this, and, after being apprised of my intention, communicated to me, at subsequent periods, many particulars of his life, which probably could not otherwise have been preserved."[12] Boswell did survive Johnson, and the eventual *Life* indeed presents itself as honoring Johnson's memory, in contrast to what Boswell believed to be the unfairly negative portraits found in Hawkins's *Life* and Hester Piozzi's *Anecdotes.* The germ of Boswell's biography is thus in his enthusiastic response to two tombs that unite and memorialize a great religious hero and his younger disciple.[13] In a Wittenberg church in the second year of their twenty-year friendship, Boswell already imagines Johnson (and himself) as dead and in need of a posthumous monument.

The advertisement to the first edition of the *Life* presents the biography in precisely these monumental terms. The dedication to Sir Joshua Reynolds and the Horation epigraph on the title page—which compares the autobiographical satires of Lucilius to a painted votive tablet—prepare the reader to think of the *Life* through the metaphor of portraiture, as what Boswell will later call his "Flemish picture" (*Life* 3:191). But Boswell's first direct address to the reader asks us to imagine the book as a monumental cairn:[14]

The delay of [the *Life's*] publication must be imputed, in a considerable degree, to the extraordinary zeal which has been shewn by distinguished persons in all quarters to supply me with additional information concerning its illustrious subject; resembling in this the grateful tribes of ancient nations, of which every individual was eager to throw a stone upon the grave of a departed Hero, and thus to share in the pious office of erecting an honourable monument to his memory. (*Life* 1:4)

There is a faint echo of Steele's account in the final *Spectator* of wishing to write a work with Addison "which should bear the Name of *the Monument, in Memory of our Friendship*"; Boswell also locates himself in the classical tradition of venerating human excellence ("immortality" in Hannah Arendt's sense) through the concentrated string of words derived from the register of Roman ritual duty with which the paragraph ends ("pious"/*pius,* "office"/*officium,* "erect"/*erigere,* "honourable"/*honorabilis,* "monument"/*monumentum*).[15] The *Life of Johnson* is presented as if it were an epitaph, a textual double of the literal Johnson monument, originally intended for Westminster Abbey but eventually placed in St. Paul's, for which Boswell collected subscriptions following Johnson's death.[16] As a monument, however, the *Life* differs from its marble double and their classical predecessors in that it comprises not a single inscription but an accumulation, a heaping up, of individual anecdotes. In the following pages, Boswell shifts to a new sepulchral metaphor, imagining the *Life* as the embalmed corpse of Johnson himself, incomplete only because not all of Johnson's intimates preserved his sayings and doings as Boswell did: "Had his other friends been as diligent and ardent as I was, he might have been almost entirely preserved" (*Life* 1:30). As Paul Alkon points out, Boswell used this conceit several times when explaining the project of the *Life* to correspondents in the immediate wake of Johnson's death, calling the book "an Egyptian Pyramid in which there will be a complete mummy of Johnson" and "a Mausoleum [containing] all of his precious remains that I can gather."[17]

The *Life of Johnson* is unprecedented in its scrupulous organization of time, filled with dated letters and documents and framed by running titles that give not only the year but, where possible, the precise date of Johnson's actions and conversations.[18] The structure of the *Life* is not only chronological—that is, sequential—but chronometric. Like the dated *Spectator* essays reprinted in volume form, the *Life of Johnson* invites its reader to reenter a past sequence of calendar time. Yet, as Alkon's study of "Boswellian Time" demonstrates, Boswell's scrupulous dating nevertheless creates a sense of timeless present, because of its disproportionate focus on Johnson in his final years, in London, in literary conversation: "Towards the end, upon completion and during subsequent readings, there is aroused a sensation that it is almost always Easter, almost always April, almost always spring.... Also contributing to such deceleration is Boswell's nonprogressive depiction of a character who does not develop or change from year to year."[19]

Easter is crucial to Boswell's diurnal yet timeless record of Johnson. As his manuscript prayers and meditations show, Easter week was the high point, beside the New Year and the anniversary of Tetty's death, in Johnson's annual round of spiritual self-examination. It was also Boswell's preferred season for visiting London. This was certainly due to the Scottish legal calendar, which kept him in Edinburgh from November to March and June to August; it may also be an expression of the seasonal vicissitudes of Boswell's hypochondria.[20] In a 1774 letter to Johnson, Boswell describes Easter in London as a pilgrimage, "like going up to Jerusalem at the feast of the Passover," which conveyed a "strong devotion" that "diffused its influence on [his] mind through the rest of the year" (*Life* 2:275). Easter is the story of a dead body in a sealed tomb turning into a living interlocutor, who appears to the disciples in order to eat with them—and Boswell carefully records the food that Johnson eats during their visits in Easter season, whether the abstemious cross buns and milkless tea of Good Friday or the "very good soup, boiled leg of lamb and spinach, a veal pye, and a rice pudding" that they eat the first time Johnson invites Boswell for Easter dinner (*Life* 2:215). Easter is at once the zenith of the Christian liturgical year, what Charles Taylor calls "higher time," and, counterintuitively, a deep source of secular time, as it was the need to set its date correctly that led to the promulgation of the Georgian calendar.[21] It is thus a metaphor for Boswell's project in the *Life* of turning a tomb with a mummy in it into a living conversationalist, the "bringing to life" that has been, I argue below, a mainstay of reader response to the *Life* for two centuries.

If Boswell's Johnson is a type of Christ, Boswell's Christ has some of the features of Johnson, as illustrated by a theological conversation from Boswell's *Journal of a Tour to the Hebrides*:

I spoke of the satisfaction of Christ. [Johnson] said his notion was, that it did not atone for the sins of the world; but by satisfying divine justice, by showing that no less than the Son of God suffered for sin, it showed to men and innumerable created beings the heinousness of it.... The effect it should produce would be repentance and piety, by impressing upon the mind a just notion of sin.... He presented this solemn subject in a new light to me, and rendered much more rational and clear the doctrine of what our Saviour has done for us, as it removed the notion of imputed righteousness.... By this view Christ has done all already that he had to do, or is ever to do, for mankind, by making his great satisfaction; the consequences of which will affect each individual according to the particular conduct of each. (*Life* 5:88–89)

Boswell simplifies this complicated revision of a mysterious doctrine with an image: "Christ's satisfaction resembles a sun placed to shew light to men, so that it depends upon themselves whether they will walk the right way or not" (ibid.). In two consecutive sentences, Johnson and Christ in turn provide light. The latter becomes not a substitute who covers man's sin but a source of true moral knowledge that shows erring man the right way, Rambler as much as redeemer. When revising his 1773 journal for publication a dozen years later, Boswell supplies a footnote explaining that this was not the view with which Johnson died: "he afterwards was fully convinced of the propitiatory sacrifice" (ibid.). But Boswell's own approval of a Johnsonian Christ whose suffering provides man with inspiration and guidance, rather than a sacrificial substitute, remains in the body of the text.[22]

Johnson as ghostly Old Hamlet, as Luther, as Roman ancestor, as preserved corpse, as resurrected Christ; each metaphor is planted in the *Life*. One more metaphor lies below the surface, offering a full synthesis of personal and literary immortality: the *Life of Johnson* as heaven itself. In 1764, desperate to secure an interview with Rousseau in his retreat at Môtiers, Boswell had attempted to impress the philosopher with an autobiographical sketch, focusing in particular on his early religious education:

My mother was extremely pious. She inspired me with devotion. But unfortunately she taught me Calvinism. My catechism contained the gloomiest doctrines of that system. The eternity of punishment was the first great idea I ever formed. How it made me shudder!... I became the most timid and contemptible of beings. However, from the age of eight to the age of twelve I enjoyed reasonably good health. I had a tutor who was not without sentiment and sensibility. . . . He set me to reading *The Spectator;* and it was then that I acquired my first notions of taste for the fine arts and the pleasure there is in considering the variety of human nature. . . . My governor sometimes spoke to me of religion, but in a simple and pleasing way. He told me that if I behaved well during my life, I should be happy in the other world. There I should hear beautiful music. There I should acquire the sublime knowledge that God will grant to the righteous; and there I should meet all the great men of whom I had read, and all the dear friends I had known. At last my governor put me in love with heaven, and some hope entered into religion.[23]

Boswell's early religious education is divided between the hellfire of Scottish Calvinism and the elegant and sociable futurity of Addisonian Anglicanism. The allurements of heaven—"beautiful music," "sublime knowledge," and meeting "great men"—satisfy appetites developed by reading the *Spectator:* "taste for the fine arts" and "pleasure . . . in considering human nature." Boswell never ceased to vacillate between these two visions of the hereafter, and between the fear and hope respectively that they elicited in him. More than any other part of his life, his spring visits to London during Johnson's life prefigure the pleasures Boswell expects from the *Spectator's* version of heaven. Even before getting to know Johnson, Boswell saw London in this way: the opening pages of his *London Journal* record that on sighting the city, Boswell recited the "soliloquy on the immortality of the soul" from Addison's *Cato* while his own "soul bounded forth to a certain prospect of happy futurity" (43–44).[24] A decade later, his diary describes an intimate dinner at General Oglethorpe's in April 1772 as though it were a beatific vision: "Mr. Johnson and Dr. Goldsmith and nobody else were the company. I felt a completion of happiness. I just sat and hugged myself in my own mind. Here I am in London, at the house of General Oglethorpe, who introduced himself to me just because I had distinguished myself; and here is Mr. Johnson, whose character is so vast; here is Dr. Goldsmith, so distinguished in literature. Words cannot describe our feelings . . . the radiance of light cannot be painted" (*For the Defense* 104).

An extensive record of the conversation, reproduced in the *Life,* follows. The topics are typical of Boswell and Johnson: current events and law cases, ghosts and dueling. Of course, Boswell's record of his own bliss to be at dinner with "great men" and "dear friends" is excluded from the *Life*. But the reader who enters into Boswell's detailed accounts of Johnson's table talk is not surprised to learn that he or she is experiencing what Boswell thought of as paradise. His most celebrated dinner scene, the meeting between Johnson and John Wilkes, "was not only pleasing at the time, but had the agreeable and benignant effect of reconciling any animosity . . . which . . . had been produced in the minds of two men, who though widely different, had so many things in common" (3:78). Boswell brings about the peaceable kingdom, in which the lion lies down with the lamb. In the closing pages of the *Life*, Boswell states explicitly that he imagines heaven as a place where he will be reunited with Johnson: "I look forward with humble hope of renewing our friendship in a better world" (4:380).[25]

For all the pleasure transmitted by the *Life's* conversational tableaux, it contains too much shade—Johnson's early disappointments, late diseases, and constant battles with melancholy—to stand in fully as a substitute for Addisonian futurity. Precisely where the biography is not a type of the blessed afterlife, however, it becomes an instrument for getting there. This is true in two senses. First, Boswell holds up Johnson as a moral exemplar; even his guarded record of Johnson's moral failings (4:395–98) is carefully calibrated to depict Johnson as the most imitable of sinners.[26] Bruce Redford points out that part of Boswell's intention in writing Johnson's life "in scenes" was to make him a vivid moral model: "He signals his intention by quoting part of a couplet from Pope's prologue to Addison's *Cato*: 'To make mankind, in conscious virtue bold, / Live o'er each scene, and be what they behold.' "[27] This is not to say that Boswell sets Johnson up as a figure for universal imitation; he is too emphatic in depicting Johnson's psychological and physical particularity for that. But the text clearly sets Johnson up as an heroic inspiration, deserving "admiration and reverence" (the final words of the *Life*, 4:430).[28] Second, the *Life* projects Johnson himself into heaven, much as *Clarissa* does its heroine, by presenting a peaceful and pious version of Johnson's death, in which he is "perfectly resigned" and "seldom or never fretful or out of temper" (4:417). Boswell seeks to rebut the insinuations of Sir John Hawkins and others that Johnson either committed suicide or scarified himself into premature death through an impious avidity for life.[29] According to the writing-makes-it-so logic of Boswellian wish-fulfillment, Johnson's last reported words, "God bless you, my dear!," should usher him into heaven (4:418).

From the exotic, gothic conceit of erecting a pyramid for Johnson (itself mingled with suggestions of Catholic veneration of relics) to the elegant Addisonian heaven of Easter in London, the *Life of Johnson* mingles multiple streams of eighteenth-century religious rhetoric. Yet it is important to recognize that Boswell's minutely documentary project is also grounded in his Scottish Enlightenment training, even as it goes beyond it. In the introduction to his *Journal of a Tour to the Hebrides*, a trial balloon for the fuller *Life* that Boswell published separately in 1785, Boswell supplies a detailed description of Johnson's face, manners, clothes, shoes, (with "silver buckles") and even his walking stick, and then states, "Let me not be censured for mentioning such minute particulars. Everything relative to so great a man is worth observing. I remember Dr. Adam Smith, in his rhetorical lectures at Glasgow, told us he was glad to know that Milton wore latchets in his shoes instead of buckles" (*Life* 5:19). Boswell heard Smith's lectures in 1759; a surviving copy of student notes taken from the 1762–63 academic year does not contain Smith's remark on Milton, but lecture 22, which discusses panegyric oratory, shows that Boswell is indeed expressing Smith's views: "The smallest circumstances, the most minute transactions of a great man are sought after with eagerness. Everything that is created with Grandeur seems to be important."[30] Though he evidently used the example of Milton's shoe-latchets when delivering the lecture to Boswell, in the surviving written text Smith gives Xenophon's panegyric on Agesilaus—a traditional celebration of the victories and virtues of that Spartan king—as his paradigmatic example of a minute description of character. But Boswell's unprecedented use of chronometric precision as well as anecdotal detail means that the completed *Life* goes beyond the model of Xenophon, just as it does Boswell's own stated classical model, Plutarch.

Diary as Mirror

Johnson knew that Boswell meant to write his life, and despite some ambivalence he was in the end a not unwilling collaborator.[31] Boswell could not claim an explicit imprimatur from his subject, but throughout the *Journal of a Tour* and the *Life of Johnson*, he shows himself in dialogue with Johnson about what kind of book the *Life* will be. He records Johnson's collaboration in his documentary legwork, noting for instance the evening on which he gathered from Johnson the "authentick information" which is "incorporated in its proper place" in the *Life* (2:441). Boswell reports Johnson's permission to publish his letters: "Nay, Sir, when I am dead, you may do as you will" (2:60). He intimates that Johnson is "secretly pleased to find so much of the fruit of his mind preserved" and "delighted . . . to find that his conversation teemed with point and energy" when Boswell reports to him in 1778 how much of the last fifteen years of his speech has been recorded in Boswell's journal (3:260).[32] The *Journal of a Tour* in particular contains a feedback loop throughout, as Boswell repeatedly records Johnson reading and praising Boswell's journal, including its records of Johnson reading and praising earlier sections.[33]

Throughout their friendship, Boswell talks with Johnson about the practice and theory of life writing and the ethics of publication. In addition to demonstrating that the project of the *Life* connects to Johnson's own interests and anxieties, these discussions provide an entrée into the relationship between the biography of Johnson and the rest of Boswell's writings, particularly his voluminous diaries and personal memoranda. The *Life* records a conversation on March 30, 1778, at Streatham, where, over coffee with Johnson, Mrs. Thrale, and Robert Barnewall (called by courtesy Lord Trimlestown, though his grandfather had lost the title for being a Jacobite), Boswell introduces the topic of an autobiographical "Life of Sir Robert Sibbald" that Boswell had purchased from his uncle John Boswell, MD.[34] He moots the possibility of publishing the manuscript, in which Sibbald, a seventeenth-century Scottish physician and geographer, recounts his return to Protestantism after a brief Catholic conversion because, as Boswell puts it, "he found the rigid fasting prescribed by the church very severe upon him." A discussion follows:

> MRS. THRALE: "I think you had as well let alone that publication. To discover such weakness exposes a man when he is gone." JOHNSON: "Nay, it is an honest picture of human nature. How often are the primary motives of our greatest actions as small as Sibbald's, for his reconversion." MRS. THRALE: "But may they not as well be forgotten?" JOHNSON: "No, Madam, a man loves to review his own mind. That is the use of a diary, or journal." LORD TRIMLESTOWN: "True, Sir. As the ladies love to see themselves in a glass; so a man likes to see himself in his journal." BOSWELL: "A very pretty allusion." JOHNSON: "Yes, indeed." BOSWELL: "And as a lady adjusts her dress before a mirror, a

man adjusts his character by looking at his journal." I next year found the very same thought in Atterbury's *Funeral Sermon on Lady Cutts;* where, having mentioned her *Diary,* he says, "In this glass she every day dressed her mind." This is a proof of coincidence, and not of plagiarism; for I had never read that sermon before. (3:228)[35]

Boswell's authorial gift for organizing conversation is on brilliant display here. Mrs. Thrale's opening is a foil for Johnson to express a characteristic gnomic truth (his rhetorical question about the smallness of "primary motives" paraphrases *Rambler* 141).[36] When Mrs. Thrale persists, Johnson subtly but decisively changes the topic, from the propriety of publishing Sibbald's *Life* to the value of a diary to the individual diary-keeper. Trimlestown earns Boswell and Johnson's applause when he picks up the submerged metaphor in Johnson's use of the word "review" by comparing a diary to a mirror; even when Johnson does not make the cleverest remark, he remains, in the *Life,* the arbiter of conversation. Finally, Boswell completes the tricolon of "review . . . glass . . . mirror" by extending the analogy from self-regard to self-improvement. Boswell atypically gives himself the last word here, perhaps because using a diary as a tool of character formation was a lifelong project for him. Indeed, the biographical resonance of this passage is equal to its dramaturgic deftness. Like Sibbald (and Gibbon and Rousseau) before him, the young Boswell flirted with Catholicism, and like Sibbald was reclaimed from Rome for reasons that do little credit to Protestantism.[37] (As Frederick Pottle puts it, in the spring of 1760 Alexander Montgomerie, Lord Eglinton "rescued Boswell from religious error by making him a libertine, in every sense of that word.")[38]

Boswell praises Trimlestown's comparison of "glass" and "journal" as "a very pretty allusion." Trimlestown and Boswell are both updating a long-standing metaphor of biographies as mirrors in which readers can see themselves—as in the Elizabethan *Mirror for Magistrates* (1559), Samuel Clarke's Nonconformist *Mirror or Looking-Glasse Both for Saints and Sinners* (1646), the Dutch Anabaptist *Martyr's Mirror* (1660), and even Richard Steele's *Conscious Lovers* (1723).[39] Boswell's ostensible classical model for the *Life,* Plutarch, uses the image in the opening of his *Life of Timoleon:* "I find that I am continuing [the *Lives*] and delighting in it now for my own sake also, using history as a mirror and endeavouring in a manner to fashion and adorn my life in conformity with the virtues therein depicted."[40] Boswell's innovation is to imagine a man's own diary, not the life record of a heroic predecessor, as the engine of self-fashioning. Johnson and Trimlestown here conceive of a diary as a source of narcissistic pleasure, Boswell as a way of adjusting "character."

Boswell kept his diary (in various forms, and with some significant hiatus) from his eighteenth year until two months before his death.[41] The segment of this massive archive that concerns his year in London from November 1762 to August 1763 (known to twentieth-century readers as the *London Journal*) begins with a programmatic statement that prepares the reader to find both Boswell's narcissistic pleasures and his character adjustments in the leaves that follow:

> A man cannot know himself better than be attending to the feelings of his heart and to his external actions, from which he may with tolerable certainty judge "what manner of person he is." I have therefore determined to keep a daily journal in which I shall set down my various sentiments and my various conduct, which will be not only useful but very agreeable. It will give me a habit of application and improve me in expression; and knowing that I am to record my transactions will make me more careful to do well. Or if I should go wrong, it will assist me in resolutions of doing better. I shall here put down my thoughts on different subjects at different times, the whims that may seize me and the sallies of my luxuriant imagination. I shall mark the anecdotes and stories that I hear, the instructive or amusing conversations that I am present at, and the various adventures that I may have. (*London Journal* 39)

Boswell's explanation exhibits the same overdetermining plenitude as his later defense of John Reid; journal-keeping is both *utile* and *dulce* because it promotes self-knowledge, is morally both prophylactic and corrective, and provides "a store of entertainment for my after life" (*London Journal* 40). Fredrick Pottle's editorial quotation marks also draw attention to a daringly repurposed citation from the book of James. The scripture reads:

> But be ye doers of the word, and not hearers only, deceiving your own selves. For if any be a hearer of the word, and not a doer, he is like unto a man beholding his natural face in a glass: For he beholdeth himself, and goeth his way, and straightway forgetteth *what manner of man he was.* But whoso looketh into the perfect law of liberty, and continueth

therein, he being not a forgetful hearer, but a doer of the work, this man shall be blessed in his deed. (James 1:22–25, emphasis added)

Instead of replacing the Plutarchan heroic model, as it will in the Streatham conversation fifteen years later, the diary replaces the word of God itself (James's "perfect law of liberty") as the mirror in which the diarist can see "what manner of person" he is.

There is, at first glance, a question-begging circularity here. Without an external standard, a diary cannot provide its own benchmark for self-assessment, much less its own norms of conduct. One thinks of "someone saying 'But I know how tall I am!' and laying his hand on top of his head to prove it" in Wittgenstein's *Philosophical Investigations*.[42] Boswell has multiple solutions to the problem of making one's own writing the source and arbiter of personal identity and value. For one, he bases both life and life records on literary models, judging himself as character and his diary as narrative by their fidelity to generic conventions. "His journal constitutes a kind of source book for stock masculine characters current in mid-eighteenth-century Britain," as Erin Mackie puts it as she documents Boswell's self-conscious play-acting of roles ranging from the urbane Mr. Spectator (and his alter egos, Addison's Cato and the "Christian Hero" Richard Steele) to the violently sexual highwayman Macheath (and *his* alter ego, the actor West Digges).[43] Boswell's role-playing has received considerable attention from critics interested in theatricality and performance, a tendency increased by the self-contained accessibility of the *London Journal*, where it is particularly prominent. But the problem of generating personal norms from a self-documenting text admits of several other solutions. Beginning on his arrival in Holland for a year of legal study in August 1763, Boswell divided his diary into two parts, a minatory/hortatory daily memorandum and a (now lost) narrative journal; he then judged himself on his perceived ability to bring practice into alignment with precept. In addition to writing down his resolutions from day to day, Boswell digested them into an "Inviolable Plan" which he in turn frequently exhorts himself to read (*Boswell in Holland*, 387–90). A year later, Boswell articulates the idea of simply taking himself as norm, with no reference to external standards, while recording his behavior at a wedding he attended while in Berlin on his Grand Tour in 1764: "I was rather too singular. Why not? I am in reality an original character. Let me moderate and cultivate my originality. God would not have formed such a diversity of men if he had intended that they should all come up to a certain standard. That is indeed impossible while black, brown, and fair, serious, lively, and mild, continue direct qualities. Let me then be Boswell and render him as fine a fellow as possible" (*Grand Tour of Germany and Switzerland* 29). The idea is repeated nearly verbatim three weeks later: "I must be Mr. Boswell of Auchinleck, and no other. Let me make him as perfect as possible." (ibid. 53).

Though "let me then be Boswell" has a familiar ring to readers located in the moment of post-1960s expressive individualism, it is far from being the telos of Boswell's experiments with writing as a form of self-fashioning. A decade later, he expresses fear lest this process of writing down a self work too well: "It occurred to me that if I keep in constant remembrance the thoughts of my heart and imaginations of my fancy, there will be a sameness produced, and my mind will not have free scope for alteration; so that I had better lay by my journal and read masses of it at distant intervals" (*Ominous Years* 219–20).

The preface to the *Account of Corsica, and Memoirs of Pascal Paoli* proposes a rather different model:

> A man who has been able to furnish a book which has been approved by the world, has established himself as a respectable character in distant society, without any danger of having that character lessened by the observation of his weaknesses. To preserve a uniform dignity among those who see us every day, is hardly possible; and to aim at it, must put us under the fetters of a perpetual restraint. The author of an approved book may allow his natural disposition an easy play, and yet indulge the pride of superiour genius when he considers that by those who know him only as an author, he never ceases to be respected.[44]

The *Account* is the first of Boswell's publications to transmute diary material into a published book; in so doing, its preface postulates, Boswell creates a fixed simulacrum that liberates him to range freely, become a Wizard of Oz slipping out from behind the curtain to spend his time drinking, gambling, whoring, or in a depressive paralysis.[45]

Boswell restates this doctrine of the author's two bodies both in the final essay of *The Hypochondriack* ("Indeed, there is nothing more delusive than the supposed character of an author, from reading his compositions") and in the *Life,* where he reprints the above-quoted paragraph from the *Account of Corsica* preface in full (*Hypochondriack* 2:300, *Life* 2:69). In the *Life,* it is both fitting and unfitting; the book exploits the distance between author and work to comic effect in its early sections, such as when Bennet Langton, on first meeting Johnson after having read the *Rambler,* expects "a remarkably decorous philosopher" and instead encounters "a huge uncouth figure" (*Life* 1:247). And Boswell can present a version of himself in which the candor and pain of the diaries have been edited out. But inasmuch as its monumental purpose is to preserve Johnson entire, the *Life* seeks to erase the space between person and text; its goal is to depict Johnson so fully that the reader cannot imagine him having an existence that is invisible to, or beyond, Boswell's tome. The idea of a simulacral Author behind whom the flesh-and-blood Boswell can hide is even more problematic in *The Hypochondriack,* with its vivid and candid accounts of emotional instability and suffering. Indeed, Boswell was influenced by Steele's *Christian Hero,* which Steele claimed to have published with his name on the title page "with the avowed purpose of obliging himself to lead a religious life," as Boswell puts it—that is, make Author and author the same.[46]

The paradigm of diurnal (or, in the case of *The Hypochondriack,* monthly) writing as a technology of edification comes to Boswell directly from the *Spectator,* with a detour through the *Rambler.* Both Boswell's *London Journal* and *The Hypochondriack* echo Johnson's fear of uncultivated time and Johnson's faith in the power of regular autobiographical writing to redeem it: "In this way I shall preserve many things that would otherwise be lost in oblivion"; "Writing such essays therefore may fill up the interstices of [men's] lives, and occupy moments which would otherwise be lost" (*London Journal* 40; *Hypochondriack* 1, 1:103). But Boswell also moves beyond these models in imagining writing not only as a preservative regimen, but as an expressive therapy. As the Horatian epigraph to the first *Hypochdriack* essay has it, *sunt verba et voces quibus hunc lenire dolorem possis*—"Words will avail to ease the wretched mind" (*Hypochondriack* 1:103). Thus *Hypochondriack* 39 (begun, Boswell's journal records, "quite in despair") records the phenomenology of hypochondria—"low and desponding" self-opinion, "indolence and shame," "extreme degree of irritability," "corrosive imagination," etc. (*Laird of Auchinleck* 276; *Hypochondriack* 2:40–46). The essay's final section proposes the palliative of religion, specifically the "habitual exercise of piety" when in good spirits, which reassures the hypochondriac that his "sufferings however severe will be found beneficial in the other world, as having prepared him for the felicity of the saints above." Boswell ends, however, with the suggestion that writing itself can be therapeutic: "While writing this paper, I have by some gracious influence been insensibly relieved from the distress under which I laboured when I began it" (*Hypochondriack* 2:46). Diagnosis becomes cure.

A Tale That Is Told

Boswell's archive thus preserves a wide variety of approaches to writerly self-fashioning—role-playing in the *London Journal,* schizoid self-discipline in Holland, "being Boswell" on the Grand Tour, hiding behind the fixed mask of authorship in the *Account of Corsica,* the writing cure in the *Hypochondriack,* and finally the synthesis of author and man in the hero of the *Life of Johnson*—that calls to mind once more his multifarious and mutually canceling attempts to save John Reid. As Boswell himself recognized, they cannot be reduced to a single coherent line of thought. His gambits do, however, share the belief that life becomes meaningful only when preserved in text, as in the passage, quoted twice before in this study, where Boswell muses that he "should live no more than [he] can record, as one should not have more corn growing than one can get in" (*Ominous Years* 265). Selfhood requires text, and text equals preservation. "Boswell" as a role or identity only has meaning when it is moored to the promise of textual lastingness, whatever the precise form of that promise may be. Thus the following diary musing, from February 3, 1777: "I had lately a thought that appeared new to me: that by burning all my journal and all my written traces of former life, I should be like a new being. . . . Were I just now to go and take up house in any country town in England, it would be just a different existence. Might it not be proper to change one's residence very frequently, so as to be literally a pilgrim upon earth? For death would not be such a violent circumstance, as one would not be strongly fixed" (*In Extremes* 84). Here Boswell sees death in its mortalist, final aspect, rather than as a transition to immortality, and holds that the unwritten life is closer to such a death than the written one.

Since Boswell thought of writing as *the* technology for creating a permanent identity, it is no surprise that he reprises the coordination of textual and theological futurity that drives both the *Spectator* and *Clarissa.* This is particularly true, as argued above, in the *Life,* but it is also implicit in the logic of Boswell's lifelong diary-keeping. As Boswell himself puts it, seeking to reassure himself of the immortality of the soul in the wake of his traumatic interview with the dying Hume in summer 1776, "My great argument for *soul* is our *consciousness* of all sensations and reflections and passions; something different from all and each of our perceptions, of whatever kind and however compounded" (*In Extremes* 22). The soul, in other words, is that whose objective correlative is a diary.[47] The *Hypochondriack* furnishes another instance. Having heard Hugh Blair preach on Psalm 90 ("We spend our years as a tale that is told. The days of our years are threescore and ten" [verses 9b–10a]) on December 22, 1782, Boswell writes two months later to the London publisher of the periodical arranging to extend the essay to seventy numbers, "the years of a man's life." The eighteenth-century periodical from Steele onward plays on the ambiguity of a proper name as belonging both to a text and to its narrator: Mr. Spectator is the *Spectator,* the Rambler is the *Rambler,* and so on. Boswell extends this line of thought by pointing to the analogy between the "life" of a periodical and the life of its narrator. The Psalmist compares life to a tale that is told; Boswell reverses the simile. He also records in his diary that he wishes to make *The Hypochondriack* into "a couple of proper volumes," that is, give it the republished afterlife enjoyed by the *Spectator.*[48] Katherine Ellison has argued that Boswell revises his diaries "to convince himself that there is an afterlife"; one might add that he wrote them in the first place and published them in the *Account, Journal of a Tour,* and *Life* for the same reason.[49]

Boswell had noted Blair's lectionary text, on life as "a tale that is told," in his journal because he summarized the sermon for the dying Lord Kames, on whom he called following the service. As is typical of his interviews with the famous and/or dying, the visit is recorded in Boswell's diary at some length. At first Kames speaks like his usual earthy self: "Oh, dinna' ask foolish questions." But when Boswell returns later on in the evening, Kames is silent: "I regretted that he did not say one word as a dying man. Nothing edifying, nothing pious. His lady told me he had not said a word to her of what he thought of himself at present" (*Applause of the Jury* 45). Boswell wishes to stage a deathbed scene, a reprise of the end of *Conjectures on Original Composition,* with Kames as a Scottish Addison. Richard B. Sher has argued that Boswell saw Kames as a second surrogate father figure, offering validation and support in professional Edinburgh just as Johnson did in literary London.[50] Thus the role of Addison's stepson Lord Warwick (whom Addison instructs in Young's account to "see in what peace a Christian can die") would be all the more natural for Boswell. But the emaciated Kames, who died five days later, does not cooperate. Having just been reminded of the idea that man's life is a tale that is told, Boswell is offended by the jurist's all too human silence.[51]

Boswell felt a tension between his lifelong fascination with death scenes (both the Youngian tableaux of such dying philosophers as Kames, Hume, and Johnson and the frisson of a Newgate hanging) and his equally enduring interest in self-formation over and through time. Put another way, he was torn between Young's Addison and Addison's Addison. A conversation with Johnson during Boswell's last visit to London before Johnson's death makes the issue clear:

> I stated to him an anxious thought. . . . Suppose a man who has led a good life for seven years, commits an act of wickedness, and instantly dies; will his former good life have any effect in his favor? JOHNSON. "Sir, if a man has led a good life for seven years, and then is hurried by passion to do what is wrong, depend upon it he will have the reward of his seven years' good life; God will not take a catch of him." . . . BOSWELL. "But does not the text say, 'As the tree falls, so it must lie'?" JOHNSON. "Yes, Sir; as the tree falls: but,—(after a little pause)—that is meant as to the general state of the tree, not what is the effect of a sudden blast." (*Life* 4:225)

The argument of Young's *Conjectures* is that the truly immortal work is the poet's pious death. The *Life of Johnson* takes the same logic and moral seriousness and applies to it Johnson's reasoning here about "the general state of the tree." Thus it narrates not just Johnson's death but the entire life, anecdote by anecdote, that preceded it. The *Conjectures* show in what peace a Christian can die, and the *Life* immortalizes Johnson by showing the mingled fortunes in which a heroic man of letters can live.

Conclusion: "My Dear and Honored Contemporary"

Boswell's project in the *Life of Johnson* is thus to preserve and memorialize his mentor in daily time and through documentary anecdote. Reader response to the *Life of Johnson* over the last two centuries has been articulated, to a striking degree, in terms of Boswell's ability to bring Johnson to life, to create a conversationalist whom readers feel as uniquely vivid.[52] I close with two nineteenth-century readers who respond to Boswell's biography in this way. The first is a well-known landmark in Boswell reception: Thomas

Babington Macaulay, writing in 1831, marveled that "Johnson grown old, Johnson in the fullness of his fame and in the enjoyment of a competent fortune, is better known to us than any other man in history," and proved it by reconstructing him, body and soul, in a list of twenty-five metonyms, from "his coat" and "his wig" through "his midnight disputations" and "his gruntings" to "his queer inmates, old Mr. Levett and blind Mrs. Williams, the cat Hodge and the negro Frank." (The passage is cited in full in my introduction.)[53] This Rabelaisian/Joycean list adds up to a Johnson whose immortality Macaulay explicitly distinguishes from that provided by his works: "What a singular destiny has been that of this remarkable man! . . . That kind of fame which is commonly the most transient is, in his case, the most durable. The reputation of those writings, which he probably expected to be immortal, is every day fading; while those peculiarities of manner and that careless table-talk the memory of which, he probably thought, would die with him, are likely to be remembered as long as the English language is spoken in any quarter of the globe."[54]

Macaulay mischaracterizes Johnson, who was in fact noncommittal about the long-term prospects of his own writings, though he did see endurance over time as the true test of literary merit. Given that Macaulay is arguing that nobody reads Johnson any more, we should hardly be surprised. But although he is harshly negative about Boswell as a human being, Macaulay has Boswell's artistic priorities, whose practice as both diarist and author lay in arresting the "transient" and seeking to transform it into the "durable," dead to rights.

For my second example, the nineteenth-century belletrist and physician Oliver Wendell Holmes, the chronological structure of the *Life* was integral to its animating power. Born in 1809, exactly a century after Johnson, Holmes began in his youth to read the *Life* every year, encountering Johnson as a companion through life with each reading. Holmes writes in 1884:

> I have just lost my dear and honored contemporary of the last century. A hundred years ago this day, December 13, 1784, died the admirable and ever to be remembered Dr. Samuel Johnson. The year 1709 was made illustrious in English biography by his birth. My own humble advent to the world of protoplasm was in the year 1809 of the present century. Thus there was established a close bond of relationship between the great English scholar and writer and myself. Year by year, and almost month by month, my life has kept pace in this century with

his life in the last century. I had only to open my Boswell at any time, and I knew just what Johnson at my age, twenty or fifty or seventy, was thinking and doing, what were his feelings about life; what changes the years had wrought in his body, his mind, his feelings, his companionships, his reputation. I feel lonely now that my great companion and friend of so many years has left me. I felt more intimately acquainted with him than I do with many of my living friends.[55]

Precisely because Boswell so scrupulously documents Johnson's progress through secular time from 1709–1784, Johnson comes alive as a "companion and friend" in the nineteenth century. (Indeed, the radical meaning of "secular" as pertaining to a *saeculum,* or century, is relevant here, since Holmes's kinship for Johnson is partially rooted in the coincidence of their birthdates.) Holmes imputes to Boswell's Johnson the same immortality that the club of Oxford students of *Spectator* 553 offered Mr. Spectator by reading his daily essays aloud in their weekly meetings. Johnson is, in Holmes's brilliantly paradoxical phrase, his "contemporary of the last century"—both a figure of the past preserved in historical particularity and a current presence. Boswell could have asked for no more.

Epilogue

Keats Imagines the Life of Shakespeare

The *Spectator* postulated a horizontal afterlife in which the daily moral formation of earthly existence would continue in a posthumous "beyond" under the superintendence of a Supreme Being. Addison's reconceptualization of the afterlife prospered in the eighteenth century: Butler's *Analogy* uses it to connect the consequences of moral choice on earth to presumed analogues after death, and it is the basis of the political theology of the Scottish deist William Dudgeon, who imagined that "the other world will be a society" because "we are creatures plainly designed for improvements in knowledge and goodness, and . . . these can only be brought about by culture, teaching, and discipline, to which converse and intercourse with others is absolutely necessary."[1] Progressive immortality finds a rather more illustrious descendant in Kant's *Critique of Practical Reason,* which postulates the afterlife as a regulative idea precisely because the human lifetime is too short for the rational being to achieve complete holiness.[2] Addison's idea, transformed yet recognizable, has yet another afterlife in the letters of John Keats, in which morality recedes as the goal of personal formation. What is at stake in Keats's insistence on human immortality and the continuity between this world and the next is individuation. Life is not the state in which we form ourselves into good moral agents; it is the state in which we form ourselves into ourselves:

> The common cognomen of this world among the misguided and su-
> perstitious is "a vale of tears" from which we are to be redeemed by a
> certain arbitrary interposition of God and taken to Heaven—What a

little circumscribed straightened notion! Call the world if you Please "The vale of Soul-making" Then you will find out the use of the world (I am speaking now in the highest terms for human nature admitting it to be immortal which I will here take for granted for the purpose of showing a thought which has struck me concerning it) I say "*Soul making*" Soul as distinguished from an Intelligence—There may be intelligences or sparks of the divinity in millions—but they are not Souls till they acquire identities, till each one is personally itself. Intelligences are atoms of perception—they know and they see and they are pure, in short they are God—how then are Souls to be made? How then are these sparks which are God to have identity given them—so as ever to possess a bliss peculiar to each ones individual existence? How, but by the medium of a world like this? This point I sincerely wish to consider because I think it a grander system of salvation than the chrystain [*stet*] religion—or rather it is a system of Spirit-creation . . . As various as the Lives of Men are—so various become their souls, and thus does God make individual beings, Souls, Identical Souls of the sparks of his own essence.[3]

Young's *Conjectures Concerning Original Composition* had argued that Addison's greatest work was his life itself, but it did so ultimately on moral grounds: Addison was able to show the Earl of Warwick "in what peace a Christian can die." Similarly, Clarissa's minutely anecdotal life is both particularly her own and an exemplar of the good Christian death. Earlier in the letter cited above, Keats offers an analogous assertion of the primacy of life over writing, but discarding Young and Richardson's moralizing framework: "Shakespeare led a life of Allegory; his works are the comments on it" (2:67).

In Keats's vale of soul-making, what counts in human experience is what he calls "circumstances":

I began by seeing how man was formed by circumstances—and what are circumstances?—but touchstones of his heart—? and what are touchstones?—but proovings of his heart?—and what are proovings of his heart but fortifiers or alterers of his nature? and what is his altered nature but his soul?—and what was his soul before it came into the world and had These provings and alterations and perfectionings?—An intelligence—without Identity—and how is this Identity to be made?

Through the medium of the Heart? And how is the heart to become this Medium but in a world of Circumstances? (2:103–4)

Appropriately, both this Socratic monologue and the rest of Keats's discussion of the vale of soul-making occur in a lengthy, diaristic letter that Keats composed to send to his brother and sister-in-law in America over the course of the spring of 1819. Keats's interweaving of gossip and circumstantial reportage with "Poetry and Theology" (ibid.) is fitting because the "world of circumstances" that he evokes is the world of anecdote and quotidian narrative. When written down, the world of circumstances becomes prose immortality.

A passage earlier from the same letter to George and Georgiana Keats exemplifies this point, as Keats's train of thought leads him from a Boswellian portrait of himself in the act of writing to an act of imaginative speculation about Shakespeare:

The candles are burnt down and I am using the wax taper—which has a long snuff on it—the fire is at its last click—I am sitting with my back to it with one foot rather askew upon the rug and the other with the heel a little elevated from the carpet—I am writing this on the Maid's tragedy which I have read since tea with Great pleasure—Besides this volume of Beaumont & Fletcher—there are on the table two volumes of chaucer and a new work of Tom Moores call'd "Tom Cribb's memorial to Congress"—nothing in it—These are trifles—but I require nothing so much of you as that you will give me a like description of yourselves, however it may be when you are writing to me—Could I see the same thing done of any great Man long since dead it would be a great delight: as to know in what position Shakespeare sat when he began "To be or not to be"—such things become interesting from distance of time or place. (2:73)

At first Keats imagines minutely detailed narration as a way of collapsing the intolerable distance between himself and his beloved brother and sister-in-law. But then his train of thought turns to the possibility that it may produce closeness in time as well as space. Keats fancies that his autobiographical "trifles" function like a spell, giving him the clairvoyance to scry George and Georgiana in "sweet sleep" and the power to transmit his presence to them: "I whisper good night in your ears and you will dream of me" (2:73–74). Unstated but logically implied is a parallel power to susurr in the ears, and enter the dreams, of posterity. What Shakespeare for his part has failed to leave behind, a diary of his writing life in its physical particularity, Keats has committed to paper. Just as familial love connects Keats to his Georgian siblings, author love transmits him to us.

Though Keats says that he would delight in a biographical tableau of "any great Man long since dead," his choice of Shakespeare as an example is highly significant. Like Laetitia Pilkington, Keats has inscribed Shakespeare's language within the book and volume of his brain, to the point that his appropriation of phrases and even individual words goes beyond allusion to what can only be called deep influence. And both Pilkington and Keats are part of the century-long process, beginning with Nicholas Rowe's edition of 1709, by which Shakespeare became, in our modern sense, Shakespeare. The sesquicentennial Shakespeare Jubilee organized by David Garrick at Stratford in 1769, where Garrick recited an ode addressing the playwright as "the god of our idolatry," is a convenient synecdoche of this deification, but it is also visible in the century's distinguished series of Shakespeare editors (Rowe, Pope, Theobald, Warburton, Johnson, Steevens, Malone), Shakespeare's prestige on the eighteenth-century stage, and the development of a generalized sense in print culture that Shakespeare was both an English national hero and an unequaled universal genius.[4]

When the critics, editors, poets, actors, and readers of the eighteenth century invented Shakespeare as a god, they felt the need to invent him as a man too. Shakespeare's sonnets are confident to the point of stridency in claiming immortality for themselves and their beloved addressee, but they are unequivocally grounded in the lyric immortality paradigm, preserving the affect of love but no concrete or verifiable biographical details. For eighteenth-century bardolators, this kind of posthumous survival was inadequate. John Britton, the antiquarian who contributed a brief life of Shakespeare to the seven-volume 1814 edition of the plays that Keats owned, complains that "the same destitution of authentic incidents marks every stage of his life."[5] Just as Shakespeare's notoriously muddled and discrepant quartos and folios have endowed an industry of textual scholarship that begins with Rowe and continues to this day, the paucity of biographical information about him created in eighteenth-century admirers and creates in us a feeling of absence which no number of biographies can fill. In each case the reason is the same: neither Shakespeare nor his contemporaries could anticipate needs—for the authoritative texts of plays, for the curriculum vitae and authenticated table talk of a playwright—that they themselves did not feel. While a skeleton of legal and economic records and a smattering of secondhand references come down to us from Shakespeare's lifetime and the pre-Restoration period when his contemporaries were still living, they are dwarfed by the speculation, embroidery, and outright fabrication that accreted thereafter.

Edmond Malone, the great Shakespeare editor who debunked a series of wish-fulfilling forgeries—letters between Shakespeare and the Earl of Southampton, a contemporary portrait, even a lost play—concocted by William Henry Ireland in the 1790s, prefaces his own unfinished biography of his subject with a lament for what we cannot know about Shakespeare:

> Of all the accounts of literary men which have been given to the world, the history of the life of Shakespeare would be the most curious and instructive, if we were acquainted with the minute circumstances of his fortunes, the course and extent of his studies, and the means and gradations whereby he acquired that consummate knowledge of mankind, which, for two centuries, has rendered him the delight and boast of his countrymen: but many of the materials for such a biographical detail being now unattainable, we must content ourselves with such particulars as accident has preserved, or the most sedulous industry has been able to collect.

Malone goes on to lament that none of Shakespeare's contemporaries took pains to document his life, and that even Nicholas Rowe's 1709 biography is painfully inadequate:

> That almost a century should have elapsed, from the time of [Shakespeare's] death, without a single attempt having been made to discover any circumstance which could throw a light on the history of his private life, that, when the attempt was made, it should have been so imperfectly executed . . . and that for a period of eighty years, during which the "god of our idolatry" ranked as high among us as any poet ever did in any country, all the editors of his works, and each successive English biographer, should have been contented with Mr. Rowe's meagre and imperfect narrative; are circumstances which cannot be contemplated without astonishment.[6]

This astonishment becomes all the more understandable when we recall that James Boswell did much of his work on the *Life of Johnson* under Malone's roof and with his active assistance.[7] It was Malone's editorial competence, moral support, and steadying day-to-day presence that gave Boswell the will to complete the work under the cloud of alcoholism, self-doubt, depressive paralysis, and professional failure that clouded his final decade. Having corrected the manuscript of the *Life* as it flowed from Boswell's pen, Malone knew better than anyone what a literary biography could be; when he weighed the surviving records of Shakespeare in the balance and found them wanting, it must have been in part because he put Boswell's two folio volumes into the other side of the scales. Precisely because it is so great, Shakespeare's surviving corpus is inadequate; Malone, as Keats was to do after him, longs for a Shakespeare who lives on after death in the paradigm of prose immortality.

NOTES

Introduction

1. *Luctus Britannici*, 11.

2. My phrasing echoes William Cowper's "The Cast-away," discussed below, pp. 12–13.

3. Brack and Kelley, *Early Biographies of Samuel Johnson*.

4. Quoted in Phillipson, *Adam Smith*, 274.

5. Bishop, *Poetical Works*, 276–77. Other examples include "Dr. Johnson's Ghost" by Elizabeth Moody (in *Poetic Trifles*, 59–62) and Peter Pindar [John Walcot], *Bozzy and Piozzi*.

6. Johnson, *Dictionary of the English Language* (1755), s.v. "superfetation." All subsequent citations of Johnson's dictionary definitions refer to this edition unless otherwise noted.

7. There is something uncanny in this vision of endless biographical rebirths—Johnson as undead, rather than Johnson enjoying his afterlife. The biographers themselves, as I will demonstrate in detail in my discussion of Boswell below, were more sanguine. Bishop's suspicions have a modern successor in the work of Aaron Kunin ("Shakespeare's Preservation Fantasy"), who argues that Shakespeare's pro-creation sonnets postulate an apocalyptic future, in which everything *but* the beautiful youth has been destroyed.

8. Arnold, *Essays in Criticism*, 23.

9. Boswell, *Boswell: The Ominous Years*, 265.

10. Sherman, *Telling Time*, 25.

11. Pocock, *Barbarism and Religion*, 51.

12. Important recent studies include, in addition to the just-cited first volume of Pocock's *Barbarism and Religion* series, the following: Charles Taylor, *A Secular Age*; Isabel Rivers, *Reason, Grace, and Sentiment*; B. W. Young, *Religion and Enlightenment in Eighteenth-Century England*; and David Sorkin, *The Religious Enlightenment*. In the sphere of literary scholarship, this study aligns itself with the goals, if not always the conclusions, of the essay collection *Theology in the Age of Johnson: Resisting Secularism*, edited by Melvyn New and Gerard Reedy, whose introduction argues that "the eighteenth century cannot be understood without a reeducation in the theology that was indeed the dominant and pervasive atmosphere in which the age lived" (xviii). Despite its title, the argument of Carol Stewart's *Eighteenth-*

Century Novel and the Secularization of Ethics has affinities with my own; where Stewart describes the process of novels taking on the role of sermons and calls it secularization, I describe the process of novels borrowing ideas from sermons and call it the enduring influence of religious discourse.

13. Arendt, *Human Condition,* 19.

14. Thus Pindar offers his services to Hieron, the tyrant of Syracuse: "My friend, do not be taken in by unworthy use of wealth, for the award of posthumous fame is the only testimony that storytellers and poets can give to the lives of the dead" (*Pythian* 1.93–95, in Pindar, *Complete Odes,* 45).

15. Sidney, *Miscellaneous Prose,* 121.

16. Here and below I cite from Horace, *Odes and Epodes,* 3.30.1–7. Compare a similar gambit in Ovid, who spends fifteen books of his *Metamorphoses* proclaiming that *cuncta fluunt* [all things are in a state of flux], then closes by setting up the poem as an exception to its own rule:

> *Iamque opus exegi, quod nec Iovis ira nec ignis*
> *nec poterit ferrum nec edax abolere vetustas. . . .*
> *nomenque erit indelibile nostrum.*
> [And now my work is done, which neither the wrath of Jove, nor fire, nor sword, nor the gnawing tooth of time shall ever be able to undo. . . . I shall have an undying name.] (15.178, 871–72, 876)

17. "On Shakespeare," lines 7–8. Here and throughout I cite from Milton, *Complete Poetry.*

18. Sonnet 18.13–14. Here and throughout I quote from the *Norton Shakespeare.* For the tradition of conferring immortality through poetry prior to Shakespeare, see Leishman, *Themes and Variations in Shakespeare's Sonnets.*

19. The phrase "erotic affect" belongs to Ramie Targoff, who used it in the question and answer period of a talk to the Harvard English Department's Renaissance Colloquium in February 2012.

20. In the seventh prolusion delivered while Milton was a student at Cambridge. Milton, *Complete Prose Works,* 1:302.

21. Thus in Horace's *Ode* 4.8, mythological heroes such as Aeacus (the grandfather of Achilles) enjoy a pleasurable afterlife in Elysium because of their own deeds *and* the celebration of poets:

> *ereptum Stygiis fluctibus Aeacum*
> *virtus et favor et lingua potentium*
> *vatum divitibus consecrat insulis.*
> [His own valour, combined with the favor and the eloquence of mighty bards, has snatched Aeacus from the Stygian waves, giving him a hallowed place in the Isles of the Blest.] (4.8.25–27)

In the twentieth chapter of Revelation, meanwhile, men receive judgment based on two sets of books, the Book of Life (mentioned throughout the Old and New Testaments) in which God has written a list of the names of his chosen, but also a more circumstantial library of books that records each person's deeds: "And I saw the dead, small and great, stand before God; and the books were opened: and another book was opened, which is the book of life: and the dead were judged out of those things which were written in the books, according to their works" (Revelation 20:12; here and throughout I cite from the King James Version).

22. Thomas, *Ends of Life*, 240–41.

23. Braudy, *Frenzy of Renown*, 28.

24. Braudy recognizes this, saying of the eighteenth century that "hope of heaven, hope of immediate fame, and hope of fame in posterity were becoming difficult to distinguish" (*Frenzy of Renown*, 379).

25. As Hunter and Wootton put it in their introduction to *Atheism from the Reformation to the Enlightenment*, "The period c. 1680–1715 was a pivotal one in the emergence of atheism. . . . The growth of explicit formulations of irreligion was a by-product of major shifts in the European sensibility of the time" (4). Wootton goes on to explain that Locke's *Essay Concerning Human Understanding*, while not itself explicitly unorthodox, is an important cause of this development (49).

26. See Martin and Barresi, *Naturalization of the Soul*. For an excellent study of the literary-historical importance of Locke's innovative theory of self and consciousness that addresses a different set of texts and issues than my own, see Fox, *Locke and the Scriblerians*. For further aspects of Locke's role as a perceived threat to Anglican doctrine, see B. W. Young, *Religion and Enlightenment*, 25–27, 91.

27. This is the thesis of Robert E. Sullivan's *John Toland and the Deist Controversy*. Sullivan's more extreme statements about Latitudinarianism—that it was so undogmatic and moralistic as to be more deist than Christian—has been challenged by Roger L. Emerson in "Latitudinarianism and the English Deists." See also Rivers, *Reason, Grace, and Sentiment*, 1:25–88. In *Literature, Religion, and the Evolution of Culture*, 105–233, Howard Weinbrot develops an allied argument, that the eighteenth-century English church moved in significant ways toward inclusiveness, persuasion, and acceptance of dissident traditions. J. C. D. Clark, as part of a larger argument for eighteenth-century England as an Anglican confessional state, points out that the complacency of the established church was an expression of strength, not weakness (*English Society, 1688–1832*, 139).

28. Early-eighteenth-century Anglicans were willing to tolerate a wide range of speculative theological convictions among their clergy and parishioners, but immortality was a nonnegotiable shibboleth. As Sullivan puts it, "Without exception churchmen persisted in seeing belief in a future state of rewards and punishments as a necessary principle. . . . Their attachment to belief in personal immortality served to limit their dogmatic suppleness" (*John Toland and the Deist Controversy*, 257).

29. James, *Varieties of Religious Experience*, 109–38.

30. Taylor, *Secular Age*, 3, 303–4.

31. In its analysis of Boswell and Johnson in particular, this argument has points of contact with Fredric V. Bogel's *Literature and Insubstantiality in Later Eighteenth-Century England*. Bogel argues that the literature of the period both enacts and confronts a sense of ontological emptiness, "the world's inadequacy to the demands of

mind and heart," a "thinning of reality's texture" due in part to "secularization and faltering belief" (17, 53). To meet "the challenge posed by insubstantiality to the solidity of perceived experience [and] to a traditional system of values and a traditional rhetoric of valuing . . . it is necessary to fashion a rhetoric capable of delivering a new, at least a newly valued, image of reality: a rhetoric of substantiality. In the Age of Sensibility the principal goal of that rhetoric is a reclamation of common experience" (47). I part ways from Bogel not only in arguing for a century-long tradition that spans his Augustan Age/Age of Sensibility divide, but more importantly in emphasizing the importance of afterlife and survival as a warrant of "substantiality" in the period.

32. Sitter, *Literary Loneliness*, 11.

33. For Addison's influence on Hume, see Phillipson, *David Hume*, 15–31.

34. Sher, *Church and University in the Scottish Enlightenment*.

35. This point is made forcefully by Adam Potkay in *The Passion for Happiness*.

36. Peter Gay makes this point well: "To remote observers, the distance between radical Protestants and deists might seem negligible, but to contemporaries it was decisive. It made all the difference if one accepted revelation, no matter how attenuated, or the Christian God, no matter how remote, or rejected both revelation and the Christian God altogether" (*Deism: An Anthology*, 11–12).

37. Indeed it is an irony of the British Enlightenment that Hume and Gibbon were *Kulturpessimisten* who thought that religious superstition and bigotry were in no danger of disappearing; their view of human progress shared much with that of Samuel Johnson.

38. Thomson, *Winter*.

39. Boswell, *Life of Johnson* (1964), 5:308. All subsequent citations of the *Life* or *Journal of a Tour to the Hebrides* are to this edition unless otherwise noted.

40. Macaulay, *Critical and Historical Essays*, 92.

41. Cowper, "The Cast-away," in *Eighteenth-Century Poetry*, 512–13.

42. See King, *William Cowper*, 89.

43. As Fairer and Gerrard point out in their headnote to the poem in *Eighteenth-Century Poetry*, Cowper read the story in *A Voyage Round the World . . . by George Anson* (London, 1748), 79–80. The biographical data that the poem imagines being conveyed to Anson are, however, absent from his text. In fact, Anson supplies less information than the poem: the "cask, the coop, the floated cord" of line 27 are Cowper's addition. Cowper, writing at the end of the century, asserts more anecdotal specificity for prose than his mid-eighteenth-century source in fact contains.

44. Brown, *Preromanticism*, 2.

45. For the Scottish clerical campaign against Hume in the 1750s, see Mossner, *Life of David Hume*, 336–55. For Boswell's anecdote, see *Life of Johnson*, 1:471.

46. Boswell, *Journal of a Tour*, 5:19.

47. Thorne, *Dialectic of Counter-Enlightenment*, 280.

48. Boswell, *London Journal*, 190–94.

49. For the argument from desire, see Robert G. Walker, *Eighteenth-Century Arguments for Immortality*.

1. The Afterlife and the *Spectator*

1. For Bickerstaff's origins, success ("a prodigy of English letters"), and development as a character, see Bond, "Isaac Bickerstaff, Esq.," 103–24, 110.

2. In *Predictions for the Year 1708, The Accomplishment of the First of Mr. Bickerstaff's Predictions, etc.,* and *A Vindication of Isaac Bickerstaff Esq.* (Swift, *Bickerstaff Papers,* 139–64).

3. Bond, ed., *Tatler,* 1:23. Further citations are to this edition and noted parenthetically in the text by volume and page number. For Swift's use of Bickerstaff, see Lowe, "Why Swift Killed Partridge." Learned readers could have recognized Steele's criterion for being alive in the *Tatler* ("Living are only those that are some Way or other laudably employed in the Improvement of their own Minds, or for the Advantage of others" [2:95]) as a paraphrase from Sallust: *is demum mihi vivere atque frui anima videtur, qui aliquo negotio intentus praeclari facinoris aut artis bonae famam quaerit (Sallust,* 2).

4. For studies that offer both good overviews and valuable interventions in the Addison-as-critic and *Spectator*-in-the-public-sphere conversations respectively, see Syba, "After Design," and Pollock, "Neutering Addison and Steele."

5. Mackie, *Market à la Mode,* 28. Habermas argues that Addison "worked toward . . . the emancipation of civic morality from moral theology" *(Structural Transformation of the Public Sphere,* 43), while Black, "Social and Literary Form in the *Spectator,*" attributes to the *Spectator* "a distinct sphere of social relations that are not defined by the duty of religion or the obligation of politics but by an ethos formed in the new public sphere" (37).

6. For early-eighteenth-century didactic literature, see Hunter, *Before Novels,* 225–302. Gregg, in "'A Truly Christian Hero',", prints a summary of the scholarly literature on early-eighteenth-century moral reform movements (25, n. 2).

7. Benjamin, *Illuminations,* 261.

8. Sherman, *Telling Time,* 34–35. Sherman refers to Anderson, *Imagined Communities.*

9. Taylor, *Secular Age,* 58–59.

10. See Sutherland, *Restoration Newspaper and Its Development,* 1–43, especially 31–32. The *Spectator,* like the *Daily Courant,* was not published on Sundays.

11. Sherman, *Telling Time,* 109–59.

12. See n. 20 below for a sampling of references to the afterlife in the *Spectator.*

13. My account is synthesized from the following sources: McDannell and Lang, *Heaven: A History*; Le Goff, *Birth of Purgatory*; Almond, *Heaven and Hell in Enlightenment England*; D. P. Walker, *Decline of Hell*; Fenn, *Persistence of Purgatory*; Ariès, *Hour of Our Death.*

14. Camden, *Remains Concerning Britain,* 350.

15. McDannell and Lang, *Heaven,* 177–81.

16. Bunyan, *Grace Abounding and Pilgrim's Progress.* See Lang, "Meeting in Heaven." According to McDannell and Lang, even the theocentric Luther encouraged his children to think about heaven in human terms, telling his son Hans that

children in heaven "sing, jump, and are merry. They also have nice ponies." (*Heaven*, 153).

17. *Spectator* 90, discussed below, features a "Platonick" hell, derived from the *Phaedo* rather than Christian orthodoxy, in which sensual habits formed in life torment men's spirits after death—a negative version of the *Spectator*'s usual call to cultivate virtuous habits over time (Bond, ed., *Spectator*, 1:380–84). *Spectator* 447, also discussed below, concludes with the same idea (Bond, ed., *Spectator*, 4:73). Subsequent citations of the *Spectator* will be to this edition; in order to examine the advertisements and other paratextual features of the *Spectator*'s original 1711–12, I have also consulted the original folio half-sheets, a complete set of which (assembled by Edmond Malone, the great Shakespearean scholar) resides in the Houghton Library of Harvard University. For the first edition printed in volumes (7 vols., 8vo, 1711–13), I have used the British Library's copy as reproduced in Eighteenth-Century Collections Online. In placing less emphasis on hell, the *Spectator* is part of a larger theological movement of its time, chronicled in D. P. Walker, *Decline of Hell*. Significantly, the religious thinkers whom Walker examines (including Origen and his seventeenth-century defenders, as well as the Cambridge Platonists, various continental Socinians and Arians, Locke and Shaftesbury, and a range of English millenarian sects) frequently connect disbelief in eternal hell torments with dynamic and progressive conceptions of the afterlife. See Walker 12–13, 68–69, 240.

18. Bunyan, *Grace Abounding and Pilgrim's Progress*, 267, 271.

19. See also Robert G. Walker, *Eighteenth-Century Arguments for Immortality*, 20–34.

20. Versions of the idea (not always systematically articulated, of course) are expressed in *Spectators* 90, 93, and 111, discussed above, as well as 143 (in its character Uranius), 159, 166, 210, 213, 215, 219, 225, 237, 257, 349, 368, 381, 441, 447, 453, 465, 471, 524, 531, and 537. These papers are overwhelmingly by Addison. Not surprisingly in a text as extensive and heterogeneous as the *Spectator*, there are also a smaller number of appeals to immortality that remain firmly rooted in the older paradigm of heaven and hell as two fixed states that follow divine judgment—see, for instance, 26, 483, and 513.

21. Scott, *Christian Life*, [xi–xii]. "On the contrary," Scott continues, "in the course of a sinful Life we by a necessary Efficiency gradually sink ourselves into the State of the Damned."

22. Sherlock, *Practical Discourse Concerning Death*, 247.

23. Tillotson, *Works*, 96.

24. Dixon, "Publishing of Tillotson's Collected Works," 155.

25. Steele, *Christian Hero*, 68.

26. Sherman, *Telling Time*, 109.

27. Steele registers the hurry of writing on deadline in a letter to his wife that Rae Blanchard tentatively dates to January 1712, when the *Spectator* was in full career: "Dear Prue . . . I am come hither and not one word ready for to-morrow. In haste, yrs Richard Steele." In a letter written two months earlier, Addison declines an invitation to the country from Edward Wortley, saying, "You know I have put my hand to

the plow, and have already bin absent from my work one Entire month at the Bath" (Steele, *Correspondence,* 275–76; Addison, *Letters,* 265.

28. The letter writer goes on to comment that "it is usual for those who receive Benefit by such famous Operators, to publish an Advertisement, that others may reap the same Advantage"; such testimonials were frequently advertised in the *Spectator.*

29. For an account of the *Spectator's* cumulative, accretive rhetoric that anticipates my own, see McCrea, *Addison and Steele Are Dead,* 56–60.

30. Quoted from *Spectator* 369, Addison's final paper on Milton (3:391).

31. For the paper's contemporary readership, which included the queen, see *Spectator* 1:lxxxiii–xcvi, 3:442 n. 2.

32. Steele reused material from his own letters to his wife, *The Christian Hero,* and the sermons of Tillotson in his papers (see nos. 142, 2:60–64; 356, 3:326–29; and 103, 1:429–32, respectively). For Addison's use of his own unpublished writings, see *Spectator* 1:xxix. There was a tradition current in the 1760s that Addison wrote some of his homiletic Saturday papers during his residence at Magdalen College, Oxford, over a decade before the *Spectator* began. See James Boswell's letter to John Johnston, written from Oxford in 1763, printed in *Correspondence of James Boswell and John Johnston,* Ralph S. Walker 71–72. Walker cites confirmatory evidence that Addison used his own unpublished writings as sources for the *Spectator*—see Crum, "Manuscript of Essays by Addison."

33. This is particularly true for papers attuned to the Christian sacred calendar, such as *Spectator* 26, a meditation on the tombs of Westminster Abbey published on Good Friday 1711.

34. In *Spectator* 124, Addison suggests that readers assembled sets by theme as well as by date: "I shall continue my *rural Speculations* to the End of this Month; several having made up separate Sets of them, as they have done before of those relating to Wit, to Operas, to Points of Morality, or Subjects of Humor" (1:507–8). Note how Addison's readers connect the papers by theme, while he organizes them with respect to time, undertaking to continue the Roger de Coverley papers "to the End of this Month."

35. "To Print Myself Out" is the title of Stuart Sherman's chapter on the *Spectator;* the quotation is taken from *Spectator,* 1:5 (*Telling Time,* 109–58). In his careful attention to the paper's form and reception as a periodical during its original 1711–12 run, Sherman emphasizes Mr. Spectator's evanescence: "Mr. Spectator can exist for only as many days as he writes" (137). But this analysis does not take into account the intertwined emphases on republication and immortality that characterize the paper throughout.

36. Steele, *Conscious Lovers,* 445.

37. Boswell, *London Journal;* Boswell, *Boswell in Holland.* See also Newman, "James Boswell, Joseph Addison, and the Spectator."

38. Franklin, *Writings,* 1305–470, 1319–21.

39. Ibid., 91.

40. Pycroft, *Oxford Memories,* 1:104.

2. *Night Thoughts* on Time, Fame, and Immortality

1. Addison, *Cato*; Young, *Conjectures.*

2. Young, *Night Thoughts,* ed. Cornford (1989), 1.193–94. Subsequent parenthetical citations are to this edition.

3. For Swindon and Whiston, see Walker, *Decline of Hell,* 39, 100. In *Night the Ninth,* Young attacks those who are "more Curious, than Devout; / More fond to fix the *Place* of Heaven or Hell, / Than studious *this* to shun, or *that* secure" (9.1852–54).

4. Although I believe that he understates Young's emphasis on eternity, John Sitter is not far from my own view when he argues that the "the significant shift" between Pope's *Essay on Man* and *Night Thoughts* "is from spatial to temporal theodicy, from proportion to process" (*Literary Loneliness,* 158).

5. See Havens, *Influence of Milton,* 149–60, who argues that Young was a terrible blank-verse poet but would have been a worse one without Milton.

6. Kind, *Edward Young in Germany,* 109.

7. Montgomery, *Lectures on General Literature, Poetry &c.,* 154.

8. Petit, "English Rejection of Young's *Night Thoughts.*"

9. Wanko, "Making of a Minor Poet"; Irlam, *Elations,* 173.

10. *Spectator* 101, 1:423–24; Fielding, *Tom Jones,* book 18, chapter 1 (2:914).

11. Forster, *Edward Young,* 163; Sterne, *Tristram Shandy,* 1:12. Pilkington also enters Mead's unusual sexual proclivities into the documentary record (*Memoirs of Laetitia Pilkington,* 1:204).

12. Parker, *Triumph of Augustan Poetics,* 227.

13. For Forster's assessment, see his *Edward Young,* 398–99.

14. Forster, *Edward Young,* 194. Forster adds a turn of the screw by remarking that "the young man apparently failed to take the usual notice of the dedication and the poet was obliged to send him a reminder in the form of a private set of complimentary verses."

15. Thus pregnancy, for instance, is a symbol of deluded procrastination in 1.378–81, as those who "spin out eternal schemes" as though they "the Fatal Sisters cou'd out-spin . . . big with life's Futurities, expire," while at the beginning of *Night the Second* it reappears as a symbol of piety for those "big / With holy Hope of nobler Time to come" (2.52–53). Similarly, in 1.213–19 the moon represents the transience and mutability of human fortune, as contrasted with "*Virtue's* sure, / Self-given, *solar,* ray of sound Delight," but in 3.20–21 becomes, in the form of "*Day's* soft-ey'd Sister," the muse who will liberate the poem from the sensual "*Phoebus* . . . Inebriate at fair Fortune's fountain-head."

16. Irlam, *Elations,* 210.

17. Though the physical constraints of papyrus were not the only determining factor, and there was variation in the length of papyrus books across eras and genres in the ancient world. See Van Sickle, "Book-Roll."

18. Such as Spenser's scheme of writing twelve books of the *Faerie Queene* in honor of "the twelve private moral virtues, as Aristotle hath devised" (715).

19. Pope, *Dunciad,* 411.

20. Thomson's progressive expansions of the poem mean that it presents daunting textual problems to the modern scholar. The standard edition is *The Seasons and The Castle of Indolence*, ed. James Sambrook.

21. Young quotes 2.683–94 in a letter to the Duchess of Portland of 3 May 1742 (*Correspondence*, 138); *Night the First* is first advertised in the *Daily Post* on 2 June (accessed via the Burney Collection of Newspapers).

22. As his verse satires from the 1720s show, Young shared his generation's extensive debt to Horatian models. Blanford Parker's claim that *Night Thoughts*, "true to Young's theory, owes little to the ancients—there may be twenty specific allusions to them in 10,000 lines" has already been refuted by D. W. Odell, but I cannot resist pointing out that one page after claiming Young does not draw on the ancients in *Night Thoughts*, Parker cites ten lines from *Night the Sixth* (680–89) that are a paraphrase of Horace, *Odes* 4.7.9–16 (Parker, *Triumph of Augustan Poetics*, 223–24; Odell, "Young's *Night Thoughts*."

23. Virtue's power to redeem time is a repeated theme in the poem; see 2.81, 84: "Virtue . . . greatens, fills, immortalizes All." Shaun Irlam points out, examining 3.370, that a line is the circumference of an infinitely large circle (*Elations*, 199).

24. For Young's imagination of the continuation of this process in heaven, see 6.462–76.

25. For a further instance of this trope, see the indignation expressed in Steele and Addison's *Guardian* at the publication of a translation of André François Deslandes's *Reflections on the Death of Freethinkers* (1713) (Stephens, *Guardian*, 122, 159).

26. Young, *Conjectures on Original Composition*, 29, 30, hereafter cited parenthetically by page number.

27. This is the *et in arcadia ego* tradition, of "a present happiness menaced by death," recovered by Erwin Panofsky, "*Et in Arcadia Ego*: Poussin and the Elegiac Tradition," in *Meaning in the Visual Arts*, 295–320 (quotation from 296).

28. Wallace Stevens, "Anecdote of the Jar," lines 3–4, in *Palm at the End of the Mind*. For two different scholarly accounts of the *Conjectures* that engage seriously with Addison's deathbed scene, though without considering the interplay of literary and personal immortality, see Odell, "Argument of Young's *Conjectures*," and Chibka, "Stranger within Young's *Conjectures*."

29. Samuel Richardson had six years previous placed a similar point in the mouth of Harriet Byron, who argues for the superiority of modern learning against the pedantic Mr. Walden of Oxford in the first volume of *Sir Charles Grandison*: "Is it not, indeed, strange, that none of the modern learned . . . notwithstanding a Revelation from Heaven . . . should have deserved a higher consideration in the comparison, than as *pygmies* to *giants*?" (1:54).

30. *Boswell in Holland*, 112; Boswell, *Applause of the Jury*, 209. Boswell dedicates several pages of *Hypochondriack* 22, on plagiarism, to documenting other poets' borrowings from Young; debtors include Goldsmith, and Gray, while Young himself borrows from Johnson and Shakespeare (*Hypochondriack*, 1:279–82).

31. Boswell, *Boswell for the Defence*, 33.

32. *Boswell for the Defense*, 32, 64; *Life of Johnson*, 5:269–71.

33. *Life of Johnson,* 4:120. The trees were limes (that is lindens), not real-life examples of the "mournful yews" evoked in the *Conjectures; see* Forster, *Edward Young,* 144, and William Chambers, *Week at Welwyn,* 20.

34. *Life of Johnson,* 4:121.

35. Ironically, filial piety was not always Frederick's forte, and Young, unlike Addison, actually refused to see his son on his deathbed. Young did offer a theatrically Addisonian "God bless him!" to the absent Frederick, duly transmitted to posterity by Young's curate, John Jones (Forster, *Edward Young,* 370).

36. Pope, "Epilogue to the Satires," 2.226, in *Imitations of Horace,* 325. Aaron Hill to Richardson: "For my part, I am *afraid* to be popular. I see so many who write to the living, and deserve not to live, that I content myself with a resurrection when dead" (Richardson, *Correspondence,* 1:3). Delaney asks Richardson, who has printed some treatises for him, to send them to the college libraries of the two universities, "where, if they are to die, they may be buried with many better works, and from whence (if they are found worthy to live) they may one day revive to more advantage" (ibid., 4:2).

37. Boswell, *Life of Johnson,* 5:269–70.

3. The Threat to the Soul

1. E. Derek Taylor, *Reason and Religion in "Clarissa,"* 1.

2. Richardson, *Clarissa,* 3rd ed. (1750), 4:350. Unless otherwise noted, subsequent citations are to this third edition, which represents, for better or for worse, Richardson's considered final view of his text. I have also consulted the first edition (1747–48) and Angus Ross's edition (1986), a modernized version based on the first edition.

3. For Lovelace's rare moments of religious seriousness, including the admission that he "never was such a fool as to disbelieve a Providence," see Taylor, *Reason and Religion in "Clarissa,"* 141–43.

4. In *The Principles of Morality,* by the Irish political pamphleteer George Ensor (Berman, "Deism, Immortality," 74). As Berman points out, even atheists like Shelley could deny God without denying immortality (77).

5. For this characterization of atheism in Elizabethan and Jacobean England, see Hunter, "Problem of 'Atheism' in Early Modern England," especially 141–43.

6. Berman, "Repressive Denials of Atheism."

7. Ibid., 218.

8. Richardson, *Correspondence,* ed. Barbauld, 2:5.

9. For Locke's chapter on identity, added in the 1694 edition of the *Essay,* see Locke, *Essay Concerning Human Understanding,* 328–48; see especially 335–44. For the context and importance of Locke's account, see Seigel, *Idea of the Self,* 87–110. Writing from a twentieth-century analytic paradigm that considers the immortal soul to be an incoherent and philosophically embarrassing notion, Antony Flew gives Locke credit for being the first philosopher to notice the problems with the

soul as a concept, though Flew does not think Locke offers much of an answer (Flew, "Locke and the Problem of Personal Identity").

10. For Bayle, see Wootton, "New Histories of Atheism," 26.

11. "Others, again, who . . . have been consider'd as mere Atheists, have yet been observ'd to practice the Rules of *Morality,* and act in many Cases with such good Meaning and Affection towards Mankind, as might seem to force an Acknowledgment of their being *virtuous.*" On the relationship between virtue and reward: "They have made *Virtue* so mercenary a thing, and have talk'd so much of its *Rewards,* that one can hardly tell what there is in it, after all, which can be worth rewarding." And against otherworldliness: "They err widely who propose to turn Men to the Thoughts of a *better* world, by making 'em think so ill of *this*" (Anthony Ashley Cooper, third Earl of Shaftesbury, *Characteristics,* 1:192, 1:55, 2:48).

12. For Collins, see Martin and Barresi, *Naturalization of the Soul,* 51–60. For the ongoing debate over Locke, see Sell, *Locke and the Eighteenth-Century Divines,* 239–67.

13. This anatomy supplies the title of Isabel Rivers's magisterial *Reason, Grace, and Sentiment,* to which I am indebted for the intellectual-historical account in this paragraph.

14. Warburton, *Divine Legation of Moses Demonstrated* (London, 1738–41), 1:36–41. All subsequent references are to this, the first edition.

15. This is the implicit but unmistakable argument of "Of a Particular Providence and Of a Future State," in Hume, *Enquiries,* 132–48.

16. My phrasing alludes to "High Windows," by Philip Larkin, which discusses, in the context of the liberalization of postwar English culture, precisely the possibility of a hedonic morality liberated from "God," "sweating in the dark / About hell and that," and "having to hide / What you think of the priest" (Larkin, *Collected Poems,* 165).

17. Hence the polemical force of Adam Smith's letter to William Strahan, which describes Hume's tranquility and resignation in the face of death and concludes that Hume, "concerning whose philosophical opinions men will, no doubt, judge variously," approached in both life and death "as nearly to the idea of a perfectly wise and virtuous man, as perhaps the nature of human frailty will permit." The letter is reprinted in Hume, *Essays Moral, Political, and Literary,* xliii–xlix, xlviii–xlix; for the indignant clerical reception of Smith's letter on its 1779 publication, see Phillipson, *Adam Smith,* 246.

18. Hume, *Enquiries,* 147.

19. See Hume, *Dissertation on the Passions and Natural History of Religion,* 37–43.

20. Hume, *Letters,* 1:278.

21. For this eighteenth-century shift, see Thomas, *Religion and the Decline of Magic,* 112.

22. Quoted in Rivers, *Reason, Grace, and Sentiment,* 2:17.

23. The anecdote is recalled three decades later in a political pamphlet by Josiah Royce, who was Butler's domestic chaplain during his Bristol episcopacy (*Humble*

Address and Earnest Appeal, 20). I found the reference in Ronald Bayne's introduction to Butler, *Analogy of Religion* (1906), xii.

24. Butler, *Analogy of Religion* (1736), 142. All subsequent parenthetical citations are to this, the first edition. Hume picks up on this point in the introduction to his *Natural History of Religion* (Hume, *Dissertation on the Passions and Natural History of Religion*, 33.)

25. For Toland's pantheism, see Sullivan, *John Toland*, 173–204.

26. For Locke's interest in justified posthumous judgment, see *Essay Concerning Human Understanding*, 347.

27. For Warburton's zero-sum, polemical approach to controversy, see Christensen, *Practicing Enlightenment*, 176–77. For his influence and controversial reception among fellow eighteenth-century Anglicans, see Young, *Religion and Enlightenment*, 171–212.

28. For priestcraft, see Rivers, *Reason, Grace and Sentiment*, 2:52–58.

29. *Articles agreed upon by the archbishops and bishops*, article 7.

30. Warburton, *Principles of Natural and Revealed Religion*, 2:115–16. For the subscription debate, see Young, *Religion and Enlightenment*, 45–80.

31. For Butler, see Mossner, *Life of Hume*, 118. For Warburton, see ibid., 325–26.

32. Targets include but are not limited to Pompanazzi, Vanini, Hobbes, Spinoza, Blount, Collins, Shaftesbury, Toland, and Tindal.

33. Hume, *Letters*, 2:244.

34. I cite from the first edition: Richardson, *Clarissa* (1747–48), 4:i–vi, vi.

35. Thomas Edwards to Samuel Richardson, 4 February 1755. In Richardson, *Correspondence with George Cheyne and Thomas Edwards*, 361.

4. The Beatified Clarissa

1. This question is considered at length in Stuber, "*Clarissa*: A Religious Novel?"

2. Ibid., 105.

3. For Coleridge's interpretation of Richardson, see Hensley, "*Clarissa*, Coleridge, Kant, and Klopstock." See also Watt, *Rise of the Novel*, 208–38; Eaves and Kimpel, *Samuel Richardson*; Eagleton, *Rape of Clarissa*; Warner, *Reading Clarissa*; Castle, *Clarissa's Ciphers*.

4. E. Derek Taylor, "Samuel Richardson's *Clarissa* and the Problem of Heaven," in New and Reedy, *Theology and Literature*, 71–89, 77. Taylor does not cite sources, but he may be referring to the Puritan reading of Watt's *Rise of the Novel*, Wolff's *Richardson and the Eighteenth-Century Puritan Character*, and Damrosch's *God's Plot and Man's Stories*; he tells me in a personal communication that he was referring to the Anglican reading of Eaves and Kimpel's *Richardson: A Biography*, 550–57; and he may have in mind the Behmenist readings of Hensley's "Thomas Edwards," Doody's "Gnostic Clarissa," and Joling-van der Sar's *Spiritual Side of Samuel Richardson*.

5. E. Derek Taylor, *Reason and Religion in "Clarissa."*

6. Doody, "Gnostic Clarissa," 51, and Hensley, "Thomas Edwards," 142.

7. "I have turned over the books I found in my closet; and am not a little pleased

with them ... Stanhope's Gospels; Sharp's, Tillotson's, and South's Sermons; Nelson's Feasts and Fasts; a Sacramental piece of Bishop of Man, and another of Dr. Gauden Bishop of Exeter; and Inett's Devotions; are among the devout books" (3:290). Though there is some political and theological diversity in this list (Robert South was a Laudian high churchman and no friend of the Glorious Revolution; Tillotson was a staunch Williamite with friends among the Dissenters), they together constitute a representative sample of the early-eighteenth-century Anglican establishment. The secular bookshelf is more diverse; Clarissa notes with approval the presence of England's two great Catholic poets, Dryden and Pope.

8. Tom Keymer also detects the theological influence of Warburton in the postscript (Keymer, Richardson's "Clarissa," 212).

9. Richardson, Selected Letters, 102.

10. Richardson, Correspondence, ed. Barbauld, 2:8; Selected Letters, 303.

11. Brewer, Afterlife of Character.

12. For Richardson's maneuver of writing Pamela in Her Exalted Condition as a defense against spurious continuations, see Albert J. Rivero's introduction (xxxi–lv). For Klopstock's ode, Echlin's continuation, and many other responses to Clarissa, see Bueler, Clarissa: The Eighteenth-Century Response.

13. Flesch, Comeuppance, 51.

14. Keymer, Richardson's "Clarissa," 213.

15. Richardson, Selected Letters, 104.

16. "I will write a Comedy, I think. I have a Title ready; and that's half the work. The Quarrelsome Lovers. 'Twill do" (4:48). Lovelace returns to the conceit on 4:308 and 6:227–28, among other places.

17. For Lovelace's failure to understand Clarissa, see Damrosch, God's Plot and Man's Stories, 249.

18. Robert G. Walker, Eighteenth-Century Arguments for Immortality, 20–22.

19. Ibid., 26–34.

20. Eaves and Kimpel, Samuel Richardson, 460.

21. Tate, King Lear, 5.6.156. in Shakespeare Made Fit, 291–374.

22. Rymer invents the term in "A Short View of Tragedy" (1692), in Rymer, Critical Works, 82–176.

23. For Clarissa as a noncoercive but unmistakable invitation to faith, see Taylor, Reason and Religion in "Clarissa," 152–54.

24. Sterne, Tristram Shandy, 1:125.

25. Richardson's theological caution parallels that of Samuel Johnson. Johnson's allegorical fiction The Vision of Theodore, Hermit of Teneriffe (1748) describes life as a mountain whose summit contains the "Temples of Happiness." But this temple is obscured by a "mist ... which is pierced only by the eyes of Religion" (Works, 16:204).

26. Hensley, "Thomas Edwards," 144.

27. Ibid., 148.

28. OED, s.v. "viaticum." George Lakoff and Mark Turner provide a brief anthology of life-as-journey metaphors in More than Cool Reason, 9–10.

29. For a close reading of this motif, see Stuber, "*Clarissa:* A Religious Novel?," 105–7.

30. Lovelace returns to the topos forty pages later, while premeditating the rape: "O Jack! what a difficulty must a man be allowed to have, to conquer a predominant passion . . . however wrong he knows it to be to resolve to gratify it! Reflect upon this; and then wilt thou be able to account for, if not to excuse, a projected crime, which has *habit* to plead for it, in a breast as stormy as uncontroulable!" (5:264). Richardson's irony, of course, is that the "uncontroulable" Lovelace is under the control of his own habits.

31. The brackets are Richardson's.

32. Richardson may here recollect fable 105, "A Hare and a Tortoise," from his *Aesop's Fables* (1739). See Richardson, *Early Works,* 212–13.

33. Budd, "Why Clarissa Must Die," 16.

34. Richardson, *Correspondence,* ed. Barbauld, 2:72; Hensley, "Clarissa, Coleridge, Kant, and Klopstock," 137.

35. For a succinct account of the genre's standard form, see Roger Sharrock's introduction to Bunyan, *Grace Abounding to the Chief of Sinners,* xxvii–xxx.

36. Sarah Fielding, *Remarks on "Clarissa,"* 48.

37. Richardson, *Selected Letters,* 77. Donald Wehrs argues that Richardson uses Clarissa's death to provide a standpoint from which the reader, "adjudicating between the conflicting claims of juxtaposed voices," can reach a stable reading ("Irony, Storytelling," 775).

38. For this point, see Spencer Jackson, "*Clarissa's* Political Theology." I discuss Jackson in greater detail at the end of this section.

39. The negative example of Mrs. Sinclair contains the opposite experience: "*I get into a better frame! I, who can neither cry, nor pray! Yet already feel the torments of the damn'd!*" (8:54).

40. For the classical origins and 1740s jestbook transmission of Lovelace's allusion to Philip II of Macedon, see Nace, "Richardson's Charnel House."

41. Hill to Richardson: ""For my part, I am *afraid* to be popular. I see so many who write to the living, and deserve not to live, that I content myself with a resurrection when dead." (Richardson, *Correspondence,* ed. Barbauld, 1:3). Delaney asks Richardson, who has printed some treatises for him, to send them to the college libraries of the two universities, "where, if they are to die, they may be buried with many better works, and from whence (if they are found worthy to live) they may one day revive to more advantage" (ibid., 4:2).

42. Richardson, *Correspondence,* ed. Barbauld, 2:33.

43. Kurt Eissler argues that the close sibling relationship contained an incestuous element in *Goethe: A Psychoanalytic Study.*

44. Goethe, *Dichtung und Wahrheit,* 1:249, translated by R.O. Moon as *Autobiography, Poetry and Truth,* 195.

45. *Faust I,* lines 2428–39, in Goethe, *Werke,* 3:87.

5. Happy Ever After in *Sir Charles Grandison*

1. Compare Frye, *Anatomy of Criticism*, 163.

2. Emily Friedman discusses the lack of a traditional end to the novel in "The End(s) of Richardson's *Sir Charles Grandison*."

3. *Rambler* 139; *Works*, 4:376.

4. Quoted in Richardson, *Sir Charles Grandison*, 3:467. All subsequent parenthetical references are to this edition.

5. This understanding of marriage has a precedent in *Clarissa*, where the repentant Belford describes himself as "very earnest in my wishes to be admitted into the Nuptial State," as though marriage were like joining the Freemasons or getting an MA (8:226). The oddness of Richardson's language here is apparent if one contrasts it with such imaginable but non-occurring alternate formulations as *"I wish to marry a virtuous woman" or *"I love Charlotte Montague."

6. To be fair, Harriet resists this line of reasoning when it is presented to her directly:

> *Lady L.* This must do, Miss Byron: Who would not wish for such a mother?
> *Harriet.* Is the mother to be the principal inducement in such an article as this?
> (1:261)

Yet only fifteen pages later, another conversation with the Earl's mother affects her as follows: "Agreeable Lady D.! thought I: My heart will not suggest a thought in favour of your *son;* but I shall easily be in love with *you*" (1:276).

7. Each of these examples or variants occurs multiple times in *Sir Charles Grandison:* see for example 1:198, 1:318, 3:408, 3:374, 2:631. Vivavsan Soni makes this point in his discussion of the eighteenth-century novel as a "trial narrative": "Marriage itself can be figured as heaven or affective bliss, and affective pleasure can be figured as heavenly transport." But Soni, who discusses *Pamela* and *Clarissa* but not *Sir Charles Grandison*, wrongly sees heaven as an unnarratable endpoint to plot: "Heaven remains the most abstract of the determinations of happiness solicited by the trial narrative. Viewed from the perspective of narrative, it is no more than a narratological placeholder. . . . It holds open a narrative place for happiness, without explaining the specific content of happiness or the nature of the experience. Heaven is supposed to defy all attempts at description" (*Mourning Happiness*, 270). Donald R. Wehrs sees the same analogy between marriage and salvation evident already in Pamela's typological use of the Psalms to describe her trials at the hands of Mr. B, though he presents it in the traditional terms of Shamelan critique: "To the extent that hope of future 'rewards' regulates present 'virtue,' the equation of 'long-term good' with 'long-term happiness' allows material well-being or worldly enjoyment to function as a metaphor for, or prefiguring of, spiritual well-being, thus opening the text to the charge of crassly figuring the pleasures of Heaven in terms of those of being a squire's wife" ("Novelistic Redemption," 6).

8. Harris, *Samuel Richardson*, 2.

9. The phrase "here and hereafter," with its Butlerian play of both analogy and

difference, appears throughout *Clarissa* as well as *Sir Charles Grandison,* most memorably in James Harlowe, Senior's curse (3:258).

10. The end of *Pamela* contains a close parallel: "Oh! what a poor thing is human Life in its best Enjoyments. . . . This, duly reflected upon, methinks, should convince every one, that this World is not a Place for the immortal Mind to be confined to; and that there must be an Hereafter, where the *whole* Soul shall be satisfy'd" (Richardson, *Pamela,* 455).

11. Butler, *Analogy,* 31–35. Hume attacks this specific argument in "Of a Providence and Future State" (in *Enquiries,* 141–42); Lovelace admits it in *Clarissa* 5:331.

12. Sir Charles makes this point again when ridding Lord W. of Mrs. Giffard: "What folly is there in wickedness! . . . But we see in my mother, and in her brother, how habitual wickedness debases, and how habitual goodness exalts, the human mind" (2:49).

13. Hume, *Essays,* 592.

14. Flynn, *Samuel Richardson,* 45–46.

15. Klopstock's ode *Die Todte Clarissa* makes this point strongly: *Lüfte, wie diese, so die Erd' umathmen, / Sind, die leiseren selbst, dir rauhe Weste* [Even the softest breezes that blow on earth are the harsh west wind to you] (Klopstock, *Ausgewählte Werke,* 61; translation mine).

16. See *Clarissa,* 8:280–87, where Richardson cites Addison and Rapin's accounts of Aristotle, whom Richardson praises as "the greatest master of reason, and the best judge of composition, that ever lived" (8.280).

17. Aristotle, *Poetics,* 1451b2–4, in *Complete Works,* ed. Jonathan Barnes. Compare to Rapin, *Whole Critical Works,* 2:185–86. Subsequent citations are to these editions.

18. Else, *Aristotle's "Poetics": The Argument,* 285.

19. Stephen Halliwell comments on this passage: "What this analogy signifies for Aristotle is not the mere sense-experience of an animal's shape and proportions, but the understanding (by teleological criteria) of the interrelated functions of its parts" (*Aristotle's Poetics,* 98). In *On Length and Shortness of Life,* Aristotle correlates the size of an animal to the length of its life (466a14–16).

20. Aeschylus, *Agamemnon,* ed. and trans. Peter Burian and Alan Shapiro, in *Complete Aeschylus,* 1:69.

21. I have not seen the allusion remarked elsewhere; Richardson refers to the *Oresteia* when quoting Rapin on tragedy in the postscript to *Clarissa* (8:286).

22. *Agamemnon,* in *Complete Aeschylus,* 1:69. I am grateful to Gregory Nagy for drawing my attention to this passage.

23. Sophocles, *Oedipus the King,* ed. and trans. Stephen Berg and Diskin Clay, in *Complete Sophocles,* 1:292.

24. Ibid., 286.

25. Sophocles, *Oedipus at Colonus,* in *Complete Sophocles,* 1:395–96.

6. Laetitia Pilkington in Sheets

1. Pilkington, *Memoirs*. The volumes are paginated continuously; all subsequent page references are parenthetical in my text.

2. Nussbaum, *Autobiographical Subject,* 178–200; Clarke, *Queen of the Wits.*

3. See Lakoff and Turner, *More than Cool Reason,* 103.

4. See, e.g., the following, from "Verses Wrote in a Library," *Memoirs* 58:

Learning can the soul refine
Raise from human to divine.
Come then, all ye sacred Dead,
Who for Virtue wrote or bled,
On my Mind intensely beam,
Touch it with your hallow'd Flame.

5. Rousseau, *Confessions,* 34.

6. Richardson, *Correspondence,* ed. Barbauld, 2:127.

7. Berens, "Sword Unsheathed," dedicates a chapter to Swift's role in forming Pilkington as a poet (81–151); her consideration of Pilkington's body is linked to her exploration of the larger theme of "wit." For "favour," see *OED,* sv. "favour" 2c.

8. Pilkington's word "Heteroclite" supplies Felicity Nussbaum with a chapter title in *The Autobiographical Subject.*

9. Berens, "Sword Unsheathed," 5.

10. Weber, *Memory, Print and Gender,* 53. Weber's case studies of the relationship between print technology and memory in the works of Cavendish, Milton, Pope, and Richardson illuminate many of the themes considered in this project; I seek to extend Weber's work both chronologically (his account of Cavendish is an excellent summation of the *status quo ante* of "lyric immortality" with which my introduction begins) and through a shift in emphasis, from the memorial archive to the theologically tinged immortality of republication and rereading.

11. Compare to Proverbs 3:3: "Let not mercy and truth forsake thee: bind them about thy neck; write them upon the table of thine heart."

12. Swift, *Poems,* 565.

13. Relke, "In Search of Mrs. Pilkington," 118–19.

14. Ibid., 120; *Memoirs,* xxxvi–viii, 597.

15. See Jakobson, "Metaphoric and Metonymic Poles."

16. Nussbaum, *Autobiographical Subject,* 189–90.

17. So, e.g., Pope: "He wins this Patron, who can tickle best" (*Dunciad* [1743] 2.196). Compare 2.191–220 and n. to 2.213; Swift's *On Poetry: A Rhapsody,* which Mary Barber delivered to Matthew Pilkington for London publication in 1733, similarly connects the patronage-seeking to prostitution: "O, what Indignity and Shame / To prostitute the Muse's Name, / By flatt'ring [Kings] whom Heaven design'd / The Plagues and Scourges of Mankind" (413–16). For Pilkington's role in the publication of *On Poetry,* see *Memoirs* 64n. (Citations are from Pope, *Dunciad,* and Swift, *Poems.*)

18. For Savage's life and Johnson's account of it, see Holmes, *Dr. Johnson and Mr. Savage*. The fullest biography of Savage is Tracy, *Artificial Bastard*.

19. For an account of this climate, see Griffin, *Literary Patronage in England*; Clarke, *Queen of the Wits*, is particularly evocative in describing this component of Pilkington's career.

20. Relke anticipates my concept of the structural double entendre by observing that "throughout the *Memoirs*, we find . . . curious business transactions that read more like metaphors for sexual solicitation" ("In Search of Mrs. Pilkington," 124).

21. *Memoirs*, 180–81. Elias does not mention that the phrase "mighty Dead" is taken from Thomson's *Winter*, where it also describes a night vision of literary-historical figures.

22. The *English Short Title Catalogue*, which attributes *The Christian's Daily Practice* in one record to John Welch and in another to Richard Alleine (both were seventeenth-century clergymen), reports editions of 24pp. in 12° (Edinburgh 1698, Edinburgh 1703), and 8pp. in 8° (Glasgow 1700, Boston 1730, Glasgow 1751), i.e., one sheet and one half sheet, respectively.

23. During two years of attending Eastern Mennonite High School in the late 1990s, I encountered a game called "between the sheets" that is in structure strikingly similar to Foote's jest. This game, which could be played alone but was best in groups, was rather more innocent than it sounds: it consisted of selecting the titles of hymns from a hymnal, adding the phrase "between the sheets," and chortling at the resulting phrase. In my case, the hymnal in question was Mennonite, but Internet research suggests that the game is played ecumenically, and indeed I suspect that wherever two or three high school students are gathered for compulsory chapel services some version of "between the sheets" will eventually develop. The results are often non sequiturs ("Guide My Feet . . . between the sheets!"), but they can be mildly salacious ("For We Are Strangers No More . . . between the sheets!") or even highly blasphemous—I will leave instances of this kind as an exercise to the reader.

24. For Ricks's concept of an anti-pun, in which "there is only one sense admitted but there is another sense denied admission," see *The Force of Poetry* (Oxford: Clarendon Press, 1984), 265–66.

25. The *Critical Review, or Annals of Literature* for May 1796 opines that "this ode possesses a very small share of poetical merit, but perhaps quite enough for the subject" (235).

26. For the history of the word "autobiography," see Folkenflik, "Introduction: The Institution of Autobiography," in *Culture of Autobiography*, 1–21.

27. Mascuch, *Origins of the Individualist Self*, 6.

28. Peter Pindar [pseud. of John Wolcot], *Bozzy and Piozzi*, 21. Mascuch mistakenly attributes *The Hero of Finsbury Square* to Wolcot (*Origins of the Individualist Self*, 207). Contemporaries were more discriminating; John Murray's *English Review* notes that the author "seems to be somewhat of kin, though not probably very *nearly* related, to his justly celebrated namesake Peter Pindar, Esq." (*English Review*, vol. 26, 1795, emphasis in original).

7. Johnson's Eternal Silences

1. For Johnson's ambivalent but ultimately collaborative role in Boswell's project, see Radner, "'A Very Exact Picture.'"

2. Helen Deutsch reports an academic panel on "Whatever Happened to the Age of Johnson?" in which "one panelist's response, however ironic, said it all: 'Ageless'" (*Loving Dr. Johnson*, 15).

3. Psychoanalytic interpretations of Johnson, particularly George Irwin's *Samuel Johnson: A Personality in Conflict,* have traced much of the psychic trauma of his life to a relationship with a distant and demanding mother. I have not seen noted the significance of Johnson's name, which W. J. Bate suggests likely came from Sarah Johnson, in honor of her brother Samuel Ford (*Samuel Johnson,* 5). In the Old Testament, Samuel is the firstborn son given to Hannah on the condition that she give him back again to God. She takes him to the temple when he is three and thereafter sees him only once a year—an echo of the Abraham and Isaac story with the emphasis shifted from the father to the mother, and from a single climactic sacrifice to a renunciation that must be repeated again every year.

4. Hawkins, *Life of Samuel Johnson,* 277. Boswell and George Steevens reported otherwise; see below, n. 50.

5. Printed as volume 1 of the Yale *Works.* Henceforth all works of Johnson in the Yale Edition will be cited parenthetically by volume and page, with a short title supplied for clarity if needed.

6. Piozzi, for instance, describes often making tea for Johnson "till four o'clock in the morning," as he "loved late hours extremely, or more properly hated early ones" (*Anecdotes,* 123–24). Boswell records Johnson recounting how he once fasted from Sunday dinner to Tuesday dinner (*Life,* 3:306; compare 1:468 and 5:284).

7. Among the few exceptions are several journals kept during periods of illness and a sequence of letters written to Hester Thrale during Johnson's tour of Scotland with Boswell in 1773 (*Works,* 1; *Letters,* 3:46–119).

8. See sermons 10 and 25 (*Works,* 14:107–15, 261–71). The *Dictionary* records a tension between the fundamental importance of the afterlife to Johnson, and the uniqueness in his mind of Christianity as an authority for its existence. Johnson's first definition of *Religion* is "Virtue, as founded upon reverence of God, and expectation of future rewards and punishments." The quotations that follow are grounded in both Christian and classicized usages, from Watts, Milton, Blackmore, and Ben Jonson's *Catiline.* His second definition, "A system of divine worship and faith as opposite to others," includes the following quotation from Tillotson: "The doctrine of the gospel proposes to men such glorious rewards, and such terrible punishments, as no religion ever did, and gives us far greater assurance of their reality and certainty than ever the world had."

9. When Johnson told Dr. William Adams that he is "afraid [he] may be one of those who shall be damned . . . sent to Hell . . . and punished everlastingly," he had six months and one day to live (Boswell, *Life,* 4:299).

10. See Deutsch, *Loving Dr. Johnson,* 122–23 and 278 n. 48, and Bate, *Samuel Johnson,* 451–52.

11. See Suarez, "Johnson's Christian Thought," 198–99.

12. Boswell, *Life,* 5:88.

13. For Bunyan's heaven, see *Grace Abounding and Pilgrim's Progress,* 269–71.

14. Potkay, *Passion for Happiness,* 200–201.

15. Ibid., 6; Bate, *Samuel Johnson,* 449; Parker, *Triumph of Augustan Poetics,* 239.

16. Kernan calls it "the Magna Carta of the modern author" (*Printing Technology, Letters, and Samuel Johnson,* 105). Compare Carlyle, *Samuel Johnson,* 59. The first chapter of Lipking, *Samuel Johnson: The Life of an Author,* begins with the letter, assuming Carlyle and Kernan's argument in its structure.

17. Johnson, *Letters,* 1:5–6.

18. To follow the full saga of the prize poem, as chronicled in the *Gentleman's Magazine* itself, see vol. 4 (1734), pp. 382 (July), 442 (August), 508 (September), 560 (October), 619 (November); vol. 5 (1735), pp. 41 (January), 227 (May), 393–436 ("Extraordinary" issue between July and August), 673 (November), 726 (December); vol. 6 (1736), pp. 59–60. *Gentleman's Magazine,* reprinted, London: Pickering and Chatto, 1998. Subsequent references are also to this reprint.

19. Barker, "Cave, Edward (1691–1754)"; *Gentleman's Magazine* 24 (1754), 59–60.

20. *Gentleman's Magazine* 5 (1735): 395.

21. In the Loeb translation, the corresponding lines read "In all the lands extending from Cadiz as far as Ganges and the Dawn, there are few people who can remove the fog of confusion and distinguish real benefits from their opposite" (Juvenal and Persius, *Works,* 367).

22. Lipking, "Learning to Read Johnson," 533.

23. DeMaria Jr., *Life of Samuel Johnson,* 138–39.

24. See Potkay, *Passion for Happiness,* 113–14.

25. Braudy, *Frenzy of Renown,* 293.

26. H. J. Jackson, "General Theory of Fame," 14.

27. For the other side of this communion, the prayers of the living for the dead, see Johnson's prayer for his mother, written within a few days of *Idler* 41 (*Works,* 1:62). For the economy of salvation in the middle ages, see Le Goff, *Birth of Purgatory.*

28. Johnson, *Letters,* 1:45–46.

29. *Gentleman's Magazine* 10 (1740): 593.

30. Lipking, *Samuel Johnson,* 38–41, traces the extent of Johnson's (acknowledged) debt to Addison, a debt, he points out, not always noted by modern Johnsonians.

31. Parker, *Triumph of Augustan Poetics,* 243.

32. The man who "treasure[s] up the papers of the day merely because others neglect them" recalls the eccentric virtuoso of *Rambler* 82, whose collection of worthless curiosities includes a Chinese snail and "sand scraped from the coffin of King Richard" (*Works,* 4:64–70).

33. For the philosophical weight carried by detritus, remnants, leftovers, and waste, see Gee, *Making Waste.*

34. Johnson expresses himself similarly in many other places, e.g., *Rambler* 151:

"Amidst all the disorder and inequality which variety of discipline, example, conversation, and employment produce in the intellectual advances of different men, there is still discovered by a vigilant spectator such a general and remote similitude as may be expected in the same common nature affected by external circumstances indefinitely varied" (*Works*, 5:38).

35. Smallwood is discussing Johnson's much later *Lives of the Poets,* but the phrase applies equally to the periodicals. ("Annotated Immortality," 77).

36. For Johnson's deep immersion in classical moral philosophy, particularly Roman ideas of the good life, see Potkay, *Passion for Happiness.*

37. Rothstein, *Gleaning Modernity,* 20.

38. Sherman, *Telling Time,* 190, 194.

39. See also Philip Smallwood, "Ironies of the Critical Past: Historicizing Johnson's Criticism," in *Johnson Re-Visioned: Looking Before and After,* ed. Smallwood (Lewisburg, PA: Bucknell University Press, 2001), 114–33. Smallwood suggests that taking Johnson seriously as a critic entails questioning the narrative of progress that relegates him to an irrelevant, neoclassical intellectual past.

40. "Whatever might be the state of female literature in the last century, there is now no longer any danger lest the scholar should want an adequate audience at the tea-table" (*Works,* 5:153).

41. *Works,* 9:122. For wider context, see Spadafora, *Idea of Progress.*

42. The idea that languages, like other things, can be preserved through literature finds more optimistic expression in Henry Flood's epitaph for Johnson, published in Boswell's *Life:*

> No need of Latin or of Greek to grace
> Our Johnson's memory, or inscribe his grave;
> His native language claims this mournful space,
> To pay the Immortality he gave. (4:424)

Boswell earlier reports that Johnson himself "would never consent to disgrace the walls of Westminster Abbey with an English inscription" (*Life,* 3:85).

43. Translations of these works follow *The Vision of Theodore* in *The Preceptor* (2 vols., 1748), an educational anthology published by Robert Dodsley (*The Vision* is 2:516–26; "The Choice of Hercules" is 2:530–40; and "The Picture of Human Life," the final piece in the volume, is 2:541–56). See also the introduction to *The Vision of Theodore* in *Works,* 16:179–93.

44. *Spectator,* 1:46.

45. *Spectator,* 3:152, 154.

46. Sachs, "Vacuity of Life," 345. As Sachs acknowledges, this article is to some extent an elaboration of the argument of W. J. Bate's *Achievement of Samuel Johnson.*

47. Sachs, "Vacuity of Life," 346.

48. *Spectator* 3:156.

49. Richardson, *Clarissa,* 8:217–22.

50. Johnson's watch was an object of great interest to his contemporaries, and has left behind a tangled historical record. Hawkins reports that Johnson bought his first

watch in 1768, for seventeen guineas, from the prestigious horologers Mudge and Dutton (Hawkins, *Life of Johnson,* 277). Hawkins gives the inscription as Νυξ γαρ ερχεται (actually, Νμξ γαρ ερχεται, since Hawkins says that the inscription has "the mistake of a letter μ for υ"). Boswell says in the *Life* (2:56) that he saw the watch in the spring of 1768, and gives the same inscription, without the mu/μ. Both Hawkins and Boswell say that he replaced the dial plate (Hawkins: "about three years after"; Boswell: "some time afterwards") because it was "pedantic" (Hawkins) or "ostentatious" (Boswell). As Redford and Goldring point out, Boswell's "paragraph on SJ's watch does not originate in JB's journal, notes, or memoranda" (*Life of Johnson: Edition of the Original Manuscript,* 2:30 n. 6). It thus seems possible that Boswell was guided by Hawkins's *Life* in dating the watch to 1768. Boswell reports a detail omitted by Hawkins: that when Johnson replaced the dial plate, the original came into possession of George Steevens (*Life,* 2:58). Neither Hawkins nor Boswell note the discrepancy between the inscription and the actual text of John 9:4, which reads simply ερχεται νυξ. Frances Reynolds presents a minority report to the effect that the dial plate was in Latin, not Greek, and that the words were *Nox enim veniet,* and that he had it removed because *enim* does not appear in the Vulgate, which reads simply *venit nox.* She claims that the entire watch, not just the plate, "was some years since in the possession of Mr. Steevens," but she does not know where it got to following his death (i.e., after 1800) (Hill, *Johnsonian Miscellanies,* 2:295). However, the Hyde Collection preserves an exchange of letters between Frances Reynolds and Steevens himself two years before his death in which she asks him about a Latin engraving and he replies that the inscription was indeed in Greek, and that he "is wholly unacquainted with any Latin Motto applied by his late Friend to a similar purpose" (Houghton Library MS Hyde 25 I.5, 1797–98). From Johnson's death there are two parallel watch traditions, consistent with the dial plate having been removed and attached to another watch. According to Aleyn Lyell Reade, at Johnson's death his watch was pocketed by John Hawkins, though it belonged by right to Francis Barber, who eventually recovered it and sold it to the Canon of Lichfield, Hugh Bailye (*Johnsonian Gleanings,* 2:53–56). Meanwhile, a cricket-playing Oxford-memoir-writing clergyman named James Pycroft wrote in to *Notes and Queries* in 1871 and again in 1885 to claim that he inherited Johnson's watch from his mother, Steevens's niece. He reports the same inscription as Boswell and Steevens (Pycroft, "Dr. Johnson's Watch"). For Pycroft's life as a Victorian stereotype, see Howat, "Pycroft, James (1813–1895)."

51. *Book of Common Prayer, 1662 Version,* 228. Damrosch, *Samuel Johnson and the Tragic Sense,* 74 n. 14, points out that Johnson also cites this verse in *Adventurer* 120, a prayer from Lent 1768, and sermons 4 and 25; it also appears in sermon 27 and *Idler* 43 (*Works,* 1:118; 2:137, 2:470; 14:50, 271, 295). Unlike the watch inscription, these uses omit the particle "for" that points back to the Book of Common Prayer.

52. Seccombe, "Mudge, Thomas."

53. One of Johnson's Bibles, for instance (Houghton Library, Hyde 2003J–SJ989) contains tabulations of the numbers of chapters in various sections of the Bible, and records of readings over the course of days and months (e.g., the inside front cover of

vol. 6, in which Johnson has written "Begun Ap 20. Easterday / Ended this Volume May 7—83"). Boswell records a similar record from 1775 in *Life,* 2:289.

54. "O my journal! art thou not highly dignified?" Boswell crows after the first such recommendation (*London Journal,* 305).

55. Sherman, *Telling Time,* 143–58.

56. Boswell, *Ominious Years,* 265. The idea stuck with Boswell; he uses it again verbatim in *Hypochondriack* 66, from March 1783 (Boswell, *Hypochondriack,* 2:258).

57. *Idler* 24 reprises Steele and William Sherlock's idea that those who lead empty lives are no better than the dead, though he places the emphasis on occupation and sensation rather than ethical conduct: "He that lives in torpid insensibility, wants nothing of a carcase but putrefaction" (*Works,* 2:77).

58. Philip Dormer Stanhope, 4th Earl of Chesterfield, *Letters,* 3:1047 (30 October 1747). Wesley quoted in Nussbaum, *Autobiographical Subject,* 88.

59. Arendt, *Human Condition,* 79–174.

60. Ibid., 83; Johnson, *Works,* 4:210–11.

61. Arendt, *Human Condition,* 136; Johnson, *Works,* 4:213.

62. Boswell may have *Rambler* 108 in mind when he justifies writing *The Hypochondriack* by arguing that "writing such essays therefore may fill up the interstices of their lives, and occupy moments which would otherwise be lost" (*Hypochondriack,* 1:103).

63. Erasmus, *Praise of Folly,* 2.

64. A definition of "time" added to later editions of the *Dictionary* is relevant here: "Life considered as employed, or destined to employment," with the following quotation from John Fell's *Life of the Most Learned, Reverend and Pious Dr. H. Hammond* (1661): "A great devourer of his *time,* was his agency for men of quality" (Johnson, *Dictionary of the English Language,* 6th ed. [1785]). Johnson has slightly altered Fell's original, which appears on page 93 of the *Life of Hammond.*

8. James Boswell, Also, Enters into Heaven

1. Hume, *Letters,* 1:173. Hume is responding to a correspondent who had attempted a refutation of his 1751 *Enquiry Concerning the Principles of Morals.*

2. Boswell, *Boswell, Laird of Auchinleck,* 283. Monboddo, here a philosophical bugbear, had been an ally five years earlier, in 1776, when Boswell was badly shaken by his deathbed interview with Hume: "My shock from having been with David Hume was not almost cured. . . . I was roused to noble hope again by an accidental conversation in the Library with Lord Monboddo, who talked of *spirit* like Plato himself, and said 'Show me anything destroyed, and then maintain the annihilation of mind'" (Boswell, *Boswell in Extremes,* 21). For yet another example of Boswell the affective philosopher, see *Boswell: The Ominous Years,* 212: "My state of mind today was still affected by Hartley and Priestley's metaphysics, and was continually trying to perceive my faculties operating as machinery."

3. Bunyan, *Grace Abounding and Pilgrim's Progress,* ed. Sharrock, 1966, 69.

4. "The Spectator mentions his being seen at Child's, which makes me have an

affection for it. I think myself like him, and am serenely happy there" (*London Journal*, 76). For Boswell's reverence of Young, see *Life*, 1:214.

5. Pottle, *James Boswell, the Earlier Years*, 92. Pottle argues that while Boswell's stated preference among novelists was Fielding, "It was Richardson . . . who first demonstrated the values of the scrupulous short-term dramatic stance which furnishes the prime characteristic of Boswell's journalizing." Notwithstanding Pottle's confidence, which he tells the reader is based on "a recent reading of *Clarissa*," I take it to be an open question whether Boswell does not record reading Richardson in his journal because he needed to read Richardson in order to be able to keep such a journal (*propter hoc ergo post hoc*); whether Boswell does not mention Richardson because he is embarrassed by the printer's bourgeois class antecedents and prefers to be an admirer of Fielding, whose genteel legal/belletristic career parallels Boswell's own (and whose humor and easygoing sexual code Boswell found congenial); or whether Boswell simply never read much Richardson and developed the same close documentary style independently. For Pilkington, see *Bibliotheca Boswelliana. A Catalogue of the entire Library of the Late James Boswell, Esq.* [i.e., Boswell's son], item 1836. Unfortunately, a thorough comparison of this 1825 catalogue with surviving records from Boswell's lifetime undertaken while working for the Yale Boswell Editions suggests to me that his son's collection contains no more than a handful Boswell's own books.

6. Freud, *Interpretation of Dreams*, 85–86. For the Reid saga, see Boswell, *Boswell in Search of a Wife*, 12; and *Boswell for the Defense*, 250–349. So committed was he to Reid's cause that he convinced himself that by virtue of his "more delicate nature," he "suffered much more than" Reid himself (ibid., 288). The cross-pressured quality of the efforts he made on Reid's behalf was not lost on Boswell: "It gave me some uneasiness to think that he was solemnly preparing himself for an awful eternity while at the same time I was trying to keep him back" (ibid., 326).

7. Turnbull, "Boswell and Sympathy," 108–9. Turnbull argues that the trauma of the Reid trial was instrumental in driving Boswell out of Scots legal practice and toward biography and London as vocation and location in the final years of his life.

8. Compare *London Journal*, 260–61, with *Life*, 1:391–95.

9. Boswell, *Boswell on the Grand Tour*, 114.

10. Because the portion of Boswell's journal that covers his embarkation from Harwich is lost, this scene (as well as Johnson's famous kicking of the stone to refute Berkeley) was composed from memory twenty-five years after the fact. Johnson's exhortation to Boswell to pray is suggestively similar to the closing paragraph of the surviving *London Journal*: "My feeble mind shrinks somewhat at the idea of leaving Britain in so very short a time from the moment in which I now make this remark. . . . Let me commit myself to the care of my merciful Creator" (333). Despite the faith of Marshall Waingrow and other Boswellians that "JB was quite capable of recalling some twenty-five years after the event noteworthy matter that he neglected to preserve at the time," it is easy to imagine that Boswell, when composing the life, transposed his own invocation to prayer into Johnson's mouth (*Boswell's Life of Johnson: An Edition of the Original Manuscript*, 1:328 n. 3). Also possible is that the

August 4 *London Journal* passage was written a few days after its assigned date, with Johnson's call to prayer at the Harwich altar fresh in Boswell's mind. Note that both Boswell's trepidation in the *London Journal* about leaving "Britain" and Johnson's reference in the *Life* to Boswell leaving his "native country" elide, in the face of his departure for the continent, the journey Boswell has already taken from Scotland to England.

11. Indeed, the *Life* is the only authority for the text of the letter. "Superstition" and "enthusiasm" were stock epithets used by Enlightenment authors to stigmatize irrational thinking, associated with Catholicism and Evangelical dissent respectively. Boswell's fear of falling into both faults at once has a slight tinge of comic hyperbole. See Hume, "Of Superstition and Enthusiasm," in *Essays,* 73–79.

12. *Boswell's Journal of a Tour to the Hebrides,* 300.

13. The typological association of Luther and Johnson implied in Boswell's 1764 letter from Melanchthon's tomb is felicitous, given the ultimate form of the *Life,* since the English word "table talk" likely entered the language as a calque for the *Tischreden* recorded by Luther's students and disciples (see *OED* s.v. "table talk").

14. For "cairn," the mot juste for the vehicle of Boswell's simile here, I thank Jane Darcy.

15. *Spectator,* 4:493.

16. Boswell, *Boswell, the Great Biographer,* 19.

17. Alkon, "Boswellian Time," 243–44. The quotations are from letters to Anna Seward and Joseph Cooper Walker and can be found in *Correspondence and Other Papers of James Boswell,* ed. Waingrow, 78–79, 91.

18. Donald Greene is fond of pointing out places where Boswell gets these dates wrong, for instancef in "Boswell's *Life* as 'Literary Biography.'" At stake for me here is Boswell's reality effect, not reality.

19. Alkon, "Boswellian Time," 250.

20. As recorded in the journals he kept from his return from the Grand Tour to his death (i.e., 1767–95), Boswell experiences substantially more "up" emotions (euphoria or restless, wakeful activity) than "down" (depression and lassitude) in February, March, and April, and more "down" than "up" in July and October–December. January, May, June, August, and September are more mixed. (My methodology consisted of reading all fourteen volumes of the trade edition of Boswell's private papers and marking his records of his mood with up and down arrows in a notebook. This is not a procedure that would satisfy reviewers for a learned journal of psychiatry, but it is suggestive.) Boswell's vernal sanguinity and aestival/brumal melancholy are consistent with patterns that modern medical researchers have observed in bipolar disorder, whose sufferers in some cases follow such a seasonal pattern as they alternate between depression and either mania or more moderate but nevertheless measurable hypomania (Goodwin and Jamison, *Manic-Depressive Illness*). I am broadly in accord with the current critical taboo against diagnosing historical figures out of our contemporary psychiatric manuals, and moreover it is certainly plausible that Boswell's high spirits in spring simply reflect the fact that going to London pleased and energized him. But the Court of Session sat from 12 June to 11 August and 12

November to 11 March—he could just as well have gone to London every Michaelmas rather than every Easter (*Boswell for the Defense*, 351). Thus Boswell may well have gone to London because he was hypomanic (he often records high spirits for some days before departure) rather than becoming hypomanic on arrival. Boswell, unlike Johnson, always maintained that the weather and time of year affected his mood; see, e.g., *Laird of Auchinleck*, 463, where he remarks on the oddness of feeling "in strong spirits" in July, "hypochondria being by some curious periodical influence always with me at that time." For a study of literary creativity and bipolar disorder whose theoretical limitations show the possibilities for further, more sophisticated interdisciplinary work, see Jamison, *Touched with Fire*.

21. Taylor, *Secular Age*, 54–59.

22. As Boswell's cautious footnote implies, the theory of atonement proposed by Johnson here enters onto fraught theological ground. From the 1690s on, conceptions of the crucified Christ as example rather than sacrifice were denounced as "Socianiasm" by orthodox Anglicans, and taken to entail the rejection of Trinitarianism and even of the establishment of the priesthood. See Champion, *Pillars of Priestcraft Shaken*, 117–19.

23. I cite, with slight modification, Frederick Pottle's translation of Boswell's French, as printed in Pottle, *James Boswell: The Earlier Years*, 2–3.

24. In a pattern that will repeat itself endlessly over the course of the *London Journal*, Boswell follows his performance as Cato with an impromptu bawdy song in the mode of *The Beggar's Opera*.

25. Boswell uses this as an argument in his interview with the dying Hume: "Would it not be agreeable to have hopes of seeing our friends again?" (*Boswell in Extremes*, 13).

26. In *Marginalia: Readers Writing in Books*, H. J. Jackson concludes that readers have indeed used the *Life* for self-help: "Boswell's readers were looking for help with their own lives and were most struck by those places in which there was something at stake for them personally" (178). Cited in Deutsch, *Loving Dr. Johnson*, 279 n. 67.

27. Redford, *Designing the Life of Johnson*, 84–85.

28. As with Boswell's construction of the *Life*'s intellectual sociability as a type of heaven, journal notes omitted from the *Life* are revealing in this connection. "I was elevated in spirit while I walked in the cloisters of an Oxford college with Dr. Johnson in the moonlight," Boswell reports in March 1776. "I said, 'This is the road to a better world'" (*Ominous Years*, 281).

29. The evidence suggests that the incisions Johnson made in his legs to drain dropsical fluid indeed hastened his death; for the controversy, see Deutsch, *Loving Dr. Johnson*, 55–56.

30. Smith, *Lectures on Rhetoric and Belles Lettres*, 132.

31. See Radner, "A Very Exact Picture."

32. Boswell had been triumphant in 1763 when Johnson encourages him to keep a diary, going home to write, "O my journal! art thou not highly dignified? Shalt thou not flourish tenfold?" (*London Journal*, 305).

33. Boswell records Johnson reading the journal "all along" on 19 September 1773

and mentions subsequent readings on 27 September (to himself while in company), 3 October, and 12 October, where Johnson supplies blanks and offers corrections— Boswell's footnote to this day's journal wonders that Johnson does not say something about Boswell's record of Johnson's tics and mutterings (*Life,* 5:226, 262, 279, 307).

34. For Boswell's acquisition of the manuscript, see *Boswell in Extremes,* 23–24.

35. In a footnote written after Boswell's death, Edmond Malone explains that Trimlestown, like Sibbald, had studied medicine; it is appropriate that Boswell ends his record of the conversation with a quotation from Francis Atterbury, because Atterbury, like Trimlestown's grandfather, lost his title (a bishopric) for supporting the Stuarts (O'Brien, "Barnewall, Robert"; *City and Country Calendar,* 85).

36. "Whoever shall review his life will generally find, that the whole tenor of his conduct has been determined by some accident of no apparent moment, or by a combination of inconsiderable circumstances, acting when his imagination was unoccupied, and his judgment unsettled; and that his principles and actions have taken their colour from some secret infusion, mingled without design in the current of his ideas" (Johnson, *Works,* 4:384).

37. In fact, Boswell's version of Sibbald's religious history is either an inexact recollection or an uncharitable extrapolation. Sibbald records that when his conversion became public he was attacked by a Protestant mob in Edinburgh and fled to London, where he found that "keeping Lent where few good fishes could be had" made him "indisposed." But he attributes his actual reconversion to dismay at the political program of James II (*Memoirs of Sir Robert Sibbald,* 93–94). Three decades after Sibbald's flight to London, the low quality of the seafood there elicited a more active response from Richard Steele, who spent much of his post-*Spectator* career promoting a scheme called the Fish Pool, which was to bring fish alive to the London market in boats designed to carry seawater in their holds (Winton, *Sir Richard Steele, M.P.,* 103–21).

38. Pottle, *Earlier Years,* 48. Lord Trimlestown, a longtime activist for Roman Catholic emancipation in Ireland, had the mortification of seeing his son conform to that island's established Protestant Church.

39. For Steele, see chap. 1, n. 36.

40. Plutarch, *Lives,* 6:261. For Boswell as Plutarchan biographer, see DeMaria Jr. "Plutarch, Johnson, and Boswell," and Dowling, *Boswellian Hero.*

41. For the "Journal of the North Circuit," of 1–19 September 1758, which was written in a series of letters to James Love, see Boswell's letter to William Temple of 16 December 1758 (printed in *Correspondence of James Boswell and William Johnson Temple,* 15–16 and n. 7). Boswell's last known journal entry (printed in *Boswell, the Great Biographer,* 311–12) dates to March 1795; he died in May.

42. Wittgenstein, *Philosophical Investigations,* §279.

43. Mackie, *Rakes, Highwaymen, and Pirates,* 84. Mackie's section on Boswell's paradoxical identification with both Mr. Spectator and Macheath extends a critical tradition, New Historicist/Foucaldian in methodology, whose founding text is Felicity Nussbaum's chapter on Boswell in *The Autobiographical Subject.*

44. Boswell, *Account of Corsica,* 14–15.

45. As Donald J. Newman points out, Boswell had already expressed this idea in a record of a conversation with Lord Kames in October 1762 ("James Boswell, Joseph Addison, and the Spectator," 21).

46. Margery Bailey, whose quotation of Boswell I transcribe, draws the connection between *The Christian Hero* and *The Hypochondriack* in her introduction to the latter (1:23).

47. It would be correct, if uncharitable, to point out that Boswell, who has recorded reading Hume's essays earlier in this same journal entry, does not seem aware of Hume's nuanced and thorough arguments against knowledge of this soul-guaranteeing *"consciousness"* (a term that has a clearly Lockean ring to it), as, for instance, in the famous part 4 of book 1 of the *Treatise of Human Nature*. For Boswell's relatively shallow engagement with the philosophical substance of Hume's thought, see Schwartz, "Boswell and Hume: The Deathbed Interview."

48. This was not to be until 1923, with Margerey Bailey's edition.

49. Ellison, "James Boswell's Revisions of Death."

50. Sher, "'Something That Put Me in Mind of My Father.'"

51. Given that Kames was a legal and economic modernizer and reformer, it is ironic that he chooses, in Boswell's account, an old-fashioned death. According to Philippe Ariès, the "tame death" of early European culture features a simple turning away, while it is the histrionic early modern "death of the self" that indulges in dying speeches (*Hour of Our Death*, 5–29).

52. The account of Johnsonian reception history below stands on the shoulders of recent scholarship; in addition to Deutsch's indispensable *Loving Dr. Johnson,* see Wiltshire, *The Making of Dr. Johnson,* and Hart, *Samuel Johnson and the Culture of Property.*

53. Macaulay, *Critical and Historical Essays,* 92.

54. Ibid., 115.

55. Quoted in Dowling, "Boswell at the Breakfast Table," 124.

Epilogue

1. Dudgeon, *Philosophical Works,* 140. The essay from which this quotation is taken, *A Letter to the Author of the State of the Moral World Considered,* was first published in 1734.

2. "Complete adequacy of the will to the moral law, however, is *holiness,* a perfection of which no rational being in the world is capable at any point of time in his existence. Since this adequacy is nonetheless demanded as practically necessary, it can be encountered only in a progression proceeding *ad infinitum* toward that complete adequacy. . . . This infinite progression, however, is possible only on the presupposition of an *existence* and personality—of the same rational being—continuing *ad infinitum* (which is called the immortality of the soul)" (Kant, *Critique of Practical Reason,* 155).

3. Keats, *Letters,* ed. Rollins, 2:102–3. Subsequent citations are to this edition;

throughout I have retained Keats's emphases and spelling while silently removing a few of Rollins's editorial indications of omitted, canceled, or torn letters.

4. Garrick's "Ode to Shakespeare" is reprinted in Ellis, *That Man Shakespeare,* 76. For the process of Shakespeare's rise to his current status, see Lynch, *Becoming Shakespeare.*

5. *Dramatic Works of William Shakespeare,* 7 vols. (Chiswick, 1814), 1:xvii. Keats's copy is now in the Houghton Library of Harvard University.

6. Quoted in Ellis, *That Man Shakespeare,* 101–4.

7. Indeed, it was Boswell's son, James Boswell Jr., who published Malone's biographical fragment after Malone's death, in 1821, as the second volume of his own twenty-one-volume edition of the plays and poems.

BIBLIOGRAPHY

Addison, Joseph. *Cato. A Tragedy.* The seventh edition. London, 1713.

———. *The Letters of Joseph Addison.* Edited by Walter James Graham. Oxford: Clarendon Press, 1941.

Aeschylus. *The Complete Aeschylus.* Vol. 1, *The Oresteia.* Oxford: Oxford University Press, 2011.

Alkon, Paul. "Boswellian Time." *Studies in Burke and His Time* 14, no. 2 (1972–73): 239–56.

Almond, Philip C. *Heaven and Hell in Enlightenment England.* Cambridge: Cambridge University Press, 1994.

Anderson, Benedict. *Imagined Communities: Reflections on the Origin and Spread of Nationalism.* London: Verso, 1983.

Anson, George. *A Voyage Round the World. . . .* London, 1748.

Arendt, Hannah. *The Human Condition.* Chicago: University of Chicago Press, 1958.

Ariès, Philippe. *The Hour of Our Death.* Translated by Helen Weaver. New York: Oxford University Press, 1991.

Aristotle. *Complete Works.* Edited by Jonathan Barnes. 2 vols. Bollingen Series 71. Princeton, NJ: Princeton University Press, 1995.

Arnold, Matthew. *Essays in Criticism: Second Series.* Edited by S. R. Littlewood. London: Macmillan, 1969.

Articles agreed upon by the archbishops and bishops of both provinces, and the whole clergy, in the Convocation holden at London in the year 1562. London, 1720.

Barker, Anthony David. "Cave, Edward (1691–1754)." In *Oxford Dictionary of National Biography,* edited by H. C. G. Matthew and Brian Harrison. Oxford: Oxford University Press, 2004. http://www.oxforddnb.com/view/article/4921.

Bate, W. J. *The Achievement of Samuel Johnson.* Oxford: Oxford University Press, 1955.

———. *Samuel Johnson.* New York: Harcourt Brace Jovanovich, 1977.

Benjamin, Walter. *Illuminations.* Edited by Hannah Arendt. Translated by Harry Zohn. New York: Schocken Books, 1969.

Berens, Kathleen Inman. "The Sword Unsheathed: Wit in Pilkington's *Memoirs.*" PhD diss., University of California, Berkeley, 1999.

Berman, David. "Deism, Immortality, and the Art of Theological Lying." In *Deism,*

Masonry, and the Enlightenment: Essays Honoring Alfred Owen Aldridge, edited by J. A. Leo Lemay, 61–78. Newark: University of Delaware Press, 1987.

———. "The Repressive Denial of Atheism in Britain in the Seventeenth and Eighteenth Centuries." *Proceedings of the Royal Irish Academy, Section C: Archaeology, Celtic Studies, History, Linguistics, Literature* 82 (1982): 211–46.

Bibliotheca Boswelliana. A Catalogue of the Entire Library of the Late James Boswell, Esq. London, 1825.

Bishop, Samuel. *The Poetical Works.* London, 1796.

Black, Scott. "Social and Literary Form in the *Spectator.*" *Eighteenth-Century Studies* 33, no. 1 (1999): 21–42.

Bogel, Fredric V. *Literature and Insubstantiality in Later Eighteenth-Century England.* Princeton, NJ: Princeton University Press, 1984.

Bond, Donald F., ed. *The Spectator.* 5 vols. Oxford: Clarendon Press, 1965.

———. *The Tatler.* 3 vols. Oxford: Clarendon Press, 1987.

Bond, Richmond P. "Isaac Bickerstaff, Esq." In *Restoration and Eighteenth-Century Literature: Essays in Honor of Alan Duglad McKillop,* 103–24. Rice University Semicentennial Publications. Chicago: University of Chicago Press for William Marsh Rice University, 1963.

Book of Common Prayer, 1662 Version. Introduced by Diarmaid MacCulloch. London: Everyman, 1999.

Boswell, James. *An Account of Corsica, the Journal of a Tour to that Island; and the Memoirs of Pascal Paoli.* Edited by James T. Boulton and T. O. McLoughlin. Oxford: Oxford University Press, 2006.

———. *Boswell: The Applause of the Jury, 1782–1785.* Edited by Irma S. Lustig and Frederick A. Pottle. New York: McGraw-Hill, 1981.

———. *Boswell for the Defence, 1769–1774.* Edited by William K. Wimsatt Jr. and Frederick A. Pottle. New York: McGraw-Hill, 1959.

———. *Boswell in Extremes, 1776–1778.* Edited by Charles McC. Weis and Frederick A. Pottle. New York: McGraw-Hill, 1970.

———. *Boswell on the Grand Tour: Germany and Switzerland, 1764.* Edited by Frederick A. Pottle. New York: McGraw-Hill, 1953.

———. *Boswell, the Great Biographer, 1789–1795.* Edited by Marlies K. Danziger and Frank Brady. New York: McGraw-Hill, 1989.

———. *Boswell in Holland, 1763–1764.* Edited by Frederick A. Pottle. New York: McGraw-Hill, 1952.

———. *Boswell, Laird of Auchinleck, 1778–1782.* Edited by Joseph W. Reed and Frederick A. Pottle. New York: McGraw-Hill, 1977.

———. *Boswell: The Ominous Years, 1774–1776.* Edited by Charles Ryskamp and Frederick A. Pottle. New York: McGraw-Hill, 1963.

———. *Boswell in Search of a Wife, 1766–1769.* Edited by Frank Brady and Frederick A. Pottle. New York: McGraw-Hill, 1956.

———. *The Correspondence of James Boswell and John Johnston of Grange.* Edited by Ralph S. Walker. New York: McGraw-Hill, 1966.

———. *The Correspondence of James Boswell and William Johnson Temple, 1756–1795.*

Vol. 1, *1756–1777*. Edited by Thomas Crawford. New Haven, CT: Yale University Press, 1997.

———. *The Correspondence and Other Papers of James Boswell Relating to the Making of the Life of Johnson*. Edited by Marshall Waingrow. 2nd ed. New Haven, CT: Yale University Press, 2001.

———. *The Hypochondriack*. Edited by Margery Bailey. 2 vols. Stanford, CA: Stanford University Press, 1928.

———. *Journal of a Tour to the Hebrides*. Edited by Frederick A. Pottle and Charles H. Bennett. New York: Viking, 1936.

———. *The Life of Johnson: Edition of the Original Manuscript*. Edited by Marshall Waingrow. 3 vols. New Haven, CT: Yale University Press, 1994–2012.

———. *The Life of Johnson: Together with Journal of a Tour to the Hebrides and Johnson's Diary of a Journey into North Wales*. Edited by George Birkbeck Hill and L. F. Powell. 2nd ed. rev. 6 vols. Oxford: Clarendon Press, 1964.

———. *London Journal, 1762–1763*. Edited by Frederick A. Pottle. New York: McGraw-Hill, 1950.

Brack, O M, and Robert E. Kelley, eds. *The Early Biographies of Samuel Johnson*. Iowa City: University of Iowa Press, 1974.

Braudy, Leo. *The Frenzy of Renown: Fame and Its History*. New York: Oxford University Press, 1986.

Brewer, David. *The Afterlife of Character, 1726–1825*. Philadelphia: University of Pennsylvania Press, 2005.

Brown, Marshall. *Preromanticism*. Stanford, CA: Stanford University Press, 1991.

Budd, Adam. "Why Clarissa Must Die: Richardson's Tragedy and Editorial Heroism." *Eighteenth-Century Life* 31, no. 3 (Fall 2007): 1–28.

Bueler, Lois E., ed. *Clarissa: The Eighteenth-Century Response, 1747–1804*. 2 vols. New York: AMS Press, 2010.

Bunyan, John. *Grace Abounding to the Chief of Sinners*. Edited by Roger Sharrock. Oxford: Clarendon Press, 1962.

———. *Grace Abounding to the Chief of Sinners, and, The Pilgrim's Progress from This World to That Which Is to Come*. Edited by Roger Sharrock. London: Oxford University Press, 1966.

Butler, Joseph. *The Analogy of Religion*. London, 1736.

———. *The Analogy of Religion*. Introduced by Ronald Bayne. London: J. M. Dent, 1906.

Camden, William. *Remains Concerning Britain*. Edited by R. D. Dunn. Toronto: University of Toronto Press, 1984.

Carlyle, Thomas. *Samuel Johnson*. London, 1853.

Castle, Terry. *Clarissa's Ciphers: Meaning and Disruption in Richardson's "Clarissa."* Ithaca, NY: Cornell University Press, 1982.

Chambers, William. *A Week at Welwyn*. London, 1873.

Champion, J. A. I. *The Pillars of Priestcraft Shaken: The Church of England and Its Enemies, 1660–1730*. Cambridge: Cambridge University Press, 1992.

Chesterfield, 4th Earl of (Philip Dormer Stanhope). *Letters*. Edited by Bomany Dobrée. 6 vols. New York: AMS Press, 1968.

Chibka, Robert L. "The Stranger within Young's *Conjectures*." *ELH* 53, no. 3 (Fall 1986): 541–65.

Christensen, Jerome. *Practicing Enlightenment: Hume and the Formation of a Literary Career*. Madison: University of Wisconsin Press, 1987.

The City and Country Calendar; or Irish Court Registry, for the Year of Our Lord 1796. Dublin, 1796.

Clark, J. C. D. *English Society, 1688–1832: Ideology, Social Structure, and Political Practice during the Ancien Regime*. Cambridge: Cambridge University Press, 1985.

Clarke, Norma. *Queen of the Wits*. London: Faber and Faber, 2008.

Cowper, William. "The Cast-away." In *Eighteenth-Century Poetry: An Annotated Anthology*. Edited by David Fairer and Christine Gerrard, 552–53. Oxford: Blackwell, 1999.

Crum, M. C. "A Manuscript of Essays by Addison." *Bodleian Library Record* 5, no. 2 (1954): 98–103.

Damrosch, Leo. *God's Plot and Man's Stories: Studies in the Fictional Imagination from Milton to Fielding*. Chicago: University of Chicago Press, 1985.

———. *Samuel Johnson and the Tragic Sense*. Princeton, NJ: Princeton University Press, 1972.

DeMaria, Robert, Jr. *The Life of Samuel Johnson: A Critical Biography*. Oxford: Blackwell, 1993.

———. "Plutarch, Johnson, and Boswell: The Classical Tradition of Biography at the End of the Eighteenth Century." *Eighteenth-Century Novel* 6–7 (2009): 79–102.

Deutsch, Helen. *Loving Dr. Johnson*. Chicago: University of Chicago Press, 2005.

Dixon, Rosemary. "The Publishing of John Tillotson's Collected Works, 1695–1757." *Library: The Transactions of the Bibliographical Society* 8, no. 2 (June 2007): 154–81.

Dodsley, Robert, ed. *The Preceptor*. 2 vols. London, 1748.

Doody, Margaret Anne. "The Gnostic Clarissa." *Eighteenth-Century Fiction* 11, no. 1 (October 1998): 49–78.

Dowling, William C. "Boswell at the Breakfast Table." *New England Quarterly* 83, no. 1 (March 2010): 124.

———. *The Boswellian Hero*. Athens: University of Georgia Press, 1979.

Dudgeon, William. *The Philosophical Works of William Dudgeon*. N.p., 1965.

Eagleton, Terry. *The Rape of Clarissa: Writing, Sexuality, and Class Struggle in Samuel Richardson*. Minneapolis: University of Minnesota Press, 1982.

Eaves, T. C. Duncan, and Ben D. Kimpel. *Samuel Richardson: A Biography*. Oxford: Clarendon Press, 1971.

Eissler, Kurt. *Goethe: A Psychoanalytic Study, 1775–1786*. 2 vols. Detroit: Wayne State University Press, 1963.

Ellis, David. *That Man Shakespeare*. Mountfield, East Sussex: Helm Information, 2005.

Ellison, Katherine. "James Boswell's Revisions of Death as 'The Hypochondriack' and in His London Journals." *Eighteenth-Century Fiction* 21, no. 1 (Fall 2008): 37–59.

Else, Gerald F. *Aristotle's "Poetics": The Argument.* Cambridge, MA: Harvard University Press, 1967.

Emerson, Roger L. "Latitudinarianism and the English Deists." In *Deism, Masonry, and the Enlightenment: Essays Honoring Alfred Owen Aldridge,* edited by J. A. Leo Lemay, 19–48. Newark: University of Delaware Press, 1987.

Erasmus, Desiderius. *The Praise of Folly.* Edited and translated by Clarence H. Miller with an afterword by William H. Gass. 2nd ed. New Haven, CT: Yale University Press, 2003.

Fell, John. *Life of the Most Learned, Reverend and Pious Dr. H Hammond.* London, 1661.

Fenn, Richard K. *The Persistence of Purgatory.* Cambridge: Cambridge University Press, 1995.

Fielding, Henry. *A Journey from This World to the Next and The Journal of a Voyage to Lisbon.* Edited by Ian A. Bell and Andrew Varney. Oxford: Oxford University Press, 1997.

———. *Tom Jones.* Edited by Martin C. Battestin and Fredson Bowers. 2 vols. [Middletown, CT]: Wesleyan, 1975.

Fielding, Sarah. *Remarks on "Clarissa."* Edited by Peter Sabor. Los Angeles: William Andrews Clark Memorial Library, University of California, 1985.

Flesch, William. *Comeuppance.* Cambridge, MA: Harvard University Press, 2007.

Flew, Antony. "Locke and the Problem of Personal Identity." *Philosophy* 26, no. 96 (January 1951): 53–68.

Flynn, Carol Houlihan. *Samuel Richardson: A Man of Letters.* Princeton, NJ: Princeton University Press, 1982.

Folkenflik, Robert. *The Culture of Autobiography: Constructions of Self-Representation.* Stanford, CA: Stanford University Press, 1993.

Forster, Harold. *Edward Young: The Poet of Night Thoughts, 1683–1765.* Alburgh, Norfolk: Erskine, 1986.

Fox, Christopher. *Locke and the Scriblerians: Identity and Consciousness in Early Eighteenth-Century Britain.* Berkeley: University of California Press, 1988.

Franklin, Benjamin. *Writings.* Edited by J. A. Leo Lemay. Library of America 37. New York: Literary Classics of the United States, 1987.

Freud, Sigmund. *The Interpretation of Dreams.* Edited by Richie Robertson. Translated by Joyce Crick. Oxford: Oxford University Press, 1999.

Friedman, Emily. "The End(s) of Richardson's *Sir Charles Grandison.*" *SEL: Studies in English Literature, 1500–1900* 52, no. 3 (2012): 651–67.

Frye, Northrop. *The Anatomy of Criticism.* New York: Atheneum, 1965.

Gay, Peter, ed. *Deism: An Anthology.* Princeton, NJ: Van Nostrant, 1968.

Gee, Sophie. *Making Waste: Leftovers and the Eighteenth-Century Imagination.* Princeton, NJ: Princeton University Press, 2010.

Gentleman's Magazine. Vols. 1–20. Reprinted. London: Pickering and Chatto, 1998.

Goethe, Johann Wolfgang von. *Dichtung und Wahrheit.* 2 vols. Cologne: Könemann,

1998. Translated by R. O. Moon as *Autobiography, Poetry and Truth from My Own Life*. Washington: Public Affairs Press, 1949.

———. *Werke*. Edited by Friedmar Apel et al. 6 vols. Frankfurt: Insel, 1998.

Goodwin, Frederick K., and Kay R. Jamison. *Manic-Depressive Illness: Bipolar Disorders and Recurrent Depression*. 2nd ed. New York: Oxford University Press, 2007.

Greene, Donald. "Boswell's *Life* as 'Literary Biography.'" In *Boswell's "Life of Johnson": New Questions, New Answers*, edited by John A. Vance, 161–71. Athens: University of Georgia Press, 1985.

Gregg, Stephen H. "'A Truly Christian Hero': Religion, Effeminacy, and Nation in the Writings of the Societies for the Reformation of Manners." *Eighteenth-Century Life* 25, no. 1 (2001): 17–28.

Griffin, Dustin. *Literary Patronage in England, 1650–1800*. Cambridge: Cambridge University Press, 1996.

Habermas, Jürgen. *The Structural Transformation of the Public Sphere: An Inquiry into a Category of Bourgeois Society*. Translated by Thomas Burger with the assistance of Frederick Lawrence. Cambridge, MA: MIT Press, 1989.

Halliwell, Stephen. *Aristotle's Poetics*. Chicago: University of Chicago Press, 1998.

Harris, Jocelyn. *Samuel Richardson*. Cambridge: Cambridge University Press, 1987.

Hart, Kevin. *Samuel Johnson and the Culture of Property*. Cambridge: Cambridge University Press, 1999.

Havens, Raymond Dexter. *The Influence of Milton on English Poetry*. Cambridge, MA: Harvard University Press, 1922.

Hawkins, John. *The Life of Samuel Johnson, LL.D.* Edited by O M Brack. Athens: University of Georgia Press, 2009.

Hensley, David C. "*Clarissa*, Coleridge, Kant, and Klopstock: Emotionalism as Pietistic Intertext in Anglo-German Romanticism." *Studies in the Literary Imagination* 28, no. 1 (Spring 1995): 125–47.

———. "Thomas Edwards and the Dialectics of Clarissa's Death Scene." *Eighteenth-Century Life* 16 (November 1992): 130–52.

Hill, G. B., ed. *Johnsonian Miscellanies*. 2 vols. Oxford: Clarendon Press, 1897.

Holmes, Richard. *Dr. Johnson and Mr. Savage*. New York: Pantheon, 1994.

Horace. *Odes and Epodes*. Edited and translated by Niall Rudd. Cambridge, MA: Harvard University Press, 2004.

Howat, Gerald M. D. "Pycroft, James (1813–1895)." In *Oxford Dictionary of National Biography*, edited by H. C. G. Matthew and Brian Harrison. Oxford: Oxford University Press, 2004. http://www.oxforddnb.com/view/article/22915.

Hume, David. *A Dissertation on the Passions and The Natural History of Religion*. Edited by Tom L. Beauchamp. Oxford: Clarendon Press, 2007.

———. *Enquiries Concerning Human Understanding and Concerning the Principles of Morals*. Edited by L. A. Selby-Bigge and P. H. Nidditch. Oxford: Clarendon Press, 1975.

———. *Essays Moral, Political, and Literary*. Edited by Eugene F. Miller. Indianapolis: Liberty Fund, 1985.

———. *Letters of David Hume.* Edited by J. Y. T. Greig. 2 vols. Oxford: Clarendon Press, 1932.

Hunter, Michael. "The Problem of 'Atheism' in Early Modern England." *Transactions of the Royal Historical Society,* 5th ser., 35 (1985): 135–57.

Hunter, Michael, and David Wootton, eds. *Atheism from the Reformation to the Enlightenment.* Oxford: Clarendon Press, 1992.

Hunter, Paul. *Before Novels: The Cultural Context of Eighteenth-Century English Fiction.* New York: Norton, 1990.

Irlam, Shaun. *Elations.* Stanford, CA: Stanford University Press, 1999.

Irwin, George. *Samuel Johnson: A Personality in Conflict.* Auckland: Auckland University Press, 1971.

Jackson, H. J. "A General Theory of Fame in the *Lives of the Poets.*" *Age of Johnson: A Scholarly Annual* 19 (2009): 9–20.

———. *Marginalia: Readers Writing in Books.* New Haven, CT: Yale University Press, 2001.

Jackson, Spencer. "*Clarissa's* Political Theology and the Alternative Modernity of God, Death, and Writing." *Eighteenth Century: Theory and Interpretation* (forthcoming).

Jakobson, Roman. "The Metaphoric and Metonymic Poles." In Roman Jakobson and Morris Hale, *Fundamentals of Language,* 76–82. Hague: Mouton, 1956.

James, William. *The Varieties of Religious Experience.* Introduced by John E. Smith. Cambridge, MA: Harvard University Press, 1985.

Jamison, Kay R. *Touched with Fire: Manic-Depressive Illness and the Artistic Temperament.* New York: Free Press, 1993.

Johnson, Samuel. *A Dictionary of the English Language.* 2 vols. London, 1755.

———. *A Dictionary of the English Language.* 6th ed. 2 vols. London, 1785.

———. *The Letters of Samuel Johnson.* Edited by Bruce Redford. 5 vols. Princeton, NJ: Princeton University Press, 1992.

———. *The Yale Edition of the Works of Samuel Johnson.* 23 vols. New Haven, CT: Yale University Press, 1958–2011.

Joling-van der Sar, Gerda. *The Spiritual Side of Samuel Richardson: Mysticism, Behmenism, and Millenarianism in an Eighteenth-Century English Novelist.* Leiden: University of Leiden, 2003.

Juvenal and Persius. *Works.* Edited and translated by Susanna Morton Braund. Cambridge, MA: Harvard University Press, 2004.

Kant, Immanuel. *Critique of Practical Reason.* Translated by Werner S. Pluhar. Indianapolis: Hackett, 2002.

Keats, John. *The Letters of John Keats, 1814–1821.* Edited by Hyder Edward Rollins. 2 vols. Cambridge, MA: Harvard University Press, 1958.

Kernan, Alvin. *Printing Techonology, Letters, and Samuel Johnson.* Princeton, NJ: Princeton University Press, 1987.

Keymer, Tom. *Richardson's "Clarissa" and the Eighteenth-Century Reader.* Cambridge: Cambridge University Press, 1992.

Kind, John Louis. *Edward Young in Germany*. New York: Columbia University Press, 1906.

King, John. *William Cowper: A Biography*. Durham, NC: Duke University Press, 1986.

Klopstock, Friedrich Gottlieb. *Ausgewählte Werke*. Edited by Karl August Schleiden. Munich: Carl Hanser, 1962.

Kunin, Aaron. "Shakespeare's Preservation Fantasy." *PMLA* 124, no. 1 (2009): 92–106.

Lakoff, George, and Mark Turner. *More than Cool Reason: A Field Guide to Poetic Metaphor*. Chicago: University of Chicago Press, 1989.

Lang, Bernard. "Meeting in Heaven according to John Bunyan in *The Pilgrim's Progress*." In *Tod und Jenseits in der Schriftkultur der Frühen Neuzeit*, edited by Marion Kobelt-Groch and Cornelia Niekus Moore, 119–37. Wiesbaden: Harrassowitz Verlag in Kommission, 2008.

Larkin, Philip. *Collected Poems*. Edited by Anthony Thwaite. New York: Farrar, Straus & Giroux, 1989.

Le Goff, Jacques. *The Birth of Purgatory*. Translated by Arthur Goldhammer. Chicago: University of Chicago Press, 1984.

Leishman, J. B. *Themes and Variations in Shakespeare's Sonnets*. New York: Harper & Row, 1966.

Lipking, Lawrence. *Samuel Johnson: The Life of an Author*. Cambridge, MA: Harvard University Press, 1998.

———. "Learning to Read Johnson: The *Vision of Theodore* and *The Vanity of Human Wishes*." *ELH* 43, no. 6 (1976): 517–37.

Locke, John. *Essay Concerning Human Understanding*. Edited by Peter H. Nidditch. Oxford: Clarendon Press, 1975.

Lowe, N. F. "Why Swift Killed Partridge." *Swift Studies: The Annual of the Ehrenpreis Center* 6 (1991): 70–82.

Luctus Britannici: or The Tears of the British Muses; for the Death of John Dryden, Esq. London, 1700.

Lynch, Jack. *Becoming Shakespeare*. New York: Walker, 2007.

Macaulay, Thomas Babington. *Critical and Historical Essays*. Edited by Hugh Trevor-Roper. New York: McGraw-Hill, 1965.

Mackie, Erin Skye. *Market à la Mode: Fashion, Commodity, and Gender in the "Tatler" and the "Spectator."* Baltimore, MD: Johns Hopkins University Press, 1997.

———. *Rakes, Highwaymen, and Pirates*. Baltimore, MD: Johns Hopkins University Press, 2009.

Martin, Raymond, and John Barresi. *Naturalization of the Soul: Self and Personal Identity in the Eighteenth Century*. London: Routledge, 2000.

Mascuch, Michael. *Origins of the Individualist Self: Autobiography and Self-Identity in England, 1591–1791*. Cambridge: Polity Press, 1997.

McCrea, Brian. *Addison and Steele Are Dead: The English Department, Its Canon, and the Professionalization of Literary Criticism*. Newark: University of Delaware Press, 1990.

McDannell, Colleen, and Bernard Lang. *Heaven: A History.* 2nd ed. New Haven, CT: Yale University Press, 2001.

Milton, John. *The Complete Poetry of John Milton.* Edited by John T. Shawcross. Rev. ed. Garden City, NY: Anchor Books, 1971.

———. *Complete Prose Works.* General editor Don M. Wolfe. 8 vols. New Haven, CT: Yale University Press, 1953–82.

Moody, Elizabeth. *Poetical Trifles.* London, 1798.

Montgomery, James. *Lectures on General Literature, Poetry &c. Delivered at the Royal Institution in 1830 and 1831.* New York: Harper & Brothers, 1838.

Mossner, Ernest Campbell. *The Life of David Hume.* 2nd ed. Oxford: Clarendon Press, 1980.

Nace, Nicholas D. "Richardson's Charnel House: Pamela, Lovelace, and 'The Skull of King Philip.'" *Notes and Queries* 57, no. 1 (2010): 89–91.

Nettleton, George H., and Arthur E. Case, eds. *British Dramatists from Dryden to Sheridan.* Revised by George Winchester Stone Jr. Carbondale: Southern Illinois University Press, 1969.

New, Melvyn, and Gerard Reedy, eds. *Theology in the Age of Johnson: Resisting Secularism.* Newark: University of Delaware Press, 2012.

Newman, Donald J. "James Boswell, Joseph Addison, and the Spectator in the Mirror." In *James Boswell: Psychological Interpretations,* edited by Donald J. Newman, 1–31. New York: St. Martin's, 1995.

The Nine Muses, or Poems Written by Nine Several Ladies upon the Death of the Late Famous John Dryden, Esq. London, 1700.

Nussbaum, Felicity. *The Autobiographical Subject.* Baltimore, MD: Johns Hopkins University Press, 1995.

O'Brien, Gerard. "Barnewall, Robert, styled twelfth Baron Trimleston (c. 1704–1779)." In *Oxford Dictionary of National Biography,* edited by H. C. G. Matthew and Brian Harrison. Oxford: Oxford University Press, 2004. http://www.oxforddnb.com/view/article/63654.

Odell, D. W. "The Argument of Young's *Conjectures on Original Composition.*" *Studies in Philology* 78, no. 1 (Winter 1981): 87–106.

———. "Young's *Night Thoughts:* Christian Rationalism or Fideism?" *English Language Notes* 43, no. 1 (2005): 48–58.

Ovid. *Metamorphoses.* Edited and translated by Frank Justus Miller. Revised by G. P. Goold. 3rd ed. 2 vols. Cambridge, MA: Harvard University Press, 1977–84.

Panofsky, Erwin. *Meaning in the Visual Arts.* New York: Doubleday, 1955.

Parker, Blanford. *The Triumph of Augustan Poetics.* Cambridge: Cambridge University Press, 1998.

Petit, Henry. "The English Rejection of Young's *Night Thoughts.*" *University of Colorado Studies: Series in Language and Literature* 6 (1957): 23–38.

Phillipson, Nicholas. *Adam Smith: An Enlightened Life.* London: Penguin, 2010.

———. *David Hume: The Philosopher as Historian.* New Haven, CT: Yale University Press, 2012.

Pilkington, Laetitia. *Memoirs of Laetitia Pilkington*. Edited by A. C. Elias Jr. 2 vols. Athens: University of Georgia Press, 1997.

Pindar. *The Complete Odes*. Edited by Stephen Instone. Translated by Anthony Verity. Oxford: Oxford University Press, 2007.

Pindar, Peregrine [pseud.]. *Ode to the Hero of Finsbury Square*. London, 1795.

Pindar, Peter [John Walcot]. *Bozzy and Piozzi, or, the British Biographers, a Town Eclogue*. London, 1786.

Piozzi, Hester Lynch. *Anecdotes of the Late Samuel Johnson, LL.D*. London, 1786.

Plutarch. *Lives*. Translated by Bernadotte Perrin. 11 vols. London: William Heinemann, 1928.

Pocock, J. G. A. *Barbarism and Religion*. Vol. 1, *The Enlightenments of Edward Gibbon, 1737–1764*. Cambridge: Cambridge University Press, 1999.

Pollock, Anthony. "Neutering Addison and Steele: Aesthetic Failure and the Spectatorial Public Sphere." *ELH* 74, no. 3 (2007): 707–34.

Pope, Alexander. *The Dunciad*. Edited by James Sutherland. London: Methuen, 1953.

———. *Imitations of Horace*. Edited by John Butt. London: Methuen, 1953.

Potkay, Adam. *The Passion for Happiness: Samuel Johnson and David Hume*. Ithaca, NY: Cornell University Press, 2000.

Pottle, Frederick A. *James Boswell, the Earlier Years, 1740–1769*. New York: McGraw-Hill, 1985.

Pycroft, James. "Dr. Johnson's Watch." *Notes and Queries*, 5th ser., 7 (March 1871): 243.

———. "Dr. Johnson's Watch." *Notes and Queries*, 6th ser., 12 (November 1883): 393.

———. *Oxford Memories: A Retrospect after Fifty Years*. 2 vols. London: R. Bentley & Son, 1886.

Radner, John B. "'A Very Exact Picture of His Life': Johnson's Role in Writing the *Life of Johnson*." *Age of Johnson: A Scholarly Annual* 7 (1996): 299–342.

Rapin, René. *The Whole Critical Works of Monsieur Rapin*. 2 vols. London, 1706.

Reade, Aleyn Lyell. *Johnsonian Gleanings*. 11 vols. New York: Octogon, 1968.

Redford, Bruce. *Designing the Life of Johnson*. Oxford: Oxford University Press, 2002.

Relke, Diana M. A. "In Search of Mrs. Pilkington." In *Gender at Work*, edited by Ann Messenger, 114–149. Detroit: Wayne State University Press, 1990.

Richardson, Samuel. *Clarissa*. 1st ed. 7 vols. London, 1747–48.

———. *Clarissa*. 3rd ed. 8 vols. London, 1750.

———. *Clarissa*. Edited by Angus Ross. London: Penguin, 1985.

———. *The Correspondence of Samuel Richardson*. Edited by Anna Laetitia Barbauld. 6 vols. London: 1804.

———. *Correspondence with George Cheyne and Thomas Edwards*. Edited by David E. Shuttleton and John A. Dussinger. Cambridge: Cambridge University Press, 2014.

———. *Early Works*. Edited by Alexander Petit. Cambridge: Cambridge University Press, 2012.

―――. *Pamela, or, Virtue Rewarded.* Edited by Albert J. Rivero. Cambridge: Cambridge University Press, 2011.

―――. *Pamela in Her Exalted Condition.* Edited by Albert J. Rivero. Cambridge: Cambridge University Press, 2012.

―――. *Selected Letters of Samuel Richardson.* Edited by John Carroll. Oxford: Clarendon Press, 1964.

―――. *Sir Charles Grandison.* Edited by Jocelyn Harris. 3 vols. London: Oxford University Press, 1972.

Ricks, Christopher. *The Force of Poetry.* Oxford: Clarendon Press, 1984.

Rivers, Isabel. *Reason, Grace, and Sentiment: A Study of the Language of Religion and Ethics in England, 1660–1780.* 2 vols. Cambridge: Cambridge University Press, 1991–2000.

Rothstein, Eric. *Gleaning Modernity: Earlier Eighteenth-Century Literature and the Modernizing Process.* Newark: University of Delaware Press, 2007.

Rousseau, Jean-Jacques. *Confessions.* Translated by Christopher Kelly. Edited by Christopher Kelly, Roger D. Masters, and Peter G. Stillman. Hanover, NH: University Press of New England, 1995.

Royce, Josiah. *An Humble Address and Earnest Appeal.* Gloucester, 1775.

Rymer, Thomas. *The Critical Works.* Edited by Curt A. Zimansky. New Haven, CT: Yale University Press, 1956.

Sachs, Arieh. "Samuel Johnson on 'The Vacuity of Life.'" *SEL: Studies in English Literature 1500–1900* 3, no. 3 (1963): 345–63.

Sallust. *Sallust.* Edited by J. C. Rolfe. London: W. Heinemann, 1921.

Schwartz, Richard B. "Boswell and Hume: The Deathbed Interview." In *New Light on Boswell,* edited by Greg Clingham, 116–125. Cambridge: Cambridge University Press, 1991.

Scott, John. *The Christian Life.* London, 1681.

Seccombe, Thomas. "Mudge, Thomas (1715/16–1794)." Revised by David Penney. In *Oxford Dictionary of National Biography,* edited by H. C. G. Matthew and Brian Harrison. Oxford: Oxford University Press, 2004. http://www.oxforddnb.com/view/article/22915.

Seigel, Jerrold, *The Idea of the Self.* Cambridge: Cambridge University Press, 2005.

Sell, Alan. *Locke and the Eighteenth-Century Divines.* Cardiff: University of Wales Press, 1997.

Shaftesbury, Earl of (Anthony Ashley Cooper). *Characteristics of Men, Manners, Opinions, Times.* Edited by Philip Ayres. 2 vols. Oxford: Clarendon Press, 1999.

Shakespeare, William. *The Dramatic Works of William Shakespeare.* With a life of the author by John Britton. 7 vols. Chiswick, 1814.

―――. *The Norton Shakespeare.* Edited by Stephen Greenblatt et al. New York: W. W. Norton, 1997.

Sher, Richard B. *Church and University in the Scottish Enlightenment: The Moderate Literati of Edinburgh.* Princeton, NJ: Princeton University Press, 1985.

―――. "'Something That Put Me in Mind of My Father': Boswell and Lord Kames."

In *Boswell: Citizen of the World, Man of Letters,* edited by Irma S. Lustig, 64–86. Lexington: University Press of Kentucky, 1995.

Sherlock, William. *A Practical Discourse Concerning Death.* London, 1689.

Sherman, Stuart. *Telling Time: Clocks, Diaries, and English Diurnal Form, 1660–1785.* Chicago: University of Chicago Press, 1996.

Sibbald, Sir Robert. *The Memoirs of Sir Robert Sibbald.* Edited by Francis Paget Hett. London: Humphrey Milford, 1932.

Sidney, Philip. *Miscellaneous Prose of Sir Philip Sidney.* Edited by Katherine Duncan-Jones and J. A. van Dorsten. Oxford: Clarendon Press, 1973.

Sitter, John. *Literary Loneliness in Mid-Eighteenth-Century England.* Ithaca, NY: Cornell University Press, 1982.

Smallwood, Philip. "Annotated Immortality: Lonsdale's Johnson." *Eighteenth-Century Life* 31, no. 3 (2007): 76–84.

Smith, Adam. *Lectures on Rhetoric and Belles Lettres.* Edited by J. C. Bryce. Indianapolis: Liberty Fund, 1985.

Soni, Vivavsan. *Mourning Happiness: Narrative and the Politics of Modernity.* Ithaca, NY: Cornell University Press, 2010.

Sophocles. *The Complete Sophocles.* Vol. 1, *The Theban Plays.* Edited by Peter Burian and Alan Shapiro. Oxford: Oxford University Press, 2011.

Sorkin, David. *The Religious Enlightenment: Protestants, Jews, and Catholics from London to Vienna.* Princeton, NJ: Princeton University Press, 2008.

Spadafora, David. *The Idea of Progress in Eighteenth-Century Britain.* New Haven, CT: Yale University Press, 1990.

Spenser, Edmund. *The Faerie Queene.* Edited by A. C. Hamilton, Hiroshi Yamashita, and Toshiyuki Suzuki. Harlow, England: Longman, 2001.

Steele, Richard. *The Christian Hero.* Edited by Rae Blanchard. London: H. Milford, Oxford University Press, 1932.

———. *The Conscious Lovers.* In *British Dramatists from Dryden to Sheridan,* edited by George H. Nettleton and Arthur E. Case, revised by George Winchester Stone Jr., 435–70. Carbondale: Southern Illinois University Press, 1969.

———. *The Correspondence of Richard Steele.* Edited by Rae Blanchard. London: H. Milford, Oxford University Press, 1941.

Stephens, John Calhoun, ed. *The Guardian.* Lexington: University Press of Kentucky, 1982.

Stevens, George Alexander. *Songs, Comic, and Satyrical.* London, 1772.

Stevens, Wallace. *The Palm at the End of the Mind: Selected Poems and a Play.* Edited by Holly Stevens. New York: Vintage, 1971.

Sterne, Laurence. *Tristram Shandy.* Edited by Melvyn New and Joan New. 3 vols. Gainesville: University Press of Florida, 1978–84.

Stewart, Carol. *The Eighteenth-Century Novel and the Secularization of Ethics.* Burlington, VT: Ashgate, 2010.

Stuber, Florian. "*Clarissa:* A Religious Novel?" *Studies in the Literary Imagination* 28, no. 1 (Spring 1995): 105–24.

Suarez, Michael. "Johnson's Christian Thought." In *The Cambridge Companion to*

Samuel Johnson, edited by Greg Clingham, 192–208. Cambridge: Cambridge University Press, 1997.

Sullivan, Robert E. *John Toland and the Deist Controversy: A Study in Adaptations.* Cambridge, MA: Harvard University Press, 1982.

Sutherland, James Runcieman. *The Restoration Newspaper and Its Development.* Cambridge: Cambridge University Press, 1986.

Swift, Jonathan. *Bickerstaff Papers: And Pamphlets on the Church.* Edited by Herbert Davis. Oxford: Basil Blackwell, 1957.

———. *The Poems of Jonathan Swift.* Edited by Harold Williams. 2nd ed. 3 vols. Oxford: Oxford University Press, 1958.

Syba, Michelle. "After Design: Joseph Addison Discovers Beauties." *SEL: Studies in English Literature, 1500–1900* 49, no. 3 (2009): 615–35.

Tate, Nahum. *King Lear.* In *Shakespeare Made Fit: Restoration Adaptations of Shakespeare,* edited by Sandra Clark. London: J. M. Dent, 1997, 291–374.

Taylor, Charles. *A Secular Age.* Cambridge, MA: Belknap Press of Harvard University Press, 2007.

Taylor, E. Derek. *Reason and Religion in "Clarissa": Samuel Richardson and "The Famous Mr. Norris, of Bemerton."* Farnham, UK: Ashgate, 2009.

Thomas, Keith. *The Ends of Life: Roads to Fulfilment in Early Modern England.* Oxford: Oxford University Press, 2009.

———. *Religion and the Decline of Magic.* London: Penguin, 1991.

Thomson, James. *The Seasons and The Castle of Indolence.* Edited by James Sambrook. Oxford: Clarendon Press, 1987.

———. *Winter: A Poem.* London, 1726.

Thorne, Christian. *The Dialectic of Counter-Enlightenment.* Cambridge, MA: Harvard University Press, 2009.

Tillotson, John. *The Works of the Most Reverend Dr. John Tillotson.* London, 1696.

Tracy, Clarence Rupert. *The Artificial Bastard.* Cambridge, MA: Harvard University Press, 1953.

Turnbull, Gordon. "Boswell and Sympathy: The Trial and Execution of John Reid." In *New Light on Boswell,* edited by Greg Clingham, 104–15. Cambridge: Cambridge University Press, 1991.

Van Sickle, John. "The Book-Roll and Some Conventions of the Poetic Book." *Arethusa* 13, no. 1 (1980): 5–42.

Walker, D. P. *The Decline of Hell: Seventeenth-Century Discussions of Eternal Torment.* Chicago: University of Chicago Press, 1964.

Walker, Robert G. *Eighteenth-Century Arguments for Immortality and Johnson's "Rasselas."* ELS Monograph Series 9. Victoria, BC: English Literary Studies, University of Victoria, 1977.

Wanko, Cheryl. "The Making of a Minor Poet: Edward Young and Literary Taxonomy." *English Studies* 72, no. 4 (1991): 355–67.

Warburton, William. *The Divine Legation of Moses Demonstrated.* 2 vols. London, 1738–41.

———. *The Principles of Natural and Revealed Religion Occasionally Opened and Explained.* 2 vols. London, 1753–54.

Warner, William. *Reading Clarissa: The Struggles of Interpretation.* New Haven, CT: Yale University Press, 1979.

Watt, Ian. *The Rise of the Novel: Studies in Defoe, Richardson, and Fielding.* Berkeley: University of California Press, 1971.

Weber, Harold. *Memory, Print and Gender in England, 1653–1759.* New York: Palgrave Macmillan, 2008.

Wehrs, Donald R. "Irony, Storytelling, and the Conflict of Interpretation in *Clarissa.*" *ELH* 53, no. 4 (Winter 1986): 759–77.

———. "Novelistic Redemption and the History of Grace: Practical Theology and Literary Form in Richardson's *Pamela* and Fielding's *Joseph Andrews.*" In *Theology and Literature in the Age of Johnson,* edited by Melvyn New and Gerard Reedy, 1–26. Newark: University of Delaware Press, 2012.

Weinbrot, Howard. *Literature, Religion, and the Evolution of Culture, 1660–1780.* Baltimore, MD: Johns Hopkins University Press, 2013.

Wiltshire, John. *The Making of Dr. Johnson.* Crowham Manor, UK: Helm Information, 2009.

Winton, Calhoun. *Sir Richard Steele, M.P.: The Later Career.* Baltimore, MD: Johns Hopkins University Press, 1970.

Wittgenstein, Ludwig. *Philosophical Investigations.* Translated by G. E. M. Anscombe. Oxford: Blackwell, 1968.

Wolff, Cynthia Griffin. *Samuel Richardson and the Eighteenth-Century Puritan Character.* Hamden, CT: Shoe String Press, 1972.

Wootton, David. "New Histories of Atheism." In *Atheism from the Reformation to the Enlightenment,* edited by Michael Hunter and David Wootton, 13–53. Oxford: Clarendon Press, 1992.

Young, B. W. *Religion and Enlightenment in Eighteenth-Century England.* Oxford: Clarendon Press, 1998.

Young, Edward. *Conjectures on Original Composition.* Edited by Edith J. Morley. Manchester: Manchester University Press, 1918.

———. *Correspondence of Edward Young.* Edited by Henry Petit. Oxford: Clarendon Press, 1971.

———. *Night Thoughts.* Edited by Stephen Cornford. Cambridge: Cambridge University Press, 1989.

INDEX

Account of Corsica (Boswell), 154, 167, 169, 170
Adair, Robin, 118, 130, 131
Addison, Joseph: on afterlife as trajectory, 28, 107; on assembled sets of the *Spectator,* 187n34; on authors as their works, 117; on benevolent creator and immortality, 84; *Cato,* 37, 51, 160, 161, 166; deathbed scene, 37, 50, 51–52; on diaries, 145, 147; on Enlightened afterlife, 4, 10; on human improvement, 110; Hume influenced by, 10; Johnson influenced by, 140, 143, 144, 200n30; and Johnson on Hell, 135; as literary critic, 21; on our souls continuing as we made them, 29; Pilkington's *Memoirs* compared with, 116; positions himself at moral and social center of British society, 16; reuses his unpublished writings, 187n32; Richardson's *Clarissa's* pastiche of, 87; social status of, 115; Steele on, 34–35; stepson Lord Warwick, 170; on virtue and resurrection, 26–27; on writing on deadline, 186n27; Young as disciple of, 37; Young's *Conjectures on Original Composition* on, 38, 50–52, 176. See also *Spectator; Tatler*
Adventurer, 142, 143
Aeschylus, 109–10
afterlife. *See* immortality
Agamemnon (Aeschylus), 109–10

Alkon, Paul, 157, 158
Analogy of Religions (Butler), 64, 66–70, 79–80, 104, 175
Anderson, Benedict, 22–23
Anecdotes (Piozzi), 2, 156
Anglicanism: Book of Common Prayer, 30, 135; Boswell and, 160; versus Calvinism and Methodism, 69; emphasis shifts to personal moral conduct, 8–9, 183n27; empiricism adapted by, 66; on immortality, 183n28; moderate worldview of, 61; on moral formation over time, 29; moral philosophy in, 64; in Pilkington's *Memoirs,* 129; in Richardson's *Clarissa,* 79, 192n7; Thirty-Nine Articles, 72; Warburton's defense of, 74, 76
Anson, George, 184n43
Apology (Cibber), 126
Arendt, Hannah, 4–5, 149–50, 157
Ariès, Philippe, 208n51
Aristotle, 107–10
Arminian Magazine, 16
Arnold, Matthew, 2
atheism, 61–62, 66, 191n11
Austen, Jane, 36, 97–98
autobiography: Boswell's hoarding of autobiographical papers, 13; concern about immortality and emergence of, 10; the *Idler* on, 148; Lackington as autobiographer, 131, 132; Pilkington as autobiographer, 118, 123, 126, 128; spiritual, 16. *See also* biography

standing and the Principles of Morals (Hume), 64, 65
epic poetry, 4, 38, 108
Erasmus, 149, 150
Erskine, Andrew, 14
Essay Concerning Human Understanding (Locke), 8, 63, 183n25
Essay on Epitaphs (Johnson), 141
eternity: British upper class abandons in favor of fame, 7; Butler's *Analogy of Religion* on, 67; Christian, 6, 22, 37, 48; fame's intersection with, 134; futurity versus, 11; heavenly, 6, 7, 41; immortality and, 6, 7, 35, 41; Johnson's anxieties about, 133–34, 135; in Johnson's *Rasselas*, 136; literary, 40; literary immortality and, 7, 8, 9; Milton on, 6; periodical, 22, 24–31, 34, 133; of progressive development, 15; Richardson's *Clarissa* on, 90; Richardson's *Sir Charles Grandison* on, 107; Shakespeare on, 6; the *Spectator* on, 22, 24, 31, 67; time versus, 6, 27, 37, 38, 133; Young's *Night Thoughts* on, 40, 41, 44, 48, 49, 188n4

Fairer, David, 184n43
fame: Boswell and, 154; British upper class abandons belief in eternity in favor of, 7; heaven inferred from desire for, 15; intersection with eternity, 134; Johnson and, 134, 139, 141, 142, 144, 150, 151, 172; literary, 8, 34, 38, 39, 41, 42, 43, 129, 134, 139; *Luctus Britannici* on Dryden's, 1–2; Milton's *Lycidas* on, 6; new conception of, 7; Pilkington and, 118, 119, 121, 122, 129; posthumous, 16, 141, 182n14; Young's *Night Thoughts* on, 38, 39, 41–43, 49, 51
Faust (Goethe), 95–96
fideism, 64
Fielding, Henry: Boswell reads, 204n5; intersection of literary and Christian

immortality in novels of, 16; *Joseph Andrews*, 98, 108; *Journal of a Voyage to Lisbon*, 148; *Tom Jones*, 39–40, 98
Fielding, Sarah, 90
Flesch, William, 82
Flew, Antony, 190n9
Flood, Henry, 201n42
Flynn, Carol Houlihan, 106
Foote, Samuel, 130–31, 132, 198n23
Forster, Harold, 42, 188n14
Four Zoas, The (Blake), 38
Franklin, Benjamin, 16, 35–36

Garrick, David, 178
Gay, John, 29
Gay, Peter, 184n36
Gentleman's Magazine, 136–38, 200n18
Gerrard, Christine, 184n43
Gibbon, Edward, 7, 73, 164, 184n37
Goethe, Johann Wolfgang von, 16, 38, 80, 94–96
Goldsmith, Oliver, 160
Gray, Thomas, 51
Greene, Donald, 205n18
Gulliver's Travels (Swift), 51

Habermas, Jürgen, 21, 185n5
Halliwell, Stephen, 196n19
Hamlet (Shakespeare), 25, 83, 84, 93, 121, 122, 155, 156
Harris, Jocelyn, 101
Hawkins, John, 2, 134, 146, 156, 161, 201n50
Hensley, David, 79, 86, 90, 192n4
Hervey, Lord, 16
Hesiod, 28
Hill, Aaron, 55, 94, 190n36, 194n41
Hill, Joe, 71
History of England (Hume), 65
Hobbes, Thomas, 8, 192n32
Holmes, Oliver Wendell, 16, 172–73
Horace: and epigraph to Boswell's first *Hypochondriack* essay, 168; and epigraph to Boswell's *The Life of*

Horace (*continued*)

Johnson, 156; Johnson cites, 142; lives through his works, 117; lyricist orientation of, 11; *Ode* 4.7, 144; *Ode* 4.8, 182n21; on poetry as monument, 5, 6, 35, 36, 47–48; the *Rambler* cites, 135, 149; test of literary excellence, 139; Young influenced by, 189n22

Hoyle, Henry, 1–2, 4

Hume, David: Addison's influence on, 10; attitude toward philosophy, 152, 153; Boswell's engagement with, 8, 10, 13, 14–15; on Butler's argument for posthumous divine justice, 196n11; death of, 49, 169–70, 171, 191n17, 203n2, 206n25; on immortality, 65–66, 105; as *Kulturpessimist,* 184n37; on moral sentiment and religion, 64, 65; opponents of, 8, 10, 13; paring away of consciousness, 150; on poetic fame, 7; on the soul, 8, 9, 208n47; on Warburton, 74; on women and mortalism, 106. *Works: Enquiries Concerning Human Understanding and the Principles of Morals,* 64, 65; *History of England,* 65; *Natural History of Religion,* 73, 192n24; *Treatise of Human Nature,* 64, 74, 208n47

Hunter, Michael, 183n25

Hypochondriack, The (Boswell), 167, 168, 169, 203n62

Idler: on autobiography, 148; Christian doctrine in, 135; on communication between living and dead, 140; and Johnson not keeping a diary, 147; no claim to originality in, 143; on personal immortality and posthumous fame, 141–42; on progress, 143; on whether the soul always thinks, 148, 203n57

immortality: Addison on, 4, 10, 28, 107; Arendt on, 5–6, 150, 157; Boswell on, 169–70; Boswell's *The Life of Johnson* on, 161; Butler on, 64, 65; changed understandings of time and, 3, 133; Christian, 16, 24–25, 38, 41, 44, 74, 98; eighteenth-century obsession with, 4; horizontal, 11, 25, 26, 27, 67, 69; Hume on, 65–66, 105; of Johnson, 172, 173; Johnson on, 84, 134–35, 138, 199n8; Johnson on literary immortality and personal afterlife, 7, 139–44; Kant on, 175, 208n2; Keats on, 175–76; literary versus personal, 3–15; marriage compared with, 102–4, 195n7; periodical, 60; Pilkington's *Memoirs* on, 118, 119, 121, 123, 129–30; progress and concerns about, 10–11; the *Rambler* on, 149; Richardson's *Clarissa* on, 15, 60–63, 80, 83–86, 91, 98, 148, 169; Richardson's *Sir Charles Grandison* on, 15, 60–61, 98, 101–7; Shakespeare on, 6; skepticism about personal afterlife, 7; the *Spectator* on horizontal, 25, 26, 27, 67, 69, 175; the *Spectator's* reimagining of, 15, 22, 24–31, 169, 175; Warburton on, 64–65, 72, 74–75, 77, 135; writing and, 2, 3, 47, 121; Young's *Night Thoughts* on, 37–38, 39–43. *See also* eternity; literary immortality; prose immortality

Ireland, William Henry, 179

Irlam, Shaun, 44, 189n23

Irwin, George, 199n3

Jackson, H. J., 139, 206n26

Jackson, Spencer, 93, 194n38

Jakobson, Roman, 123

Johnson, Samuel, 133–51; Addison and Richardson as influences, 140, 143, 144, 200n30; as adversary of atheism, 8; advises Boswell to keep a diary, 147, 203n54, 206n32; anxieties about eternity, 133–34, 135; arguments about immortality for, 9–10; attempts to keep diaries, 134, 147,

Wesley, Charles, 16
Wesley, John, 149
Whiston, William, 37
Wilkes, John, 161
Winter (Thomson), 11
Wootton, David, 183n25
Worsdale, James, 124, 127

Xenophon, 162

Young, Edward: arguments about immortality for, 9–10; on benevolent creator and immortality, 84; Boswell and, 52–53, 153, 189n30; death scene of, 190n35; as disciple of Addison, 37; on doubled conception of immortality, 94; Horace as influence on, 189n22; Milton's influence on, 188n5; mistress imputed to, 52–53; open-ended structure and proto-Romantic introspection of poetry of, 4; Pilkington's *Memoirs* compared with, 116, 129; reductive literary periodization and reputation of, 39; on Richardson's *Clarissa,* 62–63; seen as otherworldly and falsely sublime, 41; social status of, 115; on time, 37, 44. See also *Conjectures on Original Composition* (Young); *Night Thoughts* (Young)
Young, Frederick, 53, 190n35

Francesca Saggini
Backstage in the Novel: Frances Burney and the Theater Arts
Translated by Laura Kopp

Scott R. MacKenzie
Be It Ever So Humble:
Poverty, Fiction, and the Invention of the Middle-Class Home

Denver Brunsman
The Evil Necessity: British Naval Impressment
in the Eighteenth-Century Atlantic World

Jacob Sider Jost
Prose Immortality, 1711–1819